BUDDHIST MEDITATION

Meditative practice lies at the heart of the Buddhist tradition. This introductory anthology gives a representative sample of the various kinds of meditations described in the earliest body of Buddhist scripture, the Pāli canon. It provides a broad introduction to their traditional context and practice and supplies explanation, context and doctrinal background to the subject of meditation. The main themes of the book are the diversity and flexibility of the way that the Buddha teaches meditation from the evidence of the canon. Covering fundamental features of Buddhist practice such as posture, lay meditation and meditative technique it provides comments both from the principal early commentators on Buddhist practice, Upatissa and Buddhaghosa, as well as from reputable modern meditation teachers in a number of Theravadin traditions. This is the first general book on Pāli Buddhism which introduces the reader to the wide range of meditative advice in the canon. It demonstrates that the Buddha's meditative tradition still offers a path of practice as mysterious, awe-inspiring yet as freshly accessible as it was centuries ago and should be of interest to students and scholars of Buddhism as well as Buddhist practitioners.

Sarah Shaw read Greek and English at Manchester University, where she took a doctorate in English. She studied Pāli at Oxford and is on the steering committee of the Oxford Centre for Buddhist Studies. She is a mother, teacher and writer. She practises with the Samatha Association of Britain.

ROUTLEDGE CRITICAL STUDIES IN BUDDHISM

General Editors: Charles S. Prebish and Damien Keown

Routledge Critical Studies in Buddhism is a comprehensive study of the Buddhist tradition. The series explores this complex and extensive tradition from a variety of perspectives, using a range of different methodologies.

The series is diverse in its focus, including historical studies, textual translations and commentaries, sociological investigations, bibliographic studies, and considerations of religious practice as an expression of Buddhism's integral religiosity. It also presents materials on modern intellectual historical studies, including the role of Buddhist thought and scholarship in a contemporary, critical context and in the light of current social issues. The series is expansive and imaginative in scope, spanning more than two and a half millennia of Buddhist history. It is receptive to all research works that inform and advance our knowledge and understanding of the Buddhist tradition.

A SURVEY OF VINAYA LITERATURE
Charles S. Prebish

THE REFLEXIVE NATURE OF AWARENESS
Paul Williams

ALTRUISM AND REALITY
Paul Williams

BUDDHISM AND HUMAN RIGHTS
Edited by Damien Keown, Charles S. Prebish and Wayne Husted

WOMEN IN THE FOOTSTEPS OF THE BUDDHA
Kathryn R. Blackstone

THE RESONANCE OF EMPTINESS
Gay Watson

AMERICAN BUDDHISM
Edited by Duncan Ryuken Williams and Christopher Queen

IMAGING WISDOM
Jacob N. Kinnard

PAIN AND ITS ENDING
Carol S. Anderson

EMPTINESS APPRAISED
David F. Burton

THE SOUND OF LIBERATING TRUTH
Edited by Sallie B. King and Paul O. Ingram

BUDDHIST THEOLOGY
Edited by Roger R. Jackson and John J. Makransky

THE GLORIOUS DEEDS OF PURNA
Joel Tatelman

EARLY BUDDHISM – A NEW APPROACH
Sue Hamilton

CONTEMPORARY BUDDHIST ETHICS
Edited by Damien Keown

INNOVATIVE BUDDHIST WOMEN
Edited by Karma Lekshe Tsomo

TEACHING BUDDHISM IN THE WEST
Edited by V.S. Hori, R.P. Hayes and J.M. Shields

EMPTY VISION
David L. McMahan

SELF, REALITY AND REASON IN TIBETAN PHILOSOPHY
Thupten Jinpa

IN DEFENSE OF DHARMA
Tessa J. Bartholomeusz

BUDDHIST PHENOMENOLOGY
Dan Lusthaus

RELIGIOUS MOTIVATION AND THE ORIGINS OF BUDDHISM
Torkel Brekke

DEVELOPMENTS IN AUSTRALIAN BUDDHISM
Michelle Spuler

ZEN WAR STORIES
Brian Victoria

THE BUDDHIST UNCONSCIOUS
William S. Waldron

INDIAN BUDDHIST THEORIES OF PERSONS
James Duerlinger

ACTION DHARMA
Edited by Christopher Queen, Charles S. Prebish and Damien Keown

TIBETAN AND ZEN BUDDHISM IN BRITAIN
David N. Kay

THE CONCEPT OF THE BUDDHA
Guang Xing

THE PHILOSOPHY OF DESIRE IN THE BUDDHIST PALI CANON
David Webster

THE NOTION OF *DITTHI* IN THERAVADA BUDDHISM
Paul Fuller

THE BUDDHIST THEORY OF SELF-COGNITION
Zhihua Yao

MORAL THEORY IN ŚĀNTIDEVA'S *ŚIKṢĀSAMUCCAYA*
Barbra R. Clayton

BUDDHIST STUDIES FROM INDIA TO AMERICA
Edited by Damien Keown

DISCOURSE AND IDEOLOGY IN MEDIEVAL JAPANESE BUDDHISM
Edited by Richard K. Payne and Taigen Dan Leighton

BUDDHIST THOUGHT AND APPLIED PSYCHOLOGICAL RESEARCH
Edited by D.K. Nauriyal, Michael S. Drummond and Y.B. Lal

BUDDHISM IN CANADA
Edited by Bruce Matthews

BUDDHISM, CONFLICT AND VIOLENCE IN MODERN SRI LANKA
Edited by Mahinda Deegalle

THERAVĀDA BUDDHISM AND THE BRITISH ENCOUNTER
Religious, missionary and colonial experience in nineteenth century Sri Lanka
Elizabeth Harris

BEYOND ENLIGHTENMENT
Buddhism, religion, modernity
Richard Cohen

The following titles are published in association with the *Oxford Centre for Buddhist Studies*

Oxford Centre for Buddhist Studies
a project of The Society for the Wider Understanding of the Buddhist Tradition

The *Oxford Centre for Buddhist Studies* conducts and promotes rigorous teaching and research into all forms of the Buddhist tradition.

EARLY BUDDHIST METAPHYSICS
Noa Ronkin

MIPHAM'S DIALECTICS AND THE DEBATES ON EMPTINESS
Karma Phuntsho

HOW BUDDHISM BEGAN
The conditioned genesis of the early teachings
Richard F. Gombrich

BUDDHIST MEDITATION
An anthology of texts from the Pāli canon
Sarah Shaw

BUDDHIST MEDITATION

An anthology of texts from the Pāli canon

Sarah Shaw

Routledge
Taylor & Francis Group
LONDON AND NEW YORK

First published 2006
by Routledge
2 Park Square, Milton Park, Abingdon, Oxon, OX14 4RN

Simultaneously published in the USA and Canada
by Routledge
270 Madison Ave, New York NY 10016

Routledge is an imprint of the Taylor & Francis Group

Transferred to Digital Printing 2008

Typeset in Times New Roman by
Newgen Imaging Systems (P) Ltd, Chennai, India

British Library Cataloguing in Publication Data
A catalogue record for this book is available from the British Library

Library of Congress Cataloging in Publication Data
Tipiòtaka. English. Selections.
Buddhist meditation: an anthology of texts from the Pali Canon /
[selected and translated by] Sarah Shaw.
p. cm. – (Routledge critical studies in Buddhism)
Includes translations from Pali.
Includes bibliographical references and index.
1. Meditation – Buddhism. I. Shaw, Sarah, Dr. II. Title. III. Series.

BQ1172.E5S43 2005
294.3'4435–dc22 2005018530

ISBN10: 0–415–35918–X (hbk)
ISBN10: 0–415–48568–1 (pbk)

ISBN13: 978–0–415–35918–4 (hbk)
ISBN13: 978–0–415–48568–5 (pbk)

FOR CHARLES

CONTENTS

PREFACE

This introductory anthology intends to give a representative sample of the various kinds of meditations described in the Pāli canon and a broad introduction to their traditional context and practice. It is intended for two sorts of readers, though some may fit into both categories. A number of people who practise Theravāda meditation in the West are surprised to find very little to read on the subject. Apart from occasional, often privately published books on specific practices there is almost nothing of a more general kind that places meditation in the context of other teachings within the Pāli canon. As a result of this, many practising meditators find the apparent complexity and inaccessibility of the Pāli literature off-putting and so never read some of the basic texts of their own tradition. There is also no general guide to texts on the subject of meditation in the Pāli canon for those whose interest is primarily academic. This anthology is intended to supply explanation, context and doctrinal background to the subject of meditation. Meditative practice lies at the heart of the Buddhist tradition and it is hoped that this book will encourage more people to appreciate the distinctive merits of the various kinds of teachings in the Pāli canon.

The main themes of the book are the diversity and flexibility of the way that the Buddha taught meditation from the evidence of the canon. Over the forty-five years during which he taught he showed practicality, pertinence and compassion in his dealings with those to whom he offered guidance. This sense of applicability is sometimes overlooked in studies that, necessarily, extract key ideas in isolation for philosophical and intellectual discussion. Buddhist *suttas*, often richly human and humorous in tone, place a given teaching in a context where meditative practice is geared to the practitioner and to other aspects of the eightfold path. They display a great inventiveness of imagery, technique and method and often show signs of being carefully tailored to the audience or person addressed. Buddhaghosa, the chief commentator on the Pāli canon, outlined forty different meditation subjects, which are commonly taught in the East today. Although the list has no exact counterpart within the canon, it is of ancient origins and is used as a classification to order the material used in the anthology. The *suttas* themselves are reassuringly resistant to easy categorization. The Buddha exhibited a great love of lists as a teaching method but seems to have avoided the provision of a uniform system to delineate the range of meditative methods. By using the forty meditation objects as a basis, I hoped to highlight the principal features of *bhāvanā* and to show ways in which the canon sometimes differs in approach from early manuals.

This book tries to cover fundamental features of Buddhist practice that people often ask about: posture and the incidence of lay meditation, for instance. So the introductions to each meditation give quotes and comment both from the principal early commentators on Buddhist practice, Upatissa and Buddhaghosa, and from reputable modern meditation teachers in a number of Theravāda traditions. As an anthology, it is not intended to give specific teaching – as the texts emphasize, this is the job of the teacher, or the 'good friend' in meditation. I hoped, however, to provide a background to each of the different objects in its ancient and modern setting – and to communicate some sense of the continued health and diversity of meditative practice today. Preconceptions about Buddhist practice soon become challenged by looking at a variety of texts from different collections. It becomes clear for instance that from the evidence of the texts the line between *samatha*, calm meditation and *vipassanā*, insight, was much more fluid in ancient times than is commonly supposed and that the canon constantly encourages a flexibly practical approach. This can be seen both in the assignation of meditation objects to practitioners and in the way help is sometimes given to practitioners to counteract imbalances and difficulties encountered. There is a large section on the recollections. These practices, usually given to the laity for use in daily life, are found in texts that are often overlooked now.

But as well as providing a general guide to meditation practice from the texts, the anthology aims to introduce the reader to the great and diverse excellences of the Pāli canon itself. As a body of texts they show every sign of being composed with the intention of being accessible and interesting to the lay public of the time: it seems time to start appreciating the distinctive merits of each collection once more.

When this project was first suggested to me, by Richard Gombrich and Sally Cutler Mellick, our idea was to use pre-existing translations. We soon realized this would not work as translators' use of technical language is so varied. So, aiming for some sort of consistency, I have made new translations on the basis of the PTS texts. For anyone who would like to read other texts, however, PTS translations of all the ones used here are available and cited in the bibliography.

ACKNOWLEDGEMENTS

There are a number of people to whom I owe particular thanks. Professor Richard Gombrich who taught me Pāli, has been endlessly helpful and generous in teaching me for many years and kindly read sections of the book while it was being written. L.S. Cousins has taught me for even longer and I have had many conversations with him about the subject. No amount of footnotes can fully acknowledge my debt to either of them. This is also the case for my husband, Charles, who has being diligently practising *khanti*, with great good humour. Dr Sally Cutler Mellick suggested the subject to me and helped me greatly when I started the book.

There are many other people I would like to thank for varied help, encouragement and information. They include Ven Dhammasami, Ven Kusalo, Ven Wan Doo Kim, Sarah Norman, Dr Rupert Gethin, Professor Peter Harvey, Dr Sanjukta Gombrich, Professor Paul Harrison, Dr Peter Skilling, Dr Jim Benson, Dr Alex Wynne, Dr Damien Keown, Dorothea Schaefter, my family, friends in the Samatha Association, frequenters of the Oxford Sanskritists' lunch and the kindly staff at the Indian Institute Library and the Oriental Institute, Oxford.

TRANSLATOR'S NOTE

For translations of Buddhist texts, it is customary to maintain consistency in the use of technical terms. While I have not followed the guideline rigidly, a glossary of some key Pāli words used is given at the end of the book. Where the translation itself requires considerable explanation, terms have been left untranslated. The word *jhāna*, the meditative state that lies at the heart of *samatha* practice, has been left untranslated.

A word that arouses great debate is *kusala*, variously translated as good, skilful or wholesome, with connotations of all of these. As the anthology is about meditation I felt it was, for the most part, much easier to see the mind as 'skilful' or 'unskilful' rather than 'good' or 'bad', with some exceptions (e.g. S V 149–52). The sense of 'good' should not be lost, however, and is often more suitable for texts on virtue (*sīla*).

Some words, such as *kamma*, *dhamma* and *nibbāna*, have now passed into common English usage in their Sanskrit form. The word *dhamma* is, however, particularly tricky. In some contexts it means the teaching of the Buddha. In others, it applies more generally to things as they are: in the fourth foundation of mindfulness, described in the *Satipaṭṭhāna-Sutta*, a suitable translation would be 'event', 'phenomenon' or even 'something that occurs'. The translation of 'mental objects' is not quite accurate as in this text the term is used to describe any event, mental or otherwise. The word sometimes describes 'states'. It can just mean 'thing', and to leave it untranslated lends it an unjustified weight. It has, however, usually been left untranslated.

ABBREVIATIONS

A	*Aṅguttaranikāya*
AA	*Manorathapūraṇī* (commentary on A)
Ap	*Apadāna*
Asl	*Atthasālinī* (commentary on Dhs)
D	*Dīghanikāya*
DA	*Sumaṅgalavilāsinī* (commentary on D)
Dhp	*Dhammapada*
DhpA	*Dhammapada-aṭṭhakathā* (commentary on Dhp)
Dhs	*Dhammasaṅgaṇi*
It	*Itivuttaka*
Ja	*Jātaka*
M	*Majjhimanikāya*
MA	*Papañcasūdanī* (commentary on M)
Nidd 1	*Mahāniddesa*
Nidd 2	*Cūḷaniddesa*
Patis	*Paṭisambhidāmagga*
S	*Saṃyuttanikāya*
Sn	*Suttanipāta*
ThA	*Theragāthā*
ThA	*Theragāthā-aṭṭhakathā* (commentary on Th)
Thī	*Therīgāthā*
ThīA	*Therīgāthā-aṭṭhakathā* (commentary on Thī)
Ud	*Udāna*
Vibh	*Vibhaṅga*
VibhA	*Vibhaṅga-aṭṭhakathā* (commentary on Vibh)
Vin	*Vinayapiṭaka*
Vism	*Visuddhimagga*

References to texts are to PTS edition, volume and page, which are denoted by a volume number (upper case Roman numeral) and page reference. For Sn, Dhp, Th and Thī references are to verse number.

Abbreviations of translations, other works and organizations (see bibliography of translations)

BL	*Buddhist Legends* (Burlingame)
BMTP	*Buddhist Meditation in Theory and Practice* (Vajirañāṇa)
BPE	*Buddhist Psychological Ethics* (Rhys Davids, C.A.F.)
BPS	Buddhist Publication Society
CDB	*Connected Discourses of the Buddha* (Bodhi)
DB	*Dialogues of the Buddha* (Rhys Davids, T.W.)
DPPN	*Dictionary of Pāli Proper Names* (Malalasekera)
Exp	*Expositor* (Tin)
GD	*Group of Discourses* (Norman)
GS	*The Book of Gradual Sayings* (Hare, Woodward)
J	*The Jātakas* (Cowell)
JPTS	*Journal of the Pāli Text Society*
KS	*The Book of Kindred Sayings* (Rhys Davids, C.A.F., Woodward)
MLDB	*Middle Length Discourses of the Buddha* (Ñāṇamoli)
MLS	*Middle Length Sayings* (Horner)
PF	*The Path of Freedom* (*Vimuttimagga*: Ehara *et al.*)
PP	*Path of Purification* (*Visuddhimagga*: Ñāṇamoli)
PTS	Pāli Text Society
VRI	Vipassanā Research Institute CD-ROM
WD	*Word of the Doctrine* (Norman)

Key to translations

BL = DhpA
BPE = Dhs
CDB = S
DB = D
Exp = Asl
GD = Sn
GS = A
KS = S
MLDB = M
MLS = M
PD = Patis
PP = Vism
WD = Dhp

Abbreviations of dictionaries

CPD	*Critical Pāli Dictionary* (Royal Danish Academy of Sciences and Letters)
DP	*Dictionary of Pāli* (Cone, M) PTS

OED	*Oxford English Dictionary* (Compact edition)
PED	*Pāli English Dictionary* PTS
SED	*Sanskrit–English Dictionary* (Monier Williams)

References are to Pāli text and only to translations where specifically cited or quoted. The *Dhammapada* commentary is referred to throughout in its translation (BL). References to *Visuddhimagga* are to chapter and paragraph denoted by Ñāṇamoli in PP (see Ñāṇamoli).

1

INTRODUCTION

What is meditation?

If there is one image which has done the most to encourage the practice of Buddhist meditation in the modern world it is that of the Buddha himself, sitting in the meditation or *samādhi* posture, with legs in the lotus position and palms held upwards on the lap, the right hand held gently over the left. Easterners treat a Buddha figure with great respect: little street shrines can be seen in odd corners all over South East Asia, surrounded with flowers and incense. Although the figure of the Buddha is also often seen on market stalls, as backdrop to romantic films or giving atmosphere for travel brochures, its authority transcends and transforms its setting. The bodily form has become a distillation of the teaching. The shoulders are evenly balanced (*sama*), the back straight, the lower half of the body offers tranquil support to the upper, the 'lion' chest is confident and rounded without being puffed up. It is essentially a human figure, for within the Theravāda Buddhist tradition the Buddha is not regarded as a god, but as a man, who has developed to the full the human possibilities for compassion, strength and wisdom and can teach these qualities to others. The word Buddha is derived from the Pāli word for 'awake' (bujjhati); it is this quality of peaceful alertness which characterizes the seated figure, whose posture, bearing and expression bring together within the bodily form the qualities we have come to associate with the activity of *bhāvanā*, or meditation.

But what is the activity of meditation and why practise it? To explain this it is helpful to consider briefly the key events in the life of the Buddha that prompted his development of a system of meditation that forms an essential element of the eightfold path of right view, right resolve, right speech, right action, right livelihood, right effort, right mindfulness and right concentration. For six years after the renunciation of the pleasures of his palace he followed various teachers and practised two of the higher meditations, the seventh and the eighth *jhānas*, subsequently incorporated into his own system. He concluded, however, that they did not lead in themselves to peace and freedom. Joining a group of renunciates who were following the severe austerities favoured by many at the time, he attempted to find truth through self-mortification but just became ill and emaciated.

Realizing that he would never find enlightenment in this way, he ate some food and spontaneously remembered an experience that had occurred to him as a child. In the *Mahāsaccaka-Sutta*, the Buddha describes the incident that had occurred, according to the commentaries, when he was 7 years old. For the first time in his life, Gotama had been left on his own. His father, the king, was ceremonially initiating the ploughing festival by taking up the plough himself. Gotama's attention, however, falls not on the movement of the plough but, according to the commentaries, upon the object of the breath as it enters and leaves his body:

> And then, Aggivessana, this thought came to me: 'I remember that when my father the Śakyan was busy, while I was sitting in the cool shade of the rose-apple tree, quite secluded from sensual pleasures, secluded from unskilful states, I entered upon and abided in the first *jhāna*, which is accompanied by applied and sustained thought, with the joy and happiness born of seclusion. Might that be the path to awakening?' Then, following on that memory came the consciousness: 'This is the path to awakening'.
>
> 'Why am I afraid of a happiness that has nothing to do with sensual pleasures and unskilful states?' And then, Aggivessana, this thought came to me: 'I am not afraid of this happiness, for this happiness has nothing to do with sensual pleasures and unskilful states'.
>
> (M I 246–7)[1]

The Buddha's account is short but, occurring after a particularly harrowing account of the self-mortifications, is precise in its evocation of meditative experience. The incident carries a curious sense of contradiction: a state of profound peace is heightened by the proximity of an earthy, noisy and physical event, the ceremonial ploughing; the scene is companionable but also solitary, festive yet secluded and quiet. As Bronkhorst says, 'One cannot fail to be struck by the relaxed and friendly atmosphere that emanates from this passage.'[2] At the heart of the meditative teaching, later formulated within the principles of the middle way, lies an almost commonsensical assumption: that it is the mind that is at ease and at peace with itself that comes more easily to understanding than the one that is strained, and that in the grim or harsh pursuit of truth both the obvious and the subtle are lost together. Indeed the way a small or mundane event is observed with a leisured attentiveness that allows a space for things to be seen afresh reminds one of other modern myths of great discovery: Archimedes desperately trying to understand something and then allowing his attention to rest when taking a bath, Newton idly following the trajectory of an apple, or even the way a child picks up and plays with a new toy. The five factors of *jhāna*, initial or applied thought (*vitakka*), sustained thought or examining (*vicāra*), joy (*pīti*), happiness (*sukha*) and one-pointedness (*ekaggatā*) are ones we know from daily life. They are, according to *Abhidhamma* theory, present in many moments of our usual experience – but here they are unified in a refreshing state of great peace, interest and exploration.[3] All of these features underlie his teaching of the practice of *samatha* meditation.

The state does not produce enlightenment or specific soteriological insight. It is however transformatory: from that time Gotama's view of the world and his attitude to the nature of the attention and work needed to gain wisdom is changed at the root. On the basis of it he takes a step, courageous at a time when harsh austerities were considered essential for the pursuit of understanding, to follow a path that is not characterized by fear or rejection of the world of the senses. He still needs to find a way to liberation, however, and a further element, of insight, is provided by subsequent events in his search. After eating milk-rice given by Sujātā, he sits under the bodhi tree, and using the experience of the first *jhāna* as a basis, proceeds to practise the other seven *jhānas* – including the seventh and eighth which he had cultivated earlier. This confers the flexibility of mind and steadiness needed to attain insight into the corruptions that bind him and other beings to continued rebirth.

After the enlightenment the Buddha is reluctant to teach others, thinking that what he has discovered is too profound and subtle for others to understand. Lord Brahma, the ruler of the heaven realms points out to him that there are some 'with little dust in their eyes' who can benefit from this teaching. For the next forty-five years the Buddha goes on to teach: not just meditation but the system that he develops which is embodied in the middle way, the path that does not go to the extremes of sensual pleasure nor self-mortification. It is significant that it is Brahma who shows the Buddha how to use his divine eye and see the suffering of beings. According to Buddhism, Brahma is lord of the heaven realms only accessible after death to those who have attained *jhāna*, the meditation taught by the Buddha. It is through his good offices that the Buddha is able to see how his wisdom may help others. A metaphoric implication is inevitably suggested by the incident. Contact with the realm of Brahma, where beings are reborn for aeons on the basis of meditative practice, not only helps the individual to gain liberating insight, but also ensures that the mind looks on at the condition of other beings in a way that can help them. The Brahma realms were certainly regarded as realms which form the basis for rebirth, but they also suggest the available reserves of health and calmness in the mind that are needed to be able to see the suffering of others and to teach them. As modern meditation teachers point out, psychiatric hospitals are full of many who have had profound insights: no *samatha*, with its associated contentment and joy, has helped them to be able to accept them or to be able to perceive suffering around and within themselves with peace.[4]

The word meditation is a Western term for which there is no obvious counterpart in Pāli. The noun *bhāvanā*, production or cultivation, derived in Pāli from the causative of the verb to be, 'to cause to become' or 'to bring into being', is the nearest approximation (PED 503).[5] Its association with creativity suggests that the human mind can produce all the reserves it needs through self-development. As such, accompanied by the practice of giving (*dāna*) and virtue (*sīla*), it is considered fundamental to the Buddhist path. Working together, these are regarded as active qualities that help the mind to see clearly by loosening distraction, resentment and annoyance. Buddhist texts frequently cover most of the eightfold path in one *sutta* or piece of text: discussion on behaviour, meditation and insight are commonly mixed in the same discussion. This is surely not accidental, though it poses tricky problems for anyone trying to isolate material on meditation alone. It indicates that while the pursuit of *bhāvanā*, in meditation, works to purify the emotions and the area of feeling it cannot develop well without attention to behaviour in the world and 'views': the things we insist on as being right or deadening theories of mind which prevent happiness or contentment. The Buddha taught that such activities of mind, wrongly applied, prevent insight into what is actually happening in the world around: things as they really are (*yāthabhūtaṃ*). Wisdom in Buddhism is described as producing right view, release and, in the end, freedom from suffering. Some kind of emotional purification, however, provided and supported by *bhāvanā*, is needed for salvific wisdom to arise: it is necessary to see all beings and their problems, including oneself and one's own nature, without hatred, boredom or contempt. To put it another way, according to the philosophy known as *Abhidhamma*, the higher teaching, if there is not one of the *brahmavihāras* (31–5) of loving-kindness, compassion, sympathetic joy or equanimity present in the mind when any object is perceived, human or otherwise, then there is no wisdom either.[6]

Can modern science identify any benefits in meditation? There are measurable health benefits associated with Buddhist techniques. Research from the University of Wisconsin has shown that meditation affects favourably the parts of the brain associated with happiness: and it has long been proven, not only by scientists, that happiness tends to be good for people, helping to ensure health and longevity.[7] Our bodies and minds are discernibly connected in many ways, and being able to return to a point of equilibrium allows neurone receptors to replenish themselves and other aspects of the physical brain to keep active and alert. In terms of the eightfold path, meditation is usually placed in the last triad, of right effort, right mindfulness and right concentration. The search for the alertness and stillness suggested by these has a focus and challenge that could be compared to the wish to climb a great mountain, understand a problem of astrophysics or write a poem. What is so striking about Buddhist meditation, however, is that mindfulness (*sati*) and clear comprehension (*sampajañña*), the foundations of work on the mind, can also be pursued in mundane activities too: not only in seclusion but while doing the shopping, mending the computer and dealing with the usual bustle and annoyances of the day. The way the Buddha taught meditation was not intended to encourage people to ignore the world or closet themselves away, as is sometimes thought, but, with the mindfulness that is constantly enjoined, to be aware of it and participate in it more.

The early manuals

The main commentator on Buddhist meditation is Buddhaghosa, the great scholar and writer who lived in Sri Lanka in the fifth century BCE, who has left us with extensive commentaries on many of the major texts of the early Buddhist canon. The *Visuddhimagga* has been the principal means whereby the teachings on meditation from the time of the Buddha have been made practically available and accessible to later generations. It is erudite, comprehensive and in some cases, such as in the methods for the *kasiṇa* practice (1–10), breathing mindfulness (29) and the formless realms (35–8), supplies us with information that is unavailable elsewhere. Many helpful lists and guides to practice are given, such as the lists of impediments to meditation and ways of guarding the mental image (*nimitta*), the basis of *samatha* practice. Though not canonical, they appear to have emerged within the tradition as the product of years of practical experimentation and experience in dealing with meditators and their problems (see Vism III 29–56 and Vism IV 34–41). Buddhaghosa's systematic and discursive approach has seemed over elaborate to some, but through these means he covers endless contingencies, methods and potential problems, exhibiting a wish characteristic of much Indian commentarial literature to explore any given subject with exhaustive attention to detail. This is partly, it appears, for the sheer pleasure of the exercise, but also to fulfil his evident concern to provide a manual that encompasses all possible difficulties and choices facing a practising meditator. This has been more than invaluable: it is unlikely that the meditative tradition could have survived in such a healthy way, if at all, without his detailed lists and exhaustive guidance. His manual is so constantly used and quoted throughout Buddhist Theravāda countries that it is often regarded as the principal text on the subject of meditation, even to the exclusion of canonical sources.[8]

The other important early manual is Upatissa's *Vimuttimagga*, known in the West through its translation, *The Path of Freedom*. Upatissa is a mysterious figure, and we do not know where or when he lived. We do not even know in which language he wrote; his work has come to us via a Chinese translation from Pāli or some form of Buddhist Sanskrit.[9] Comparison with Buddhaghosa is interesting and tantalizing, as much of what they say accords to similar patterns. A study of the two by Bapat has shown that we cannot be certain who came first, but the little evidence we have suggests that Upatissa's work was known to and precedes Buddhaghosa: Bapat concludes that Buddhaghosa may have wanted to improve upon him. Upatissa quotes at greater length from original texts, adopts a more streamlined approach in his breakdown of meditation subjects and writes in an easy and uncluttered style that, even after translation into English, seems much simpler and more expressive than that favoured by Buddhaghosa. Buddhaghosa in certain places disagrees with other teachers who represent views that we may find in Upatissa and he does supply much more detail as regards method, though his quotes from the canon tend to be shorter. Both make extensive use of simile and metaphor, though Upatissa possibly places more emphasis on this by arranging some sections around a single simile. Buddhaghosa exhibits a great love of the *nirutti*, the elucidatory pun that plays with elaborate 'etymologies', which Upatissa does not seem to share.[10] For the modern reader both works complement one another: Buddhaghosa provides more detailed and thorough analysis of each meditation object and the work carries the reassuring weight and authority of what has become by the fifth century CE a highly developed meditative tradition. Upatissa's natural and unaffected style, however, seems to bear the imprint of a practitioner, though it would be difficult to prove this in any way. For some meditations, his accounts are refreshingly simple: the meditation on light (9), the recollection of the *dhamma* (22) and that of peace (30) are particularly noteworthy (PF 128, 149–50 and 177–9). His analysis of dependent origination, one of the most difficult areas of Buddhist doctrine, in terms of his own simile of the seedbed and the production of rice, is one of the most succinct explanations of this profound teaching that one could encounter anywhere (see PF 259–61). It is not the place here to analyse the distinguishing features of the two commentators' approaches in detail: they accord on most major issues and differ in emphasis and tone rather than practice. Both works are essential in helping our understanding of the canon, which curiously omits for some meditations methods for pursuing each one in practice.

The classification of meditation objects

This leads us to objects for meditation and how they are chosen. One of the most revealing areas in any project is considering the difficulties which are encountered at the initial stages, for this can bring to the surface important and even defining features of the nature of the subject involved. For an anthology of Buddhist meditation, this intriguing problem arises when one tries to find some sort of classification of the material. This is not because the Buddha failed to leave behind lists of subjects and practices: on the contrary, there are many, usually arranged in a standard way, sometimes as groups or described in detail by pericopes, extended descriptions transported from one *sutta* to another in precisely the same form. Groups such as the *kasiṇas* (1–10), the recollections (21–30) and divine abidings (31–4) are distributed from text to text in an often unchanged form. There is no set order in which the groups themselves appear, though the order of items within each list remains for the most part the same. We have a wide selection of these groups, collected together in many apparently endless patterns or permutations, so that one would be hard put to find a complete compilation of all the relevant lists which is reasonably comprehensive – and manageable as the basis for an anthology. It is rather like standard motifs rearranged in different ways in a mosaic or an embroidery, to create larger patterns and more intricate lists: any one *sutta* may have some, but not others, while some include so much else that they are not practicable to use as a means of classification. Sometimes designs and patterns not exclusively related to meditation are also being incorporated and woven in too. For instance the largest and most exhaustive compilation of lists, the *Jhānavagga* in the *Aṅguttaranikāya*, through its description of 101 subjects, communicates a sense of the manifold nature of meditative practice (A I 34–40). It is perhaps the best example of the way that clusters of subjects, that usually remain themselves intact, are placed with others. In such lists, features of one group sometimes appear in another, like an overlap between designs: the formless realms, for instance, appear in the standard list of the deliverances (*vimokkhā*) and on their own; the subject of death appears both as a recollection and twice as a perception. This list is worth exploring for its inclusiveness of meditation states, approaches and subjects: the four right efforts are there, which can be applied to any meditation. The very range of this text, however, renders it tricky to use as a guide to sorting texts. Other compilations of lists within the canon include elements that happen to be excluded from others, or omit some found elsewhere. Each compilation tends to have its own quirk or idiosyncrasy – perhaps one group not found or some list incorporated which one might not expect. The *Mahāsakuludāyi-Sutta* lists seventy-five features but inexplicably omits the divine abidings (31–5) (M II 524). The *Dhammasaṅgaṇi*, an early work of *Abhidhamma*, itemizes under the methods for inducing *jhāna* the deliverances and the spheres of transcendence (*abhibhāyatanāni*). It happens to exclude, however, the ten recollections, some of the most important meditations described by the Buddha: here they were perhaps taken for granted as preliminaries or felt to be included under other headings.[11]

One can only speculate about reasons for this fluid approach: many lists are possibly that way as the result of a choice made once by someone chanting a particular *sutta*, that just happened to stick. It rather appears though that the Buddha himself taught meditation as an activity that could, sometimes, be outlined in great detail but did not think in terms of rigid classification and, if anything, tended to avoid it: the many lists can seem open-ended and even organic, with new elements tacked on to suit the occasion. Any one is likely to include or leave out groups found in other lists.

The modern mind likes clear classification though – and we do need some arrangement for an anthology. So the one used here is the list of meditation subjects used to this day in all Theravāda Buddhist countries, Buddhaghosa's forty *kammaṭṭhānas*. The word *kammaṭṭhāna*, which means basis for work, is a post-canonical term, and while it is a useful designation we should always bear in mind that there is no classification that is quite the same in the texts.[12] The list of these takes each object as the basis for the practice of calm meditation, which is then used for insight, though, as we shall see, even this can be a far less clear-cut distinction than it seems.

These are:

1–10: ten devices (*kasiṇa*)
11–20: ten meditations on the foul (*asubha*)
21–30: ten recollections (*anussati*)
31–34: four divine abidings (*brahma-vihārā*), immeasurables (*appamāṇā*)
35–38: four formless spheres (*a(r)rūpa*)
39: perception of loathsomeness in food (*āhāre paṭikkūlasaññā*)
40: defining of the four elements (*catudhātuvavatthānam*).

Upatissa's list is in effect the same: although the *Vimuttimagga* lists thirty-eight subjects, it describes in the text, oddly enough, exactly the same ones that Buddhaghosa does. Both of these substitute light (*āloka*) and limited space (*paricchedākāsa*) for the space and consciousness found in the canon where ten *kasiṇas* are described.[13] The spheres of infinite space and infinite consciousness, excluded from the summary, are described by Upatissa after the earth *kasiṇa* (PF 113–17).[14] An indication of the antiquity of this list of thirty-eight, and perhaps also of an earlier date for Upatissa's work, is that it features in the introduction to a Jātaka story: the Buddha is asked by a group of monks for a *kammaṭṭhāna*, 'for release from *saṁsāra*'. He 'pondered over the thirty-eight *kammaṭṭhānas* and expounded one that was suitable to them' (Ja I 316).[15]

The treatment of meditation in the canon hints at a landscape that we cannot fully see now: and many questions are raised as to the nature of meditation objects at the time of the Buddha that we simply cannot answer. How were the deliverances and spheres of transcendence used in practice? Do their presence suggest some use of natural objects as the basis for practice? Or was the *kasiṇa* practice always undertaken in the way it is described in the commentaries, using a device in a manner apparently described by the *Cūlasuññatā-Sutta* (M III 104–9)? The presence of visualization practices in the canon suggests that sometimes no external object was needed for some meditations. In addition some subjects for meditation are described only once in the canon, there may well have been invented on the spot for a particular person, and do not happen to be discussed by the commentaries. A recollection on good friends (*kalyāṇamittā*), given instead of the recollection of the *saṅgha* after the usual recollection of the Buddha and *dhamma* to the layman Nandiya, is a striking example (see A V 336). The space element within the body is described in a *sutta* where the elements within the body are described as five rather than the usual four: this could indicate other contemporary ways of undertaking practice on the elements.[16] Meditation on the radiance of the sun and the moon, presumably some sort of variation on the perception of light, is mentioned in a canonical *Jātaka* verse.[17] These are just a few examples of meditations not listed in either manual that indicate a great diversity of approach. The Buddha seems to have seen the need for applicability and originality in a given situation when addressing a particular audience or person. As Vajirañāṇa says, 'these subjects which are to be found in the wide range of the Buddhist system of meditation are almost limitless; for they were adopted in accordance with the variety of the mental dispositions of the aspirants' (BMTP 75).

Different temperaments

Some texts in the *suttas* show that the Buddha assigned specific meditations for particular problems or hindrances, the obstacles to meditation: the practice of loving-kindness (31) is given for ill-will, meditation on the foul (11–20) for desire and the perception of light for sloth and torpor.[18] Various hindrances are described as occurring to people on separate occasions: the different practises given to the apparently luckless Tissa at different stages, also discussed in the section on hindrances, are examples of this.[19]

There is an underlying understanding of character however, found to a certain extent within the canon and developed more systematically by the time of the meditation manuals, that people are divided into different temperaments, or basic human types, and that some meditation practices suitable for some may not be for others. Some suit most temperaments. The earliest account of these types may be found in the canonical *Mahāniddesa* (see Nidd 1 360). The text says that the Buddha can discern the potential of different individuals as if looking at a lotus pond, where some lotuses remain submerged in the mud, some emerge a little and some manage to rise right above the water. He discerns six character types (*carita*): desire (*rāga*), hatred (*dosa*), delusion (*moha*), the one who applies the mind (*vitakka*), faith (*saddhā*) and wisdom (*ñāṅa*). To the one disposed to desire he teaches the foul meditations (11–20) and to the one disposed to hatred, loving-kindness (31). For the ignorant or deluded person he recommends asking questions at the right moment, listening to *dhamma* talks at the right moment and conversation about *dhamma*, as well as living near a teacher. To the one who applies his mind he teaches breathing mindfulness (29), to the one who has faith he teaches the sign that inspires confidence (*pasādanīyaṃ nimittaṃ*): the Buddha, the *dhamma* and the *saṅgha* (21–3) and one's own *sīla* or good conduct. For the one with wisdom, he teaches the three signs of existence: impermanence (*anicca*), unsatisfactoriness or suffering (*dukkha*) and not-self (*anattā*).

This method is developed and elaborated by Upatissa and Buddhaghosa (see PF 54–62 and Vism III 74–103). Buddhaghosa says that the first three types are less developed than the second three but have affinities with their counterpart – desire seeks out the good and so is like faith, but the objects it grasps are of the sense sphere, while faith grasps the 'good', that is, objects likely to lessen desire. Hate sees faults and so is like wisdom, but it is directed in the former to beings, in the latter to formations. The speculative temperament has affinities with the deluded as *vitakka*, or thinking about things, may be unnecessary; although the former is of a higher type it shares some characteristics with the deluded type. Both Buddhaghosa and Upatissa give descriptions of ways in which the types may be recognized from the way they sleep, sweep the floor, walk and perform other activities.[20] Buddhaghosa says that for those with desire the foul objects (11–20) or mindfulness of body (28) are suitable; for those of hating disposition the colour *kasiṇa* (5–8) or the divine abidings (31–4); for the deluded and the intelligence type mindfulness of breathing (29) can be given while the perception of loathsomeness in food (39), the determining of the four elements (40), mindfulness of death (27) and mindfulness of peace (30) are, for their profundity, suitable for the intelligence type (see Vism III 121–2). Upatissa gives fourteen types – by varying combinations of the three and giving two or three characteristics to each (see PF 55). He also matches meditation subject to type, noting the ones each should not practise: the divine abidings may be unsuitable for someone with strong desire, for instance, and the foul meditations may be unsuitable for someone with strong hatred (see PF 68–70).

It is notoriously difficult to tell what type one is oneself, or what meditations are suitable; the *sutta* given later on Meghiya is a famous illustration of this problem in the canon (see Ud 34–7). In practice, many people are given a selection, which might change in different circumstances. For this reason, meditation subjects in the Theravāda tradition are often given to the meditator by someone called the good friend, or the friend in what is good.

Finding a teacher or good friend

At the time of the Buddha, the sense of debate and the even argumentative nature of contacts between proponents of various views indicate that there were all kinds of teachers around, and a practitioner might go from one to another.[21] Special emphasis is given in the canon, however, to the *kalyāṇamitta*, the 'good' or 'lovely friend' or 'the friend in what is lovely', who may give guidance and encouragement in meditation.[22] The 'good friend' is important as someone in whom one can place trust and to whom one can talk openly about the meditation practice and problems connected with it: the nun Uttamā describes her teacher, Paṭācārā, as trustworthy (*saddhāyikā:* Thī 43). Upatissa says that someone who goes on the path without such a guide is like someone setting out alone on a distant journey, or an elephant without a goad. The good friend, however, is compared variously to an elephant trainer, a good road, a doctor, rain from heaven, a nursing mother, a father, parents that protect their children or a teacher who guides his or her pupils. As suggested by the last analogy, he or she is to a certain extent identified with the teacher (*ācariya*), though as we see from this and the texts later on, a rather more companionable as well as independent relationship is being described. A stress on seclusion in Buddhist texts is constantly balanced by a sense of the community: loving-kindness towards the local *saṅgha*, the community of monks where one is staying, for instance, is recommended by Buddhagosa as a practice suitable for everyone; he also suggests the meditation on death (28), with its solitary implications, as an accompaniment to this (see Vism III 58). As an antidote to each one of the hindrances to meditation, one text recommends contact with a good friend and identifies one of the stages in meditation practice when a teacher is likely to be needed.[23] The Buddha often visits struggling meditators after perceiving their problems with the 'divine eye', such as in a text in Chapter 3, where he recommends to Moggallāna various methods for overcoming sloth and torpor (see A IV 84–8).

The early manuals describe how one should search for such a person. Upatissa suggests that one should find one of two kinds of 'merit fulfiller' (PF 49–50): someone who has understanding of the three 'baskets' of texts, or one who understands the seed of *kamma*, has beneficient worldly knowledge and knows the four noble truths. If such a person cannot be found one should go to a friend who has seven qualities, listed in one of the texts in Chapter 2 of this book.[24] Buddhaghosa says that one should look for a teacher who is an arahat, failing that a non-returner, and so on down to the ordinary man who has attained *jhāna*, or, lastly, one who is familiar with one group of texts. His final words, suggesting the need for some pragmatism whatever the situation, give a helpful 'bottom line': 'Hence the ancient elders said three times "One who is conscientious will guard it" ' (Vism III 64/PP 100).[25]

Some protections are provided within the canon against the misuse of the position of teacher. Monastic rules forbid any monk from taking money for any activity, including teaching.[26] This rule extends in practice to lay teaching too, and while donations may and usually are given for the upkeep of the monastery, rental of a room and for its own sake, teachers themselves do not accept money for what they do. The fourth *Vinaya parājika*, which regards wrongful boasting about one's spiritual attainment as an offence for a monk or nun as radical as stealing or sexual intercourse also tends, in theory at least, to guard against spiritual 'one-upmanship'.[27] In practice this has meant that most monks are reluctant to lay claims to any spiritual attainment: it is striking that experienced meditation teachers avoid overt mention of the success or level of their own spiritual practice. This may sound enigmatic, for all kinds of reports inevitably circulate about different teachers, but it does mean that grand claims can be regarded with suspicion. If a teacher claims enlightenment, requests a large donation or promises enlightenment after a six-week course, he or she is unlikely to be acting in the Buddhist tradition!

In practice, confidentiality is another characteristic of the way meditation instruction is given. This is not formally prescribed by the canon, though it is implied: the *Sīgalovāda-Sutta* says of friendship in general that the mark of a good friend is that he or she does not betray secrets (see D III 187). It is assumed, however, throughout the East that discussion with one's meditation teacher is confidential and that a sense of privacy will be maintained. An ex-monk told me that he could have been in the next-door room to another for years and not even know that person's *kammaṭṭhāna*.[28]

The commentaries also outline ways that the person wishing to learn meditation should look after and honour teachers in a monastic context; teachers are accorded great respect to this day in the east.[29] Early Buddhism, however, was unusual in its attitude towards the place of the teacher. Theravāda Buddhism is not a 'guru' tradition: the practitioner takes refuge in the Triple Gem (21–4) when he or she wishes to develop meditation, either as a monk, in which case the ordination procedure follows, or as a lay person, in which case the practitioner undertakes the five precepts (see Khantipālo 1981: 142). This does not indicate any lack of respect for the role of teacher but rather the importance attached to the *dhamma* as something to be known 'by the wise'. According to Buddhaghosa, it should be visible not 'in the way that an ornament on another's head is, but rather it is visible only in one's own mind' (Vism VII 85/PP 235). But a teacher is needed to help this to happen, rather like a singing teacher would be needed to train a voice, or a good friend might be particularly helpful over a problem period in one's life.

Vajirañāṇa writes: 'It is for beginners especially that association with a teacher is an indispensable support; for the immediate success of meditation is largely due to a capable teacher who is a guide on the path of emancipation' (BMTP 97). Perhaps the main point to emerge from the atmosphere created by the texts in this anthology is that the relationship with the teacher and others following the path needs to have good heart. The teacher should, to a certain extent, be a friend; one's friends on the path are, to a certain extent, one's teachers. In one *sutta*, Ānanda suggests to the Buddha that having good friends is half the holy life. The Buddha disagrees, saying rather that 'good friendship, good companionship, good association are the entire holy life' (S I 89).

Laypeople and the practice of meditation

Another subject of interest to modern readers is that of lay practice. One of the most notable developments of the last twenty-five years of Buddhist practice has been the movement of Buddhism to the West, particularly through the practice of meditation.[30] A meditator today may well be a busy teacher, a businessman or a mother of young children trying to fit in a meditation practice as well as getting on with other daily affairs. For anyone in the position the question inevitably arises: is there any counterpart to my own way of practising in the canon? Does the Buddha address any of his teachings on meditation specifically to the laity?

The first thing that needs to be said is that the Buddha considered the monastic life as the best way to practise meditation: the general assumption in the texts is that the meditator is a monk. The 'open air' of the holy life is free from the 'path of dust' of the lay life (see S V 351). Lay practice, conversely, has traditionally been associated with keeping the precepts, generosity, treating one's family and friends with care and finding mindfulness and pleasure in daily business.[31] A favourite text throughout Buddhist countries, specifically addressed to the laity, the *Sigālovāda-Sutta*, enjoins activities such as care for one's teachers, servants, spouses and relatives and suggests the best ways of fulfilling them.[32] There are also festive and devotional practices which are specifically lay, often peculiar to one country, that link to local customs and traditions: the classical dances in homage to the Triple Gem, for instance, are among the most courtly and graceful of Thai rituals, with homage paid in precise and expressive ways through each gesture *(mudrā)*. It is not performed in front of monks, who do not watch shows or dances, but their permission is asked first at festivals in temples when it is performed, which is on many ceremonial occasions. Songs or sung chants – for monks do not sing either – are composed and performed in Thailand as well by the laity. One monk formulated this sense of Buddhism as a creative enactment of principle as much as a philosophy in a different way: it is the duty of lay people to be happy and they tend to support the *saṅgha* much better when they are.

The lay life, although not considered the highest, is accorded deep respect. The *suttas* derive much of their life and practicality from similes regarding the skilful woodturner, goldsmith, cook and the herdsman, a landscape that reflects the underlying appreciation of the daily round of the laity who supported the work of the *saṅgha*.[33] The *saṅgha* are dependent on the laity for food, lodgings and sustenance, just as the laity need the *saṅgha* for teaching and encouragement. The lay practice of giving food and alms to monks and nuns creates a continued, enlivening exchange which is felt to give merit to all involved and whose vitality depends upon the dynamic between two different ways of life. Ceremonies such as a *dāna*, in which food is offered to monks, require considerable mindfulness and attention to detail, and usually involve chanting as well. As is discussed in Chapter 8, separating the benefits of such activities from the first six recollections (21–6) is not always easy or even desirable, for the texts place considerable emphasis on bringing awareness into daily life and establishing a healthy starting point for the development of the mind. Within the *saṅgha* also it is certainly not the case that all monks and nuns practise meditation: a separate point, but one that indicates the difficulties involved in quantifying what is often a personal and little discussed affair.[34]

From the evidence of the *suttas*, many lay practitioners at the time of the Buddha did practise meditation. In the *Kandaraka-Sutta* the lay son of an elephant tamer, Pessa, says, 'From time to time, sir, we lay people, dressed in white, also abide with our minds well established in these four foundations of mindfulness' (M I 340). Some practices, such as mindfulness at all times, are frequently recommended in all bodily activities in daily life. In one instance concerning a layman, the cultivation of *jhāna* is explicitly mentioned. The householder (*gahapatī*) Citta, considered by the Buddha pre-eminent amongst his lay followers in teaching the *dhamma*, discusses his own proficiency in all eight *jhānas*.[35] He is elsewhere praised as one of the chiefs of laymen: he was a stream-enterer and never became a monk, attaining enlightenment on his deathbed.[36] Indeed the list in which Citta is cited as the foremost teacher amongst the laity, which occurs at the beginning of the *Aṅguttaranikāya*, is a good source for us to gain some sort of picture of the spread of the practice of *bhāvanā* at the time of the Buddha. The Buddha names members of all the four assemblies of monks, nuns, male and female layfollowers, who have pre-eminence in some area (*etadaggaṃ*). The list assigns the greatest number of pre-eminences to the first category of monks, less to the other assemblies.[37] The lay followers are frequently praised for lay excellences, such as that of almsgiving and generosity, but meditators do feature. The laymen include Citta, while the women include Sāmāvatī, pre-eminent amongst women who practise loving-kindness (*mettāvihārīnaṃ*), and Uttarā, foremost amongst those with meditative power (*jhāyinaṃ*). In both lay assemblies, there is one pre-eminent in unwavering confidence (*aveccapasannānaṃ*). Monks and nuns may have been in a better position to practise meditation and take the exercise to a higher level, but lay people were not completely excluded.

Early Buddhist discourses on meditation are routinely introduced with the address *bhikkhave*; the meditator is described throughout in the masculine form as a monk. But the use of the word *bhikkhu* does not exclude others, male or female, and seems to be a formal generic term based upon the most usual kind of practitioner. In one *sutta* the nun Dhammadinnā is questioned closely by the layman Visākha, who had once been her husband. Throughout this debate on meditation, even when discussing the state of cessation (*nirodha samāpatti*), she employs the usual *bhikkhu* (see M I 299–305). As an arahat, she would be talking from experience; at the end of the *sutta* her arguments are approved by the Buddha as those he would have put forward himself. The word *bhikkhu*, however, cannot apply either to her or her lay ex-husband. The commentary for the *Satipaṭṭhāna-Sutta* also recommends some general applicability for the term. Praising the people of Kuru, to whom the *sutta* is addressed, Buddhaghosa stresses that the instructions pertaining to *bhikkhus* are applicable to all four assemblies, which, he said, had been present when the *sutta* was delivered. Glossing the term *bhikkhave* he notes, 'he who follows the teaching, be he a shining one [*deva*] or a human, is indeed called a monk' (MA I 227/Soma 1981: 17–18).

Lay meditation in practice

So how much lay practice has occurred in the recent development of Buddhism? Both historically and geographically its incidence has never been quantified and has presumably varied: it has probably always needed a strong base of encouragement within the *saṅgha* in order to flourish. Certainly, there seems to be some cultural difference between Buddhist countries, though the situation may be changing now in response to Western interest. For instance in Sri Lanka, where folk tradition has held that the *dhamma* is in decline and that there are no arahats, the practice of meditation was, until recently, supposed to be forbiddingly difficult, a belief which seems to have promoted some cultural resistance to its pursuit.[38] Interestingly the situation has now changed, possibly in response to the large number of Westerners visiting Sri Lanka to learn meditation: many middle class lay people now visit monasteries for days of practice. A strong lay chanting tradition also exists. In Thailand, there have been popular meditation movements, particularly amongst the young, which suggest that meditation is a simple and natural process.[39] Burma seems to have a fairly active tradition of lay practice.[40] Which atmosphere produces more long-term meditators? Short meditation practices are given in schools in most Buddhist countries and we cannot know the extent to which these are followed in daily life or at a time of crisis, such as at the approach of death.

Amongst the old the practice of meditation seems always to have been encouraged, following the traditional Indian pattern of the *sannyāsin*, the one who leaves home at the fourth and last stage of life. In Sri Lanka, very old people, notably women, have always been a familiar sight on *poya* days in temples. In Thailand, groups of older laywomen like to go and sleep at a monastery for these days (*non-wat*). It is not exclusively a female activity, though a visitor to Thailand may gain that impression: some monasteries, particularly in forest areas, only allow men to stay. In modern times, and in the West, the practice of meditation is the aspect of the Buddha's teaching that has often attracted most initial interest. Clearly, without a native background in the Buddhist tradition, this involves some care that one consults with teachers and finds others who meditate. Ven. Buddhadāsa, one of the most highly regarded teachers of meditation in the last fifty years, was committed to teaching meditation to Western and Eastern laity as well as to the *saṅgha*:

> A growing number of people are practising *ānāpānasati* in some form, as well as other kinds of meditation, but do not always have regular access to qualified teachers. Everyone shares in the same joys and difficulties you meet with in your practice. To join with some of the many meditators – they are everywhere, even in your area – to form a sitting group will be of great benefit to you, not to mention to the wider community. Sitting groups need not be large. It isn't necessary that be 'Buddhists' or that everyone practice in the same way, as long as you sit quietly. The important things are mutual friendship, respect, and support, and that the groups meet regularly, say, once a week. Such groups can help keep you going when times are rough or your spirit is weak. Further, they are a source of the community or *saṅgha* that we all need, especially in our hyper-individualistic, alienated modern societies.
>
> (Buddhadāsa 1997: 127)

From the evidence of the texts the best way to practise meditation and to live as an arahat, or enlightened person, is as a monk, or a nun. According to the Buddha's own testimony, the evidence of the texts, and general practice in Buddhist countries, this does not exclude others from taking time off from the daily routine, finding the roots of a tree or some 'empty place' and practising meditation themselves:

> There are not only one hundred, Vaccha, or two, three, four or five hundred, but many more men layfollowers, disciples of mine, dressed in white, who enjoy the pleasures of the sense [and yet] carry out my instruction, listen to my advice, have gone beyond doubt, become free from uncertainty, have found complete confidence, and become independent of others in the dispensation of the teacher.
>
> (M I 491)

The formula is repeated for women lay followers.

Sitting posture

The canon can be surprisingly silent on some subjects: one striking omission is the issue of posture, a subject which probably prompts more initial questions than any other in someone new to meditation. While it is outside the scope of this book to discuss the practicalities of different modern meditation schools, which vary considerably in their attitude towards the actual posture to be used and the way the body should be held, it is useful to consider what few things the canon does offer us and what we can infer from more general remarks and assumptions.

The posture (*iriyāpatha*) advocated for most meditation practice is that of sitting, though all of the four postures of walking, sitting, lying-down and standing, are used on occasion and are mentioned in the texts. For the most part in modern practice where a meditation requires sustained attention and seclusion from daily activities, as in the practice of *jhāna*, the sitting posture is recommended. The *samādhi* posture shown in many Buddha images is cross-legged in a half-lotus or full-lotus position with the right hand resting gently upon the left on the lap. This is a stable posture, which after some practice can be maintained for a long time.

From a practical point of view when meditation is taught today, particularly in a Western context, care sometimes needs to be put into finding a way to sit that neither imposes too much strain nor encourages sleepiness. Modern Westerners and many modern Easterners do not routinely sit on the ground in the way that was taken for granted in ancient India. It is not even clear whether seats were used at all in ancient India, though one or two canonical references suggest that they did exist.[41] So the flexibility and strength in the lower part of the body that would have been taken for granted where most sitting was cross-legged, and where the most basic bodily functions are performed squatting, have often been lost. In Sri Lanka it is quite usual to sit on a stone floor without a mat for hours just listening to chanting: problems, where this habit has been ingrained from childhood, do not really arise. We do not know if people were given much advice about posture at the time of the Buddha: I have not been able to find much discussion of the matter. Buddhaghosa recommends a 'suitable posture'.[42] Instructions given in the *suttas* are sparse: that one should sit 'cross-legged' and 'with straight back'.[43] In the canon, this instruction is applied specifically only for breathing mindfulness, though from custom we can infer that it applies to other *jhāna* practices. For the most part a half-lotus, with the right foot tucked into the top of the left leg and the left foot on the ground, is recommended or, if this is impossible, a cross-legged position – perhaps with a cushion.[44] Other variations include sitting with legs folded to one side, which is particularly popular with women in Thailand. Different traditions of meditation emphasize different elements of bodily posture: the position of the hands and whether for instance the eyes are closed, which is more common, open or half open, can vary according to the type of meditation. In *samatha* meditation the right hand is usually placed over the left on the lap in the classic *samādhi* posture; in Zen practice the left hand tends to be placed over the right.

For meditative exercises that can be carried out during daily activities, which are not exclusively associated with *jhāna* practice, such as the recollections (*anussatis*) and the practice of mindfulness and clear comprehension in daily life, all postures may be used. The recollections in particular tend to be taught as part of a walking practice.[45] Insight practices are also sometimes associated with walking. We often hear in the texts of the Buddha or his monks walking up and down as a practice, interspersed with the other postures.[46] Walking meditations, interspersed with sitting practices, are practised using a set length of walking space. The object may be the recollections, but is also commonly the act of walking itself; for instance observing the sensation and flow of the rise and fall of the foot as it moves, which is regarded as a practice in itself. Although we do not know exactly what practices were associated with this posture at the time of the Buddha, there are many references to monks walking with mindfulness, and the *Satipaṭṭhāna-Sutta* emphasizes arousing mindfulness and clear comprehension at all times in all postures (M I 56–7). There are a number of practical advantages in a walking meditation: it is less intense than a sitting posture, ensures that the meditator does not neglect physical exercise and that there is some variety in a day of meditation.[47] The Buddha recommends it, for instance, to Moggallāna when he is suffering from the hindrance of sloth and torpor.[48]

The posture of lying-down is also described in the canon. It is undertaken by lying on the right side and is also recommended by the Buddha to Moggallāna as a means of overcoming sloth and torpor.[49] In the *Mahāsaccaka-Sutta*, the Buddha is criticized for having a rest during the day. He defends this on the grounds that in hot weather, 'mindful and clearly comprehending, I fall asleep on my right side' (M I 249). Obviously most of us associate this posture with having a nap, but it can suggest alertness and readiness too. There is a particular quality of restful attentiveness and, surprisingly, energy that may be seen in statues of reclining Buddhas: the reclining figures at Wat Po in Bangkok and at Polonnoruwa in Sri Lanka are particularly fine examples of this. In these examples, the posture is used to show the Buddha at the approach of death, his *parinibbāna*.

The standing posture is not mentioned separately as a meditative posture in the canon. After the enlightenment, however, the Buddha is said by the *Jātaka* commentary to have stood in contemplation of the Bodhi tree (see Ja I 77). The authority and sense of reassuring ease suggested by this pose can be seen in examples of standing Buddha images to be found in temples in the East. The Buddha image carved in granite at the rock shrine at Polonnaruwa in Sri Lanka, which is over seven metres tall, is an impressive example of the tranquillity that may be communicated by this. The arms, as is usual in depictions of this pose after the enlightenment, are crossed gently below the chest.[50] Other standing Buddhas show gestures such as holding a hand out in front of the body with the palm faced out, in the *abhāyā mudrā*, associated with dispelling fear.

Ānanda, the reassuringly imperfect follower of the Buddha, famously attained enlightenment in none of these postures. A post-canonical story about his enlightenment relates that he was banned from attending the First Council after the Buddha's death as he had not attained the goal, and only arahats were permitted to attend. Ānanda, desperate to take part, made repeated attempts to progress, but was so unsuccessful that he gave up and admitted failure the day before the meeting. That night, he gained enlightenment while getting into bed: this was, according to the commentators, technically neither the lying-down nor the standing posture. This story is constantly told to this day as encouragement to those experiencing difficulty in meditation who feel like giving up; it may also be taken as a reminder not to take forms of these things too seriously.[51]

Compared to other traditions of practice Buddhist meditation schools maintain a low-key attitude towards the position of the body in meditation. It is possible that the yogic use of posture in the Indian subcontinent is very ancient: Harappan tiles show a figure in a cross-legged posture, with toes just touching. It is not quite the same as the classic *samādhi* pose, but suggests the great antiquity of experimentation with posture in ancient India.[52] Many yogic traditions explore the complexity of posture in a way that is not found in Theravāda Buddhist meditative practice.[53] One writer suggests that the lack of prescriptive advice about posture from the Buddha was a response to the extreme harshness of much contemporary asceticism.[54]

From the meditator's point of view what is important is that for a sitting practice a clear adoption of a posture, in reasonable seclusion, helps to mark the beginning and end of a meditation sitting, and so contributes in the preparatory stage to the process of settling the mind. For this, the half-lotus is the most stable, but may need a bit of daily practice to become comfortable.[55] And as a reminder against harshness, it is worth remembering that the Buddha did not advocate self-mortification. The fact that the postures are so often mentioned as a group of four assumes that change of posture in the course of the day and frequent movement between different postures is to be encouraged. The Buddha on several occasions asked Ānanda or Sāriputta to give a talk on his behalf when he had backache, so that he could lie down.[56] We can infer from such detail that it is better not to strain the body: the middle way between two extremes presumably applies also to the efforts of modern meditators struggling to find a practicable way to sit with a firm basis on the ground.

Samatha and *vipassanā*

We should, finally, consider kinds of practice. The two main strands of modern meditation practice in Buddhism are calm (*samatha*) and insight (*vipassanā*). *Samatha* is usually equated with concentration (*samādhi*) and the purification of the emotions. *Jhāna*, the meditation state that is the product of concentration is derived from the word *jhāyeti*, to meditate, and is regarded as a landmark in the development of calm.[57] The factors present in the first *jhāna* are initial thought (*vitakka*), sustained thought or examining (*vicāra*), joy (*pīti*), happiness (*sukha*) and one-pointedness (*ekaggatā*). From the *Abhidhamma* point of view these can be present in any activities in daily life where there is interest, collectedness and some vitality, even those as mundane as playing tennis, washing the car or doing the garden: the mind and body are engaged, there is a sense of pleasure and a wish to do what one is doing (DhS 7–11). In meditation, they can be developed further, in seclusion, to become factors that become strong enough to direct and guide the mind to the meditation object and the first *jhāna*. Here the hindrances that characterize much of our experience are temporarily abandoned, and it is possible to see the potential of the mind when it comes to settle on a single object. Only after Gotama remembers this unificatory state does he become sufficiently refreshed and balanced to abandon excessive asceticism; he practises all eight *jhānas* on the night of his enlightenment. The first is regarded as the healthy basis for the others, which are nearly always mentioned in order after it: the four, and sometimes eight, are usually described as a progression.[58] As the mind becomes more settled four of the five factors are gradually dropped, so that the second loses initial and sustained thought, the third, joy and the fourth, happiness. The fourth *jhāna*, characterized by equanimity and one-pointedness, is the point from where it is possible to develop the higher powers of the mind (*iddhis*), the further four formless *jhānas*, which examine the nature of the attention that is placed on the meditation object, or to develop insight. Eight *jhānas* are usually described but there is a ninefold system too: the *Abhidhamma* method describes a second *jhāna* where there is *vicāra* but no *vitakka*.[59] As Cousins has shown, the extent to which *jhāna* is developed before insight and vice versa varies according to temperament and school of meditation (see Cousins 1984a: 56–66). Many variations and combinations are indicated in canonical texts.

According to the commentaries, some *samatha* practices are aimed at the attainment of *jhāna*, and some are intended to arouse the factors associated with it in a general way in daily life.[60] Some of the *anussatis* (21–6), for instance, are not necessarily linked to a secluded practice or *jhāna*. Others, such as the *kasiṇas* (1–10) and the *asubhas* (11–20), require a sustained attention that needs seclusion and tend to be practised in a monastic context or on a period of extended meditation practice. Breathing mindfulness (29) and body mindfulness (28) can be developed in daily life and as a *jhāna* practice. Mindfulness of body is said to lead to the first *jhāna* if pursued as a *samatha* practice and mindfulness of the breath to four *jhānas*. The cultivation of the *brahmavihāras* (31–4) in activities in the world is encouraged but they may be developed as a *jhāna* practice too. Neither the perception of loathsomeness in food (39) nor that of the defining of the four elements (40) is said by the commentaries to lead to *jhāna*. The formless realms (35–8) actually comprise the fifth to the eighth *jhānas*. As this short summary suggests, there is great variety and scope amongst the meditation subjects; each is assigned according to temperamental needs and each are considered in turn in this anthology, both from a canonical point of view and from that of traditional practice. The approaches even within one broad heading vary considerably. For most *samatha* meditation, though, of whatever kind, a sitting practice separated from daily business is usually recommended. All the practises outlined in this anthology are considered ways of arousing the enlightenment factors and making the mind concentrated (*samahita*), manageable (*kammanīya*) and purified (*parisuddha*): the comparison is sometimes made to gold, which when purified and molten can be shaped in any way (see S V 92–3).

Insight meditation is concerned with the area of the mind associated with identification or perception (*saññā*). It works on ignorance and the *saṅkharā*, formations or volitional activities, through the way that the world is viewed and understood. The three signs of impermanence (*anicca*), unsatisfactoriness (*dukkha*) and not-self (*anattā*) are considered. There is sometimes less emphasis on sitting practice. As we shall see from the texts discussed here, elements of both characterize many of the *kammaṭṭhānas* and both are encouraged. In practice, there may be important points at which the emphasis of a school that is predominantly *samatha* based may differ from one that is predominantly *vipassanā*. A *samatha* school tends to encourage the development of calm and joy first, while a *vipassanā* one may put more emphasis on letting go and insight: *samatha* is sometimes today called the 'wet' way and *vipassanā* the 'dry'. Cousins has shown there is a 'real difference in approach between the individual who works from the side of *samatha* and one who adopts pure insight as his vehicle. This seems to be partly a matter of what is helpful or natural to an individual of a particular temperament or character type and partly a matter of personal predilection'.[61]

The moment of path is described by the *Abhidhamma* as a moment of *jhāna*, and so necessarily has an element of *samatha*, though it is above the world (*lokuttara*), and frees the mind at that time irrevocably from some defilements (see DhS 277–364). At this point, there is a union of *samatha* and *vipassanā* practice. Ajahn Chah, the greatly revered modern meditation teacher from the forest tradition of Thailand, said,

> Meditation is like a plank of wood. Let's say *vipassanā* is one end of the plank and *samatha* is the other. If you were to pick the plank up, would just one end come up or would both of them? Of course, when you pick up the plank, both ends come up together. What is *vipassanā*? What is *samatha*? They are the mind itself.
>
> (Chah: 1998)

It seems that anyone who practises meditation needs calm and insight. Both ways of practice need mindfulness, the quality of alertness and clear comprehension. The helpfulness of the company of others, some seclusion and some work on *sīla*, good behaviour in the world, are also constantly reiterated. As if to encourage adaptability and a sense of appropriateness to the person and occasion one text describes four times or seasons: 'hearing *dhamma* at the right time, discussion of *dhamma* at the right time, *samatha* at the right time, *vipassanā* at the right time' (A II 141).

2

MEDITATION

Introductory texts

In this chapter a variety of texts have been chosen to communicate a flavour of the early Buddhist attitude towards meditation and to demonstrate the range of genres and approaches associated with it.

Enlightenment (1)

This verse is taken from a collection of utterances made by, or to, elder monks. Cittaka was given a meditation object by the Buddha, which he then went and developed in a lonely woodland. It is uttered on his attainment of enlightenment and, like many of the verses of the elders, communicates a delight and appreciation of the natural world that seems heightened rather than diminished by the attainment of freedom.[1] The trumpeting of peacocks makes the most extraordinary din: it is a beautiful but full-blooded image.

Cittaka
Blue, with beautiful necks, crested peacocks fill Karambiya with sound; playing in the cool breeze they awaken the listener to meditation!

(Th 22)

Enlightenment (2)

Sirivaḍḍha came from a rich family in Rājagaha and, after seeing the Buddha, joined the order to meditate in a forest. At the breaking of a storm, cooled by the rain, he is able to attain enlightenment. The story associated with this verse introduces us to a feature to be found in many forms of Buddhism, the surprise event or shock in the outside world that brings a meditation state to fruition. Part of the work of meditation is methodical, such as regular practice and getting the instructions right. Another part is waiting for the moment: some vivid lines in the *Therīgāthā* for instance describe the nun Paṭacārā gaining enlightenment as she pulls down the wick and extinguishes the flame of a lamp.[2] Commentarial stories to the *Dhammapada* also give us many accounts of a balance coming about through a surprise change in events.[3] In some schools the external cause comes to be regarded as a necessary preliminary to enlightenment.[4]

Sirivaḍḍha
Lightning flashes strike upon the cleft of both Vebhāra and Paṇḍava, but in the cleft in the trees, the son of the incomparable one pursues his meditation.

(Th 41)

Enlightenment (3)

These verses come from a companion collection to the one mentioned earlier, which contains some of the earliest religious texts in the world composed by women.[5] Spoken by nuns or addressed to them, the verses show that in early Buddhist texts women are described as attaining enlightenment, uttering spontaneous verses on the basis of that and, as described in the verses here, teaching meditation too. Uttamā's past lives are described by the commentary: she is reborn variously as a servant, a *deva*, a queen and, in this lifetime, in a banker's family.[6] She attains enlightenment after practising for seven days on the instructions of Paṭācārā, a nun who arouses faith in her (*saddhāyikā*: ThīA 48–9).[7] The verses suggest liberation neatly through the physical detail of stretching the legs after the extended period of cross-legged practice that has accompanied the attainment of enlightenment. No one is of course advised to sit for seven days now, but the ease and release of that moment will be recognizable to everyone who has tried a sitting practice.

Uttamā
42. Four times and five times I left the place where I was staying;
I could not find peace of mind and had no control over the mind.
43. I approached a nun whom I could trust.
She taught me the *dhamma*: the aggregates, the sense spheres and the elements.
44. I listened to the *dhamma* from her while she instructed me.
For seven days I sat in one cross-legged position, possessed by joy and happiness.
On the eighth day I stretched my legs, having destroyed the great mass of darkness.

(Thī 42–5)

Seclusion

This extract is taken from the *Itivuttaka*, a collection of 112 short discourses of the Buddha, in both poetry and prose. According to the commentarial tradition, the collection was made by the woman disciple Khujjuttarā, a servant of Sāmāvatī, queen of King Udena. After encountering the Buddha she becomes a stream-enterer and makes a practice of going to hear the Buddha's sermons, which she would then repeat to all the women in the palace.[8] The statements at the beginning and the end of the *sutta*, found in each of the discourses, were apparently inserted by the girl, to emphasize that she was not their author: hence the title to the collection of *Itivuttaka*, 'this is what was said'.[9] The collection, which provides us with some useful and concise texts for those interested in meditation, is grouped numerically, like the *Aṅguttaranikāya*, with this piece being taken from the book of 'twos'. As is the case with many key concepts in Buddhism, the idea of seclusion has levels of association ranging from the literal and physical, in the 'empty places' recommended for practice, to the spiritual. The word used here, *paṭisallāna*, is explained by the commentary as the physical solitude (*kāyaviveka*) which is suggested as a prerequisite of meditation, though the emphasis of the poem appears to include a meditative seclusion, in the freedom from senses and freedom from the factors leading to rebirth too.[10]

The seclusion sutta
'Live enjoying seclusion, monks; live delighting in seclusion, engage in practising the calming of the mind, do not neglect meditation, possess insight and frequent empty places. If you live enjoying seclusion, monks, live delighting in seclusion, engage in practising the calming of the mind, do not neglect meditation, possess insight, and frequent empty places one of two fruits is to expected: final knowledge here and now or, if there is some residual defilement, the state of non-return.'

The Exalted One explained the meaning and this was said too:

'Those who, with a mind calmed, discerning,
Are mindful and practise meditation,
See what is true with insight,
Disregarding sense pleasures.

Those who, with mind calmed, delight in carefulness,
And see danger in carelessness,
Are incapable of falling away:
They are surely close to *nibbāna*.'

This is the meaning of what was said by the Exalted One: so I have heard.
(It 39–40)

Meditation

The 423 verses of the *Dhammapada* are the most famous formulation of the Buddha's teaching, giving a distillation of theory and practice which has repeatedly challenged the skills of translators in many languages. Many of the verses occur elsewhere in the canon; some arise from a store of Indian folklore and wisdom that found its way into other texts such as the *Mahābhārata*.[11] A commentarial story is associated with the circumstances leading to the recital of each verse or group of verses: these pleasingly intricate tales often exhibit narrative twists that give context and meaning to the verses.[12] The verses here are pronounced on the occasion of the conversion of a group of 900 cunning thieves, who have been plotting to break and enter a heavily fortified house. Successful in their aim, they are amazed at the aplomb of the woman owner of the house, who carries on listening to her son giving a *dhamma* talk while they conduct their business. This practical vindication of the efficacy of Buddhist teachings at first terrifies and then converts them: they all decide to change their livelihood and ask the son to ordain them as monks. Each is given a meditation subject, each goes out to the mountain nearby, finds his own tree under which to meditate and each sets about his task. The Buddha, perceiving with divine vision what has happened, sends an image of himself to teach: these are four of nine verses he pronounces after the thieves have left the house to practise meditation. The image of the house is imbued with associations, metaphorical and literal, within the Buddhist tradition. The one who goes forth leaves the house behind; the house is also frequently employed as a means of communicating the idea of the body, personality and 'self'. When the Buddha becomes enlightened he exclaims that he has found and destroyed the 'builder of the house'.[13]

Verses from the 'Monks Chapter'

Meditate, monk! Do not be careless. Do not let your mind whirl in the strand of sensual pleasures. Do not, being careless, swallow a lead ball. As you burn do not cry out 'O, this is suffering!'

There is no meditation in one who is without wisdom, no wisdom in one who does not meditate. In whom there are both meditation and wisdom: he is, indeed, close to *nibbāna*.

When a monk has gone into an empty place, and has calmed his mind, experiences a delight that transcends that of men, seeing the *dhamma* truly.

Whenever he reflects upon the rise and fall of the aggregates, he obtains joy and gladness. To those who know, that is the deathless.

(Dhp 371–4)

Starting meditation

This famous text emphasizes some basic points regarded to this day as essential prerequisites for anyone wishing to practise meditation, in any tradition. Much of its subtlety lies in the craft of its construction and the Buddha's tactful treatment of a novice: Meghiya's first request for permission to go to Jantugāma for alms is given immediately and he is told do as he thinks fit; the second request, for permission to go and meditate in the mango grove, is cautiously granted only after it has been made three times. The reasons for this reticence soon become clear. There is no other monk in the grove where Meghiya hopes to meditate, he has not asked for help and does not yet know what to do. Meghiya himself is soon appalled that, despite his faith, he is beset by various kinds of sensual, malevolent and cruel thoughts (*kāmavitakka, vyāpādavitakka, vihiṃsāvitakka*) and returns to question the Buddha. The Buddha says that five things are needed for 'ripening' (*paripākāya*) what is 'unripe' when 'deliverance of mind' (*cetovimuttiyā*) is immature: a good friend, keeping *sīla* (the *Pātimokkha*, or the monastic code), talk which opens the heart and leads to the path, purpose and wisdom. These last four may be expected in one who finds the first.

Having fulfilled these five conditions, four more must be cultivated or 'made to become by him' (*bhāvetabbā*): reflection on foulness (11–20), to abandon desire; on *mettā* (31) to abandon ill-will (*byāpādassa*); on mindfulness of the breath (29) to cut off distraction (*vitakkupacchedāya*), and the thought of impermanence to uproot the conceit 'I am' (*asmimānasamugghātāya*). The commentarial story concerning this passage relates that Meghiya had, in a former lifetime, ruled as king from that very mango grove. By returning to the particular site of his former palace he has laid himself open, as the Buddha had presumably anticipated, to fantasies of all the beautiful dancing girls he had known there and to memories of the acts of cruelty he had perpetrated during his reign. The commentary, noting that his mind had become engulfed by these restless recollections says 'thus it was that he became encircled, surrounded, by unskilled thoughts as might a tree by a network of creepers or a hive by honey bees' (Masefield 1994b: II 569).

So the *sutta* introduces the idea of the need for a good friend who can give direction, help and encouragement in meditation: trying to meditate without help and guidance, as in the case here, can just be sterile and frustrating. This starting point is also closely linked in the tradition to the way that meditation subjects are particularly chosen to suit temperament. Although, as we have seen, this is systematized according to types in the *Mahāniddesa* and by the commentators Buddhaghosa and Upatissa, the canonical *suttas* give patterns for this.[14] This *sutta* is also representative of the *manner* in which meditation subjects are often given in the canon, with a small group of subjects suggested to a particular person to encourage and develop different faculties and deal with different problems. Such groups of subjects vary enormously, presumably because the problems of many different temperaments are being addressed. Such an approach provides some variety of method for the meditator and also possibly prevents potential imbalances: the meditation on the foul (11–20) and the perception of loathsomeness in food (39), for instance, are almost always given accompanied by other practices, as we shall see in the sections of this anthology that concern them. A radically different slant to a particular practice may also be given simply by context, as seen in this anthology in the section on the practice of the four elements within the body (40).[15]

This is worth noting when considering apparent 'inconsistencies' in the Buddha's method.[16] The fact that the Buddha often assigns a selection of meditation practices, when addressing particular people, suggests that from the earliest days of the tradition meditation practices were perceived and given rather like medicines might be, intended to act with one another, or complementing one another. It is always worth taking into account the context in which a practice is given in any discourse.

This text is taken from the *Udāna*, a collection whose *suttas* end with an 'inspired utterance'.

Meghiya sutta[17]

Thus have I heard. At one time the Exalted One was staying at Cālikā on Cālikā Hill. At that time the Venerable Meghiya was the Exalted One's attendant. And Meghiya approached the Exalted One, and after paying homage to him stood to one side and said, 'I wish to go into Jantugāma to collect alms, sir'. The Exalted One replied, 'Do now, Meghiya, what you think fit'.

Then Meghiya, when he had put on his robe in the morning, took his bowl and outer robe with him and went into Jantugāma to perform the almsround. After he had eaten he returned from the almsround and approached the bank of River Kimikālā. As he was strolling and wandering up and down on the bank of the river to stretch his legs he saw a delightful and pleasing mango grove. On seeing it he thought, 'This mango grove is very delightful and pleasing. It is just the right place for a man of good family to put in some effort to pursue his aims. If the Exalted One were to give me permission, I would come and put in some effort in this mango grove.'

Then Meghiya went up to the Exalted One, and after paying homage to him, sat down to one side and said, 'Sir, when I had put on my robe . . . I saw a delightful and pleasing mango grove. On seeing it I thought, "This mango grove is very delightful and pleasing. It is just the right place for a man of good family to make an effort to pursue his aims. If the Exalted One were to give me permission, I would come and make some effort in this mango grove." '

When he had said this, the Exalted One replied, 'We are on our own, Meghiya, so stay until some other monk arrives'.

A second time Meghiya spoke, saying, 'The Exalted One has nothing more that needs doing and there is nothing to add to what he has done . . . . If the Exalted One were to give me permission, I'd go and put in some effort in that mango grove.'

When he had said this, the Exalted One replied, 'We are on our own, Meghiya, so stay until some other monk arrives'.

A third time Meghiya spoke, saying, 'The Exalted One has nothing more that needs doing . . . . If the Exalted One were to give me permission, I'd go and put in some effort in that mango grove.'

'What can I say to you, Meghiya, when you announce that you would like to put in some effort? Do now, Meghiya, what you think fit.'

And so Meghiya rose from his seat, paid homage to the Exalted One, and keeping his right side towards him, entered into the mango grove. And when he had got there he sat down at the foot of a certain tree to spend the time for rest in the middle of the day.

But when Meghiya was staying at the mango grove, he was beleaguered by the three kinds of harmful, unskilful thoughts: thoughts of sensuality, thoughts of ill-will and thoughts of cruelty.

Meghiya then reflected, 'Well, it is extraordinary! It is amazing! Although I have gone forth out of faith from home into the homeless state, even so I am dogged by these three kinds of harmful, unskilful thoughts: thoughts of sensuality, thoughts of ill-will and thoughts of cruelty.' Then Meghiya emerged from seclusion in the late afternoon, approached the Exalted One and after prostrating and sitting to one side, said, 'When I was staying at that mango grove I was beleaguered by the three kinds of harmful, unskilful thoughts: thoughts of sensuality, thoughts of ill-will and thoughts of cruelty. And I reflected, "Well, it is extraordinary! It is amazing! Although I have gone forth out of faith from home into the homeless state, even so I am dogged by these three kinds of harmful, unskilful thoughts: thoughts of sensuality, thoughts of ill will and thoughts of cruelty." '

'When deliverance of the mind is not yet ripe five things lead to its ripening. What are they?

'Here a monk has a good friend, a good companion, a good comrade. This is the first thing that leads to the ripening of deliverance of mind when it is unripe.

'Furthermore a monk is virtuous, lives restrained by the restraint of his code (*Pātimokkha*), is endowed with good conduct and a good resort, sees danger in even the smallest fault and trains himself in the training rules he has accepted. This is the second thing that leads to the ripening of deliverance of mind when it is unripe.

'Furthermore a monk engages in talk concerned with austerity, which is a help in opening the heart, which conduces to complete turning away, dispassion, cessation, peace, knowledge, awakening, *nibbāna*: talk about wanting little, about contentment, about seclusion, about keeping to oneself, about stirring energy, about virtue, about concentration, about wisdom, about deliverance, about the knowledge and vision of deliverance. Such talk he obtains when he wishes for it, without difficulty and without trouble. This is the third thing that leads to the ripening of deliverance of mind when it is unripe.

'Furthermore a monk lives with energy stirred, abandoning unskilful states, arousing states that are skilful; he is steadfast, vigorous and persevering with regard to skilful states. This is the fourth thing that leads to the ripening of deliverance of mind when it is unripe.

'Furthermore a monk is wise, is endowed with the noble wisdom that sees into the arising and falling away of phenomena, penetrating the way to the complete destruction of suffering. This is the fifth thing that leads to the ripening of deliverance of mind when it is unripe. When deliverance of the mind is not yet ripe these five things lead to its ripening.

'It is to be expected that a monk who has a good friend, a good companion, a good comrade will be virtuous . . . that a monk who is virtuous will engage in talk concerned with austerity, that helps in opening the heart . . . that a monk who engages in talk concerned with austerity that helps in opening the heart will live with energy stirred . . . that a monk who lives with energy stirred will be wise, endowed with the noble wisdom that sees into the arising and falling away of phenomena, penetrating the way to the complete destruction of suffering.

'When a monk is well grounded in these five things he should also cultivate four more: he should cultivate the meditation on the foul to overcome desire; he should cultivate loving-kindness to overcome ill-will; he should cultivate breathing mindfulness to cut off distracting thoughts and he should cultivate the perception of impermanence for the removal of the conceit "I am". In one who perceives impermanence, the perception of not-self becomes established. And the one who perceives not-self attains the removal of the conceit "I am" and finds *nibbāna* in this very life.'

And the Exalted One, understanding the matter, gave forth this inspired utterance:

'Petty thoughts, subtle thoughts,
Follow into exhilaration for the mind.
The wandering mind rushes from one existence to the next.

Knowing these thoughts in the mind,
Ardent and mindful, he restrains them;
These thoughts that follow into exhilaration:
The awakened one forsakes them.'

(Ud 34–7)

The good friend

This short *sutta* introduces the idea of the good friend in conjunction with the enlightenment factors, qualities that both lead to and characterize the awakened mind.[18] These factors, which occur as a list in the thirty-seven constituents of enlightenment (*bodhipakkhiyādhammā*), are considered of particular importance in the development of meditation. The *Saṃyuttanikāya*, the collection from which this is taken, is composed of a series of texts which are meshed together through slight variations on themes in a kind of woven pattern: it is difficult to ascertain where one ends and one begins.[19] Within this *saṃyutta*, or section, they are juxtaposed against the hindrances which obstruct meditation practice as positive attributes to be cultivated as much as the hindrances are to be suppressed. Merely the mention of each one in turn is said to release an arahat from physical sickness.[20] They describe reserves which, through meditation, can be made available to the mind when they are needed: they are, for instance, compared to a wardrobe of different coloured clothes, which a king or a royal minister can choose to wear at different times of day (see S V 71–2). The commentary to the *Vibhaṅga* says that they are present both in *lokiya jhāna* – the 'worldly' meditations described in this volume – and in the *jhāna* associated with enlightenment itself (*lokuttara*).[21] In the *Bojjhaṅgasaṃyutta* it is said that if the mind is too passive and sluggish it can be roused by investigation of *dhamma*, effort and joy; if over-energized or excited it can be stilled by tranquillity, concentration and equanimity. It concludes with the first item in the list: 'But mindfulness, monks, I say is always useful' (S V 115).

The simile of the sun

Just as, monks, the dawn is the forerunner and herald of the sun, so too, monks, for a monk, good friendship is the forerunner and herald of the arising of the seven factors of enlightenment. When a monk has a good friend, it is to be expected that he will develop and cultivate the seven factors of enlightenment.

And how does a monk who has a good friend cultivate and make much of the seven factors of enlightenment? Here, monks, a monk develops the enlightenment factor that is mindfulness, which is based upon seclusion, dispassion, and cessation, maturing in release... he develops the enlightenment factor that is investigation of *dhammas*.... that is strength... that is joy... that is tranquillity... that is concentration... that is equanimity, which is based upon seclusion, dispassion and cessation, maturing in release. It is in this way, monks, that a monk who has a good friend cultivates and makes much of the seven factors of enlightenment.

(S V 78)

The second training sutta

This was said by the Exalted One, spoken by the arahat, so I have heard.

'For a monk who is a learner, monks, who has not attained perfection but lives aspiring for the unsurpassable security from bondage, I do not perceive another single factor, in regard to outside conditions, that is so helpful as good friendship. Monks, a monk who has a good friend abandons what is unskilful and develops what is skilful.' The Exalted One explained the meaning and this was said too:

'When a monk has good friends,
And is reverent and respectful,

Following his friends' advice,
Clearly comprehending and mindful,
He may, step by step, attain
The destruction of all of the fetters'.
This is the meaning of what was said by Exalted One: so I have heard.
(It 10–11)

Companionship

This group of verses is ascribed to the arahat Mahānāga, who is said to have admonished six monks famous for their contempt for their fellows.[22]

Mahānāga
The one who is not respectful to his companions in the holy life
wastes away in the *dhamma*, like a fish in little water.
The one who is not respectful to his companions in the holy life
Fails to grow in the *dhamma*, like a rotten seed in a field.
The one who is not respectful to his companions in the holy life,
is far from *nibbāna* in the teaching of the king of *dhamma*.
The one who respects his companions in the holy life
is like a fish in alot of water, or a good seed in a field:
He is near to *nibbāna* in the teaching of the king of *dhamma*.
(Th 387–92)

Seven qualities of a good friend
Upatissa gives some amplification of this text and the qualities it describes, regarding them as indicators to look out for, if one cannot find the two kinds of merit 'fulfillers' to teach meditation.[23] The preceding text in the *Aṅguttaranikāya* gives another list of seven: [The friend] 'gives what is hard to give, does what is hard to do, endures what is hard to endure, reveals his own secrets, guards the secrets of others; he does not forsake one at times of need and does not despise one for any loss' (A IV 30).

A monk, monks, should cultivate, follow and honour a friend who is endowed with seven things, even if he drives him away. What seven?

He should be dear and pleasing; he should be respected and just as he should be; he should be someone who speaks up; he should be kindly in speech and he should be someone who discusses things in depth. He does not urge without a reason.[24]

A monk should cultivate, follow and honour a friend who is endowed with seven things, even if he drives him away.[25]

Dear and valued, just as he should be, kindly in speech, he speaks to the depths.

He does not urge without reason.
The one in whom these qualities are found:
This is the friend for the one who desires a friend,
Compassionate and wishing for one's welfare:
He is the one to be followed, even if he drives him away.
(A IV 32)

The mind

Essential to early Buddhism is the understanding that the mind has a natural radiance, which can be rediscovered through the practice of meditation (*bhāvanā*). This notion of the luminosity of the human mind, stressed further in later Buddhist traditions, is associated with the idea that a human rebirth is a fortunate realm (*sugati*) and the result of good *kamma*. The Buddha said that once lost, it is as difficult to obtain as the chance of a blind turtle surfacing from the ocean, putting his head through a small yoke set on the surface of the sea (S V 456–7). The idea of an underlying skilful base to the mind is developed further in the *Abhidhamma*, which analyses the constituents of consciousness in detail. For a human rebirth to have occurred, the *bhavaṅga*, or consciousness to which the mind returns at rest, is skilful, whether with the two roots of non-greed and non-hatred, or more usually, with three roots, of wisdom, non-greed and non-hatred.[26] This consciousness will be present whenever the mind enters *bhavaṅga*, either momentarily at the end of each thought-process, or during deep sleep. For all born as humans, the state of *bhavaṅga* is a reflection of the skilful state of mind that must have been present at the moment of death as a governing factor for the relinking consciousness. It is passive, however, and this predisposition needs active cultivation during waking life.[27] Only when skilful consciousness is present during daily life, or during meditation, does the mind become actively bright and radiant. According to the theory this happens, for instance, at the moment of giving, of being alert and interested or when practising *jhāna*: the active part of the thought-process (*javana*) is then free from defilements. Those practising meditation are 'bringing into being' a consciousness which is thought to be a kind of birthright, but which needs cultivation. In Buddhist countries the human realm is considered particularly important for spiritual work. Birth in heaven realms is pleasant but lacks the suffering to encourage spiritual work; the realms of animals, ghosts and hell beings are considered far too painful for the path, and it is difficult, though not impossible, for such beings to find a skilful rebirth. It is said that the Buddha always has a human birth as his last existence after many lifetimes spent preparing to teach others. One *sutta* compares rebirth in a hell realm as entering into a pit of coals, that of a heaven realm to a stay in a luxurious mansion. The human realm, however, is like a man sitting in the shade of a tree in a hot climate, also the classic conditions for the practice of meditation (see M I 76–7).

The finger-snap

This mind, monks, is radiant, but is defiled by impurities which come as visitors from outside.[28] But people who have not heard the teaching, ordinary people, do not understand how this is. Therefore, I say that for people who have not heard the teaching, the ordinary people, there is no development of the mind.

This mind, monks, is radiant, but is freed from impurities which come as visitors from outside. The noble disciple, who has heard much, knows this as it actually is. Therefore, I say that for the noble disciple, who has heard much, there is development of the mind.

If, for as much as the lasting of a finger-snap, monks, a monk pursues a mind with loving-kindness: such a man is to be called a monk.[29] His meditation is not empty of result. He lives practising the doctrine of his teacher. He follows his teacher's advice. He does not eat his almsfood in vain. What should I then say of someone who makes much of this!

If, for as much as the lasting of a finger-snap, monks, a monk develops a mind with loving-kindness: such a man is to be called a monk. His meditation is not empty of result.... What should I then say of someone who makes much of this!

If, for as much as the lasting of a finger-snap, monks, a monk gives full attention to the mind of loving-kindness: such a man is to be called a monk. His meditation is not empty of result.... What should I then say of someone who makes much of this! Whatever states, monks, are unskilful, have a part in unskilfulness, are on the side of unskilfulness: all these have mind as their forerunner. Mind is the first of these states, followed by unskilful states.

Whatever states, monks, are skilful, have a part in skilfulness, are on the side of skilfulness: all these have mind as their forerunner. Mind is the first of these states, followed by skilful states.

I do not know, monks, of any other single thing, which is so responsible for causing unarisen unskilful states to arise or for unarisen, skilful states to fall away, as carelessness.[30] In one who is careless, unarisen unskilful states will arise and arisen skilful states will fall away.

I do not know, monks, of any other single thing that is so responsible for causing unarisen skilful states to arise or for unarisen, unskilful states to fall away, as care. In one who is careful, unarisen skilful states will arise and arisen unskilful states will fall away.

I do not know, monks, of any other single thing that is so responsible for causing unarisen unskilful states to arise or for unarisen, skilful states to fall away, as laziness.[31]

In one who is lazy, unarisen unskilful states will arise and arisen skilful states will fall away.

(A 1 10)

The skilful mind and body

This extract is part of a list describing the skilful mind (*kusala citta*) that opens the first of the seven books of *Abhidhamma*, the *Dhammasaṅgaṇi*. According to the commentarial tradition the Buddha taught *Abhidhamma* to his mother, who, after death was reborn in the *Tusita* realm, a sense-sphere heaven. She came down to the heaven of the Thirty-Three Gods, the heavenly realm frequently employed as a setting for discussion and debate, to hear her son, who ascended on a jewelled ladder from the realm of humans to teach her.[32] As its name indicates, *Abhidhamma* is regarded as the higher teaching and is different in style, content and emphasis from the *suttas*. Its method works through lists and delineation of states, taking each moment of consciousness as a discrete whole; its primary concern is the close examination of the mind and its relationship with matter. The third 'basket' of the teaching is not always appreciated by modern Western scholars, some of whom feel that it focuses too much on the reification of moments of consciousness through the aspect of 'momentariness' and that its precision is too dry. The practice of chanting the texts ensures that this is not the case, and in a context where it is part of a living tradition it arouses great depth of feeling and encourages clarity of thought.[33] In Burma in particular it is regarded as the source material for major points of doctrinal debate. The twenty-four aspects of the *Paṭṭhāna*, for instance, the seventh book of the *Abhidhamma*, are often arranged into a decorative flower painted on fans which can be bought at street markets: the embodiment of what is considered the highest form of the teaching is just considered lucky.[34] When chanted, an *Abhidhamma* text suggests impermanence through a kind of *rāga* of slightly different 'notes', as a few basic patterns of factors are varied to create a complex delineation of the relationship between the factors that link together mind, mental states and matter at any given moment. Even without any knowledge of the philosophy behind the system, this fluidity of movement and sense of process can be sensed by listening attentively to these subtle variations and patterns of words. Cousins points that out the intention of *Abhidhamma* is to arouse insight into not-self (*anattā*) 'so as to undermine mental rigidity' (Cousins 1984b).

The passage here describes some of these notes: the 'six pairs', factors that are always present together in the mind and body in skilful consciousness in the sense sphere. Like other factors of the first skilful state of mind (*citta*), they are also found in the first *jhāna*.[35] This passage can be read quite literally as the experience of the physical body.[36] Whether in daily life or in meditation this state of mind is also always characterized by one of the *brahmavihāras* (31–3), of loving-kindness, compassion or sympathetic joy, which can be present in daily life or as aspects of *jhāna*.[37] Equanimity and the fourth *jhāna* are associated with the fifth skilful *citta*, also characterized by these pairs.

The six pairs

40. What at that time is tranquillity of body? At that time the tranquillity, the full tranquillity, the composure and the collectedness of the aggregate

of feeling, of the aggregate of perception and of the aggregate of formations – this, at that time, is tranquillity of body.

41. What at that time is tranquillity of mind? At that time the tranquillity, the full tranquillity, the composure and the collectedness of the aggregate of consciousness – this, at that time, is tranquillity of mind.

42. What at that time is lightness of body? At that time the lightness which is there on that occasion, the lightness in changing state, the absence of sluggishness, or inertia of the aggregate of feeling, of the aggregate of perception and of the aggregate of formations – this, at that time, is lightness of body.

43. What at that time is lightness of mind? At that time the lightness which is there on that occasion, the lightness in changing state, the absence of sluggishness, or inertia of the aggregate of consciousness – this, at that time, is lightness of mind.

44. What at that time is softness of body? At that time the softness, the gentleness, the absence of harshness or stiffness of the aggregate of feeling, of the aggregate of perception and of the aggregate of formations – this, at that time, is softness of body.

45. What at that time is softness of mind? At that time the softness, the gentleness, the absence harshness or stiffness of the aggregate of consciousness – this, at that time, is softness of mind.

46. What at that time is manageability of body? At that time the manageability, the manageability for use, the state of being manageable of the aggregate of feeling, of the aggregate of perception and of the aggregate of formations – this, at that time, is manageability of body.

47. What at that time is manageability of mind? At that time the manageability, the manageability for use, the state of being manageable of the aggregate of consciousness – this, at that time, is manageability of mind.

48. What at that time is proficiency of body? At that time the proficiency, the healthiness, the proficient state of the aggregate of feeling, of the aggregate of perception and of the aggregate of formations – this, at that time, is proficiency of body.

49. What at that time is proficiency of mind? At that time the proficiency, the healthiness, the proficient state of the aggregate of consciousness – this, at that time, is proficiency of mind.

50. What at that time is straightness of body? At that time the rightness, straightness, the absence of twistedness or crookedness or bentness in the aggregate of feeling, of the aggregate of perception and of the aggregate of formations – this, at that time, is straightness of body.

51. What at that time is straightness of mind? At that time the rightness, straightness, the absence of twistedness or crookedness or bentness in the aggregate of consciousness – this, at that time, is straightness of mind.

(DhS 40–51)

Dispositions

One of the most effective means by which Buddhist philosophy and practice is distilled and embodied for subsequent generations is through the characters, behaviour and excellences of the principal arahats, whose life stories, problems in attaining enlightenment and special skills would be well known to those hearing the *suttas*. A popular Thai protective chant, which places a different arahat in each of the eight directions, with the Buddha at the centre, indicates the extent to which it is assumed that the teaching, while of 'one taste', may find different expression through various temperaments and approaches.[38] This *sutta* also gives us some acknowledgement of the variety of modes of practice within the Buddhist tradition: there are certain recognizable stages, of stream entry, once return and never return, which lead to enlightenment and arahatship, but as a way of progress different skills and kinds of paths may be suitable for different people. Some of the figures described appear throughout the texts. Sāriputta is the master of insight, and regarded as the Buddha's chief disciple while Moggallāna is renowned for his psychic powers and for his expertise in *samatha* meditation. Ānanda cared for the Buddha and memorized his teachings. Kassapa was an upholder of ascetic practices. Upāli, a low-caste barber, became the leading expert on monastic discipline (*Vinaya*). Anuruddha possessed the divine eye, the ability to see beings near and far.[39] Puṇṇa Mantānaputta was said by the Buddha to be the foremost of those that taught *dhamma*: the famous discourse on insight, the *Rathavinītasutta*, describes a discussion between him and Sāriputta, while Ānanda notes that he was a great help to him and to other novice monks.[40] The warning sting in the tail is provided by the last figure, Devadatta, the Buddha's cousin who tried to kill Gotama when young and then to cause a schism amongst the Buddha's followers. His jealousy is traced through countless past lives and he is constantly represented in canonical texts as an envious and dark parody of the Buddha, with his own powers, attendants and views.[41] The *sutta* is chosen for its atmosphere of companionship and leisurely practice: the only other of the eight who is not enlightened at that time is Ānanda; he attains arahatship on the night before the First Council.[42]

> *Walking up and down*
> At one time the Exalted One was staying at Rājagaha on Mount Vulture Peak. Now at that time, not far from the Exalted One, Venerable Sāriputta was walking up and down with a number of monks; Venerable Moggallāna was walking up and down with a number of monks. Venerable Kassapa . . . Venerable Anuruddha . . . Venerable Puṇṇamantāniputta . . . Venerable Upāli . . . Venerable Ānanda was walking backwards and forwards with a number of monks. Not far from the Exalted One, Devadatta was also walking backwards and forwards with a number of monks.
>
> Then the Exalted One addressed the monks. 'Monks, do you see Sāriputta walking up and down with a number of monks?'

'Yes, sir.'

'All those monks are of great wisdom. Do you see Moggallāna walking up and down with a number of monks?'

'Yes, sir.'

'All those monks are of great spiritual power. Do you see Kassapa walking up and down with a number of monks?'

'Yes, sir.'

'All those monks are those who defend the ascetic life. Do you see Anuruddha walking up and down with a number of monks?'

'Yes, sir.'

'All those monks possess the Divine Eye. Do you see Mantāniputta walking up and down with a number of monks?'

'Yes, sir.'

'All those monks are expounders of the *dhamma*. Do you see Upāli walking up and down with a number of monks?'

'Yes, sir.'

'All those monks are those who uphold the monastic discipline. Do you see Ānanda walking up and down with a number of monks?'

'Yes, sir.'

'All those monks are those who have heard a great deal of teaching. Do you see Devadatta walking up and down with a number of monks?'

'Yes, sir.'

'All those monks are those who wish harm.'

People gravitate and come together, monks, by way of elements. Those of an inferior disposition gravitate and come together with those of an inferior disposition. Those of a good disposition gravitate and come together with those of a good disposition. In the past they have done this, in the future they will do so. In the present they are doing so too.

(S II 155–7)

Two elephant kings

The curious incident that prompts this *sutta* is one of many such comic interludes within the canon that are easy to overlook in appraisal of the Buddha's doctrine.[43] The lightheartedness that characterizes this scene renders it however particularly appropriate as a comparison of the two great traditions of meditation practice, for it concerns two of the Buddha's chief disciples: Sāriputta, of 'golden complexion', the leading exponent of *vipassanā* and Moggallāna, whose complexion is the colour of 'blue uppala', who is the leading exponent of skills arising from *samatha* meditation. They are termed by the commentary: 'brilliant like two moon-discs or two sun-discs stationed in one and the same place in the heavens' or like two lions, or two tigers, 'alighted upon one and the same level of arousal' or like two elephant kings who had 'entered the same sāla-grove in full blossom'.[44]

The *sutta* is not one of the major texts of the tradition and not cited much. It is included because it demonstrates an approach characteristic of much of the material within the canon that gives added dimension and depth to, for instance, doctrinal difference or discussion of fine points of meditative practice. With its mutual acknowledgement of expertise it illustrates a number of points about the healthy regard that clearly existed between these two masters: it shows for instance that the chief exponent of *vipassanā*, was himself able to attain a considerable degree of concentration. The commentary suggests three possible interpretations of his state: that he had perfected the *brahmavihāra* of equanimity (34), that he had attained cessation (*nirodha samāpatti*), or that he was experiencing the fruit of a formless state (35–8). The commentary also feels obliged to excuse the 'slight pain' in his head, arguing that he should not really have experienced anything at all.[45]

The canon seems designed to be memorable, as well as easily memorized: it is full of such incident and *suttas* such as these should not be underestimated.[46] The badinage between the arahats, a mildly comic supernatural element combined with a strong sense of drama, all contribute to a piece of theatre as telling in its own way as those *suttas* whose content is more literal and overtly didactic. The mutual respect implied in this interchange is also highly suggestive of the Buddha's intention regarding the proper relationship between two great strands of spiritual practice and between exponents of different methods.

The yakkha blow sutta

Thus have I heard. At one time, the Exalted One was staying at Rājagaha, at the Squirrels' Feeding Ground in the Bamboo Grove. At that time Sāriputta and Moggallāna were staying at Kapotakandarāya, the Dove Clearing. And on that occasion Sāriputta was sitting in the open air, at night time, in the moonlight, with his head newly shaved. He had just attained a certain meditative state.

At that time two yakkhas who were friends were going south from the north on some business or other in the night and saw Sāriputta, in the moonlight, with his head newly shaved. On seeing him one yakkha said to the other, 'It has just occurred to me, my friend, to give that ascetic a blow on his head'. When he had said this the other yakkha replied, 'Watch out, my friend, do not strike that ascetic: he is very eminent. He has great powers and psychic potency!' And a second time . . . And a third time that yakkha said this to the other. And a third time the yakkha replied, 'Watch out, my friend, do not strike that ascetic: he is very eminent. He has great powers and psychic potency!'

Then that yakkha, ignoring the warning of the other yakkha, gave Sāriputta a blow on the head. And it was such a great blow that it might have brought down an elephant of seven or seven and a half feet[47] or split a great mountain peak. Whereupon that yakkha fell into a deep hell crying out, 'I am burning, I am burning!'

Then Moggallāna, with his purified divine eye, surpassing that of men, saw the yakkha giving Sāriputta a blow on the head. On seeing this he went up to Sāriputta and said, 'Are you bearing up, venerable sir, are you alright? Is there any pain?' 'I am bearing up, sir, I am alright: but I do just have a slight pain in my head', said Sāriputta.

'Well, it is wonderful, dear Sāriputta, it is extraordinary, dear Sāriputta! How great is Venerable Sāriputta's great power and psychic potency. A yakkha, dear Sāriputta, has given you here a blow on the head. And it was such a great blow that it might have brought down an elephant of seven or seven and a half feet or split a great mountain peak. And Venerable Sāriputta just maintains, 'I am bearing up, sir, I am alright: but I do just have a slight pain in my head'.

'Well, it is wonderful, dear Moggallāna, it is extraordinary, dear Moggallāna! How great is Venerable Moggallāna's great power and psychic potency, that he can see a yakkha at all. Now I wouldn't be able to see even a mud spirit.'

Meanwhile the Exalted One, with his Divine Ear, surpassing that of men, heard the conversation that was going on between the two great men. And the Exalted One, understanding the matter, gave forth this inspired utterance:

'He whose mind is like a rock, steadfast, does not quiver,
Is free from passion in the midst of enticing things,
And not disturbed when he might be angered.
When his mind is cultivated in this way, from where can suffering come to him?'

(Ud 39–41)

3

THE FIVE HINDRANCES

Sooner or later everyone practising meditation, in whatever tradition, notices that the mind does not necessarily want to focus on the object it has been given and disturbances seem to crowd in. The main obstacles to meditation, that prevent the mind from experiencing calm and alertness, are termed hindrances (*nīvaraṇā*). The texts indicate that work on these obstructions needs to occur in daily life, but they are particularly associated in the canon with the preparatory stages of *samatha* meditation. Technically opposed to *jhāna*, they take many and often quite subtle forms: the last vestiges are only finally removed at the attainment of arahatship, when they are cut off like a 'palm stump' (S V 327). They are called defilements (*upakkilesā*): 'obstructions, hindrances, defilements of the mind that weaken wisdom' (S V 92–3). While the *suttas* and the *Abhidhamma* reveal many different difficulties and obstructions that can cloud the mind at different levels of practice, all are associated with this 'heap of bad things' (A III 63):

1 Longing (*Abhijjhā*) or desire for objects of the five senses (*kāmacchanda*)
2 Ill will (*vyāpāda-padosa*)
3 Sloth and torpor (*thīna-m-iddha*)
4 Restlessness and worry (*uddhacca-kukkucca*)
5 Doubt (*vicikicchā*)

In order to understand the hindrances we need to think of the practice of meditation as an exercise which not only works on cultivating certain states but which also, as a necessary preliminary, averts and, in the final stages of insight, eradicates from the mind the presence of elements which in some way distort or defile perception so that things as they are are not seen clearly.[1] In one famous image the mind is compared to a pool which may be troubled or made muddy in different ways. The five hindrances prevent the water from being clear in various ways: with dye (desire) it is no longer clear, with heat it becomes turbulent (ill-will), with a covering of mosses it becomes brackish (sloth and torpor), with a flurry of wind it is not settled (restlessness and worry). In the case of doubt, the bowl is placed in the dark and made troubled (A III 229–36). With the eradication of the hindrances, the water is clear and pellucid.

Upatissa says, 'Thus all defilements are included in the attachment to the five hindrances' (PF 92).

The hindrances can be seen in the setbacks one might encounter in acquiring any trained skill which requires continued practice, training and time. They can be compared to the difficulties found in learning to sing or play a musical instrument, which also need regular practice and development. Other things start to seem much more interesting, irritation can arise with oneself and the instrument, the teacher or anyone else around when it does not go well, one can feel sleepy just at the thought of doing it or one cannot get on with it by being overexcited at how one is doing or too depressed; doubts of course about one's ability or one's teacher can come at any time.[2] The *nikāyas* reflect this sense of the presence of hindrances in everyday life. Some texts describe them operating while walking, sitting, lying down or just going about one's daily business.[3] Clearly in whatever we do we can find problems: we do not want to do what we are doing, desire for something else arises, we become annoyed, tired, restless, excited and then doubt that what we are doing is the right thing: the circle of dependent origination permeates human activity. In the *suttas* images derived from skilled crafts, however, are frequently employed for the mind that is composed (*samāhita*), purified (*parisuddha*) and manageable (*kammanīya*) once the hindrances have been removed: it is, for instance, like gold ready to be used to make any ornament or piece of jewellery.[4] If we bear in mind that the word that is so difficult to translate, *kusala*, has connotations of goodness, health and skilfulness we have some sense of the constriction or distortion that characterizes the mind that is unskilful or unwholesome.[5] The five hindrances are the impurities that prevent the mind being what it could be; they make the mind unsuccessful or weak. The Buddha compares them to the weakness of a man unable and unwilling to fight (see S I 99–100). Conversely, according to the *Abhidhamma*, *kusala citta* is also possible in daily life: it just requires skill and care.

Definition of each hindrance

The first, covetousness or longing (*abhijjhā*), is, as the Pali English Dictionary (PED) points out, almost identical in meaning to greed (*lobha*) and includes desire for the senses (*kāmacchanda*).[6] Such desire, a part of human existence, is not entirely weakened until stream-entry. As an obstruction it is compared to being in debt, if the images in the *Sāmaññaphala-Sutta* order of the hindrances are taken to denote each one in turn. In the *Abhidhamma*, it is said that at the moment greed *citta* arises, there is always pleasant or neutral feeling, though it is often linked to discontent in the *suttas*.[7] Ways of counteracting *abhijjhā* are described in the *Sāmaññaphāla-Sutta*, included later in this anthology, under the section on guarding the sense doors.

The second, ill-will, covers a range of states from mild irritation and petulance to great malevolence. The *Sāmaññaphala-Sutta* compares it to a serious illness, which prevents one from enjoying things. According to the *Abhidhamma*, it is synonymous with the hatred (*dosa*) that constitutes one of the unskilful roots and, like greed, may form an underlying orientation of a particular personality type. It is, according to the *Abhidhamma*, always characterized by unpleasant feeling (see Dhs 413–20).

The third hindrance is sloth and torpor, which may have originally meant 'increase of sleepiness' but soon comes to be seen as a compound meaning two qualities of sloth and torpor, affecting the mind and the body separately.[8] The *Sāmaññaphala-Sutta* compares it to imprisonment.

The fourth hindrance, restlessness and worry, is compared in the *Sāmaññaphala-Sutta* to enslavement. In the *Abhidhamma* list of unskilful states of mind both are associated with the weak consciousness based solely on ignorance, but the two are distinguished from one another in that worry characterizes the eleventh and restlessness the twelfth kind of unskilful consciousness.[9]

The fifth hindrance, the 'desire to discern' or 'incapacitating doubt', is not the healthy questioning of the word that it may have once denoted, but, as Cousins has shown, a state of incapacitation that always sheers away from the object.[10] In the *Sāmaññaphala-Sutta* it is related to being lost in a wilderness.

It has probably become clear by now that the hindrances are very much part of the round of our usual existence. Considering them can be reminiscent of the man in Jerome K. Jerome's *Three Men in a Boat* (1889) who finds a medical textbook and becomes convinced that he suffers from everything except housemaid's knee![11] The canon is rich in its pejoration of these powerful forces in the mind: as well as being hindrances, and obstructions, they 'cause blindness, loss of vision and ignorance; they obstruct insight, associate with pain and do not lead to *nibbāna*' (S V 97). They are seen as huge trees, with tiny seeds but large trunks and branches, which encircle other trees, so that the other trees become bent, cracked and split (see S V 96). In the *Mahāgovinda-Sutta*, where they are included amongst more variegated description of ailments of the mind, they are said to give off a bad smell (see D II 242). In these images the hindrances are grouped together, but there are some, if fewer, texts in which one is isolated and taken on its own, with methods suggested for dealing with it. At the end of this section two texts are given for one hindrance, sloth and torpor.

The world of the senses

The practice of meditation is not the same as the theory, but in the case of the hindrances some knowledge of the theoretical background is essential to keep these problems of the mind in some sort of perspective. According to a text discussed in Chapter 2 the mind is described as naturally pure and radiant.[12] In the *Abhidhamma* system, the *bhavaṅga*, or stream to which the mind goes when at rest, is in all humans pure and bright. Governed by the moment of consciousness at the moment of death, this continuum is established in all humans at the moment of conception; three – and occasionally two – roots of skilfulness must be present for a human birth to take place. On going to sleep, and even at the end of each thought process, the mind returns to *bhavaṅga* and the state of non-hatred (*adosa*), equated with loving-kindness (*mettā*), non-greed and, for most humans, wisdom (*amoha*).[13] Although the human mind has an inherent predisposition towards health and brightness, the sleeping mind is passive (*vipāka*): in waking consciousness the mind is generating new *kamma*, which may be coloured by the hindrances. It is the job of meditation to suppress and finally, with insight eradicate these, so that the mind is freed and the path can be realized.

Some indication of the hydra-headed complexity and diverse nature of the hindrances is given by a Pāli word used to describe them: *papañca*, the proliferation of going in five directions. While the hindrances take many more forms, as in *Abhidhamma* lists of unskilful mental states (*cetasikas*) and in the multiplicity of ways various defilements are described in the *suttas*, it is simple involvement with the world and the five senses that causes them to appear much of the time.[14] They are an *almost* inevitable product of participation in the world of beings and are perhaps more like a manifestation of original sin in the Christian sense than any specific sin. In Indian philosophy the number five is often associated with a descent into the world of the senses and to participation in *saṃsāra*: simply by living in the human world our minds are liable to proliferation.[15] Buddhist lists of five reflect this underlying attitude: there are five bundles or heaps of craving (*pañcupādānakkhandhā*): form, feeling, identification, formations and consciousness, the basic constituents of any being taking rebirth in the sense sphere. It is, however, possible to participate and act in the world without *papañca*. Arahats act, speak and conduct themselves in various ways, and yet have no vestiges of the hindrances, as indeed can ordinary people if there is mindfulness and the hindrances are temporarily suppressed.

Operation in the fivefold sense sphere is conducive to obstacles of all kinds, and is a seed-bed for greed, hatred and delusion. According to the texts, however, it is an arena in which it is possible to live, with mindfulness, without the hindrances. This is the beginning of the use of the sense sphere as a place for the practice of meditation. As a reflection of this possibility, there are two lists of five in the thirty-seven *bodhipakkhiyādhammā* that have decidedly positive connotations: the five faculties (*indriyāni*) and the five powers (*balāni*), which comprise the body of factors required for the attainment of *jhāna*. The *Abhidhamma* description of the five *jhāna* factors of initial and sustained thought, joy, happiness and one-pointedness as five-limbed (*pañcaṅgikaṃ*) also supports this idea of a 'body' that is used for meditation, rather than participation in the sense sphere (see DhS 83). The sense sphere and a human body may be the ground in which the hindrances are very likely to occur, but it is also where the conditions for the cultivation of the mind and enlightenment itself are most favourable. The practice of meditation is related to the gradual development and nourishment of a body of skills, enabling the mind to be free from the world of the senses: a number of texts employ imagery associated with food to describe this process.[16]

Dealing with the hindrances in practice

But how does the canon recommend living in daily life, and in the preliminary practice of meditation? Certainly the texts do not encourage feelings of failure when faced with the various problems in the mind. Meditation is taught in the *suttas*, and often in the modern day, in contexts where there would be considerable goodwill and mental preparation before coming to sit and practise. Amongst the laity in the East it is undertaken on full moon days, where the meditator would have put aside problems for the day, or on an extended period of practice where much is done in the way of ensuring that the meditator feels at home and is welcome. The very act of trying to meditate is to this day in the East regarded with great respect as an adventurous and challenging exercise. Any monk who can experience any meditational state, even for a finger snap, is said to be worthy of offerings (A I 38–42). This sense of the worth of the undertaking informs not just the preliminaries to meditation but the attitude to taking an object for the practice itself. The meditation object is regarded as 'special'.[17]

It also should be noted that modern meditation teachers and practitioners, following the spirit and content of so much of the canon, often make jokes about the hindrances. Walpola Rahula has pointed out the central place of humour in the canon.[18] I have heard the hindrances variously described with analogies that range from the 'manure' or 'crap' of the mind to 'the kind of guest you cannot get rid of'. One epithet of wisdom, appropriate in this context, is that it is 'smile-producing' (*hāsapaññā*) (Patis II 199–200). To this day considerable attention is paid in all meditative schools to ways in which the hindrances may be recognized and guarded against, in sitting practice and daily life. From the point of view of establishing mindfulness or awareness in daily life, this is achieved primarily through the constant reiteration of the practice of awareness at all times. In the *suttas*, texts that work through constant repetitive allusion to each of the senses were presumably intended to arouse mindfulness at the appropriate sense door in turn as each is mentioned.[19] Sumedho comments: 'It is only in the moment when a hindrance actually arises that we can really penetrate it and have insight' (Sumedho 1992: 57).

The five hindrances

Thus have I heard: At one time the Exalted One was staying at Sāvatthī, in the park belonging to Anāthapiṇḍika at the Jetavana Grove. There he addressed the monks, saying, 'Monks'. 'Sir,' they replied.

'There are five obstructions, hindrances, which grow like parasites[20] on the heart and hinder wisdom. What five? Sense desire, monks, grows like a parasite on the heart and hinders wisdom. Ill-will . . . sloth and torpor . . . restlessness and worry . . . doubt, monks, grow like a parasite on the heart and hinder wisdom. These five obstructions, hindrances, grow like parasites on the heart and hinder wisdom.

If, monks, a monk does not abandon these five obstructions, the hindrances that grow like parasites on the heart and hinder wisdom, through lack of strength and weakened wisdom, he will not know what is good for himself, he will not know what is good for another, he will not know what is good for both of these and he will not be able to experience for himself the excellence of the noble knowledge and vision that surpasses that of men: it cannot be so. It is like a mountain stream, going from one place to the next, flowing swiftly, taking everything in its path with it. A man might make inlets on both sides. Then, monks the current in the middle of the stream would be made turbulent, swirled and diverted, and the stream would not go from one place to the next, flow swiftly and take everything in its path with it. In this way, monks, a monk who does not abandon these five obstructions, the hindrances that grow like parasites on the heart and hinder wisdom, through lack of strength and weakened wisdom, will not know what is good for himself, will not know what is good for another, will not know what is good for both of these and will not be able to experience for himself the excellence of the noble knowledge and vision that surpasses that of men: it cannot be so.

If, monks, a monk does abandon these five obstructions, the hindrances that grow like parasites on the heart and hinder wisdom, he will know, with strong wisdom, what is good for himself, he will know what is good for another, he will know what is good for both of these and he will be able to experience for himself the excellence of the noble knowledge and vision that surpasses that of men: this has to be so. It is like a mountain stream, going here and there, flowing swiftly, taking everything in its path with it. A man might close it on both sides. Then, monks, the current in the middle of the stream would not be made turbulent, not be swirled and diverted, and the stream would go from one place to the next, flowing swiftly, taking everything in its path with it.

In this way, monks, a monk who does abandon these five obstructions, the hindrances that grow like parasites on the heart and hinder wisdom, with strong wisdom, will know what is good for himself, will know what is good for another, will know what is good for both of these and will be able to experience for himself the excellence of the noble knowledge and vision that surpasses that of men: this has to be so.

(A III 62)

Vijitasena

The preliminary stages of meditation practice are sometimes compared to taming an incalcitrant animal. Buddhaghosa describes the practitioner as a 'skilled cowherd' (Vism VIII 192). The image employed in these verses is pertinent, for, according to post-canonical stories, Vijitasena was born into a family of elephant trainers, and had two uncles who were also mahouts before joining the order. After seeing the twin miracle performed, he subsequently attained arahatship under their tutelage.[21]

355. I shall tie you, mind, as an elephant to a little gate
I shall not urge you on to harm, you net of desire, born of the body.
356. When fastened, you will not go, like an elephant not finding the gate open.
Dark mind, you will not wander, using force, again and again, able to delight in harm.
357. Just as one who wields a hook turns back an untrained, newly captured elephant,
Against his will, in this way I will turn you back.
358. Just as a noble charioteer, skilled in breaking horses, tames a thoroughbred,
So I, established in the five powers, will train you.[22]
359. Restrained myself, I'll bind you with mindfulness,
Curbed by the yoke of energy, you will not go far from here, my mind!
(Th 355–59)

Purification

This short text is a neat and precisely expressed example of the way in which one image may be explored as a means of understanding a particular selection of qualities. The mind is compared to gold, whose strength and manageability depends upon the removal of taints in a molten condition. Five impurities (*upakkilesā*) of gold (*jātarūpa*, or unworked gold) are described, which prevent it from being soft, pliable, shining, not easily broken up or fit for perfect workmanship. The *sutta* occurs in a section where short texts of this kind on the five hindrances are interspersed with those on the seven factors of enlightenment, the latter in various ways supplanting or superseding the former.[23]

The impurities of gold

There are, monks, these five impurities of gold, tainted by which gold is neither soft, nor manageable, nor shining, but brittle and not ready for working. What are the five?

Iron, monks, is an impurity of gold, tainted by which gold is neither soft, nor manageable, nor shining, but brittle and not good for working. Copper is an impurity of gold . . . tin . . . lead . . . silver is an impurity of gold, tainted by which gold is neither soft, nor manageable, nor shining, but brittle and not good for working. There are, monks, these five impurities of gold, tainted by which gold is neither soft, nor manageable, nor shining, but brittle and not good for working.

In the same way, monks, there are five impurities of the heart, tainted by which the mind is neither soft, nor manageable, nor shining, but brittle and not properly prepared for the elimination of the corruptions. What are the five?

Sense desire, monks, is an impurity of the heart, tainted by which the mind is neither soft, nor manageable, nor shining, but brittle and not properly prepared for the elimination of the corruptions. Ill-will . . . sloth and torpor . . . restlessness and worry . . . doubt is an impurity of the heart, tainted by which the mind is neither soft, nor manageable, nor shining, but brittle and not properly prepared for the elimination of the corruptions. These are the five impurities of the heart, tainted by which the mind is neither soft, nor manageable, nor shining, but brittle and not properly prepared for the elimination of the corruptions.

(S V 92)

Six hindrances

This list gives more detailed description of the effects of each of the hindrances and how they may be identified: it includes a sixth, ignorance (*avijjā*). The technicality of *Abhidhamma* material can appear, at first sight, bemusing and even unreadable. However, if it is consulted as one would an encyclopaedia, or even a dictionary, it is constantly helpful for its examination of each state of consciousness (*citta*) and mental factor (*cetasika*) in a more exhaustive way than is attempted in the *suttas*. This list of hindrances gives a description that is in part an account of the kind of deliberation that may be present in the mind when each hindrance is present. What is a particular hindrance? What are its symptoms? One suspects an element of humour in some of the lengthy explanations.

What are the hindrances?

1152. There are six hindrances: the hindrance of sense desire, of ill-will, of sloth and torpor, of restlessness and worry, of doubt and of ignorance.

1153. What, here, is the hindrance of sense desire?

The desire for sense pleasures in the senses, the passion for senses, delight in the senses, craving for senses, affection for senses, the fever of the senses, infatuation with the senses, grasping of the senses – this is called the hindrance of sense desire.

1154. And what, here, is the hindrance of ill-will?

When annoyance springs up at the thought: he has done me harm, is doing me harm, will do me harm; he has done harm, is doing harm will do harm to someone dear and loved by me; he has given a benefit, is giving a benefit or will be giving a benefit to someone not dear and disliked by me. Or when annoyance springs up without any grounds: all such annoyance, resentment, aggression, enmity, hostility, irritation, agitation, indignation, aversion, rejection, abhorrence, disorder of temper, detestation, antipathy, fuming, wrath, hate, hatred, hating, disorder, grumpiness, losing one's temper, opposition, anger, churlishness, abruptness, discontent in the heart: this is called the hindrance of ill-will.

1155. And what, here, is the hindrance of sloth and torpor?

There is sloth and there is torpor.

1156. And what, here, is sloth?

That which is a malaise, a lack of manageability in the mind, the sluggishness, stolidity, dullness, sticking, sticking to, stickiness, sloth, that is a stiffening, rigidity of mind: this is called sloth.

1157. And what, here, is torpor?[24]

That which is a malaise, a lack of manageability in the body, a clouding, enveloping, a barricading within, the torpor that is sleep and sleepiness, sleepiness, dozing, somnolence: this is called torpor.

This is the sloth and this the torpor that make up the hindrance that is called sloth and torpor.

1158. And what, here, is the hindrance of restlessness and worry?

There is restlessness and there is worry.

1159. And what, here, is restlessness?[25]

That restlessness of mind that lacks peace, disturbance of the mind, turmoil of the mind: this is called restlessness.

1160. And what, here, is worry?[26]

The perception that something is lawful where it is not, the perception that something is not lawful where it is, the perception that something is a fault where it is not, the perception that something is not a fault where it is: all this sort of worry, worreting, agonising, regretting and scratching of the head:[27] this is called worry.

This is the restlessness and this the worry that make up the hindrance that is called restlessness and worry.

1161. And what, here, is the hindrance of doubt?[28]

He is uncertain about the teacher, he doubts; he is uncertain about the *dhamma*, he doubts. He is uncertain about *saṅgha*, he doubts;... the training... the past... the future... the past and the future... he doubts: whatever there is that is uncertain, being uncertain, the state of uncertainty, perplexity, doubt, being in two minds, stuck at the crossroads, being unsure, being undecided, indecisiveness, hesitancy, lack of commitment, obstinancy and scratching of the head: this is called the hindrance of doubt.

1162. And what, here, is the hindrance of ignorance?

Lack of knowledge of suffering, lack of knowledge of the origin of suffering, lack of knowledge of the cessation of suffering, lack of knowledge of the way leading to the cessation of suffering. Lack of knowledge of the past... the future... and of both past and future... of the causal relationship of things which have arisen through dependent origination: lack of knowledge which is lack of vision, lack of penetration, lack of understanding, the state of being unawakened, lack of insight, lack of grasp, lack of commitment, lack of reflection, lack of reviewing, lack of realization, foolishness, silliness, lack of clear comprehension, delusion, bewilderment, deludedness, ignorance, the flood of ignorance, the yoke of ignorance, the predisposition to ignorance, the obsession

with ignorance, the barrier of ignorance, the delusion that is the root of the unskilful: this is called the hindrance of ignorance.
These are the hindrances.

(DhS 1152–62)

Abandoning the hindrances (*nīvaraṇappahāna*)

In the canon part of the work on the hindrances is simply acknowledging their presence. They are discarded, however, not just by relinquishing the unwholesome, or ensuring that what is not wholesome is not encouraged – the first two right efforts – but also through the last two right efforts, which involve introducing and sustaining skilful states.[29] The neatest account of the abandonment of each hindrance through meditation is in the *Sāmaññaphala-Sutta*, discussed in Chapter 4, which gives a short but economically worded means of dealing with each one in turn. Buddhaghosa says that they are all abandoned by the five factors of *jhāna*, which direct the mind, and dissolve the hindrances by their refreshing sense of contentment and unificatory effect (Vism IV 104–6).

This *sutta* introduces the idea of 'proper' or 'systematic' attention, the appropriate application of the mind on objects likely to arouse skilfulness; for each hindrance, a judicious placing of attention is suggested. The term is discussed in the *Abhidhamma* text, the *Vibhaṅga*: unwise attention sees the impermanent as permanent, suffering as happiness, the selfless as self and the foul as beautiful: this ignorance engenders the whole chain of dependent origination with regard to any object.[30] The text here also demonstrates a pattern of antidotes for hindrances.[31] The practice of proper or judicious attention for doubt is worthy of note: presumably some subjects or problems are liable to become amplified through doubt, which is weakened through the careful application of attention.[32]

Abandoning hindrances
I know of no other single thing, monks, of such power to cause the arising of sense desire, if not already arisen, or if arisen, to cause its growing great and increase as the beautiful image.[33] In the one who gives unwise attention to a beautiful image unarisen sense desire arises and arisen sense desire grows great and increases.

I know of no other single thing, monks, of such power to cause the arising of ill-will, if not already arisen, or, if arisen, to cause its growing great and increase, as the repugnant object. In the one who gives unwise attention to a repugnant image unarisen ill-will arises and arisen ill-will grows great and increases.

I know of no other single thing, monks, of such power to cause the arising of sloth and torpor . . . as discontent, laziness, yawning, surfeit after meals and mental inertia. In the one who has mental inertia unarisen sloth and torpor arises and unarisen sloth and torpor grow great and increase.

I know of no other single thing, monks, of such power to cause the arising of restlessness and worry . . . as lack of calm. In the one whose mind is not calmed unarisen restlessness and worry arise and unarisen restlessness and worry grow great and increase.

I know of no other single thing, monks, of such power to cause the arising of doubt . . . as proper attention. In the one who does not give proper attention to things unarisen doubt arises and unarisen doubt grows great and increases.

I know of no other single thing, monks, of such power to prevent the arising of sense desire, if not already arisen, or, if it has arisen, to cause its abandonment, as the image of the foul.[34] In the one who gives proper attention to the image of the foul sense desire, if it has not arisen, does not arise and if it has already arisen, is abandoned.

I know of no other single thing, monks, of such power to prevent the arising of ill-will if not already arisen, or if it has arisen, to cause its abandonment, as the deliverance of the mind through loving-kindness. In the one who gives proper attention to the deliverance of the mind by loving-kindness, ill-will, if it has not arisen, does not arise and, if it has already arisen, is abandoned.

I know of no other single thing, monks, of such power to prevent the arising of sloth and torpor . . . as the element of the stirring of effort, the element of exertion and the element of striving. In the one whose effort is stirred up, sloth and torpor, if they have not arisen, do not arise and if they have already arisen, are abandoned.

I know of no other single thing, monks, of such power to prevent the arising of restlessness and worry . . . as a calmed mind. In the one whose mind is calmed, restlessness and worry, if they have not arisen, do not arise and if they have already arisen, are abandoned.

I know of no other single thing, monks, of such power to prevent the arising of doubt . . . as proper attention. In the one who applies proper attention, doubt, if it has not arisen, does not arise and if it has already arisen, is abandoned.

(A I 3)

Asking for help

In this *sutta* instances are given when one should consult with a monk who is experienced in meditation and has cultivated the mind (*manobhāvanīya*). The *Aṅguttaranikāya* is a collection of *suttas* involving a number, so that 'ones' are grouped together, 'twos' and so on until the number eleven. In this text, from the 'sixes', six problems or stages in meditation are addressed. This text, typical of the practicality that can be found in many *suttas* from this *nikāya*, groups together the five hindrances with a stage in the practice of *samatha* meditation when the hindrances have been partially suppressed.[35]

This gives a slightly technical slant to the notion of the good friend, of which there are some instances in the canon. In the commentaries, as in the canon, contact with the good friend and the company of others practising the path is considered one of the best antidotes to the hindrances (see Vism IV 65, S V 34). This text also indicates the importance of guidance in the development of the mental image, a crucial stage in the development of *samatha* practice for the attainment of *jhāna*. In *vipassanā* schools any image which arises is left undeveloped, because the intention is to develop insight rather than calm. Because of the popularity of *vipassanā* meditation in the modern Western world it is common to encounter in books about meditation the enjoinder not to pay attention to any images of any kind – an instruction that is often given by a *samatha* teacher too if it is not the right time. For *samatha* practice, however, development of the image is encouraged but the role of the teacher may be very important in helping the meditator to feel peaceful and in the right frame of mind. Too much forced attention can give a headache, but ignoring images completely can undermine confidence: as in a skill like singing, the conditions need to be right. Saddhatissa suggests not chasing after images, like Alice: 'While concentrating on the *nimitta* one must be careful to keep the attention taut – neither too slack nor too tense' (Saddhatissa 1971: 77).

> *The first occasion* sutta
> A certain monk approached the Exalted One, paid respects to him and sat down to one side. So seated, he asked the Exalted One, 'What are the times, sir, when one should go and see a monk who has cultivated the mind?'
>
> 'There are six times, monk, when one should go and see a monk who has cultivated the mind.
>
> What are the six? Here, monk, at a time when a monk is obsessed in his mind by sense desire, overcome by sense desire, and knows no refuge, as it really is, from sense desire as it arises: that is the time when he should visit a monk who has cultivated the mind and say to him, 'Good sir, I am obsessed in my mind by sense desire, overcome by sense desire, and know no refuge, as it really is, from sense desire as it arises! It would be very good for me if you, sir, were to give me a teaching to get rid of it.' Then the monk who has cultivated the mind gives him a teaching to get rid of it. This, monk, is the first time that one should go and see a monk who has cultivated the mind.
>
> Again, monk, at a time when a monk is obsessed in his mind by ill-will… sloth and torpor… restlessness and worry… or by doubt… and knows no refuge from what has arisen. That is the time when he should visit a monk who has cultivated the mind and say to him: 'I am obsessed in my mind by ill-will, sir,… sloth and torpor… restlessness and worry… or by doubt… It would be very good for me if you were to give me a teaching to get rid of it.' Then the monk who has cultivated the mind gives him a teaching to get rid of it. This, monk, is the

second . . . third . . . fourth . . . fifth time that one should go and see a monk who has cultivated the mind.

Again, monk, at a time when a mental image comes and, although he pays attention to it, there is no freedom from the corruptions and he does not know the image: that is the time when he should visit a monk who has cultivated the mind and say to him, 'Although I pay attention to the mental image that has come, sir, there is no freedom from the corruptions and I do not know the image. It would be very good for me if you were to give me a teaching to destroy the corruptions.' Then the monk who has cultivated the mind gives him a teaching to destroy the corruptions.

This, monk, is the sixth time that one should go and see a monk who has cultivated the mind.

(A III 316)

Assessing one's own mind

The *sutta* is a delightful instance of explication by means of a simple simile: there are many such texts in the canon, which provide small but helpful points about meditative practice not easily categorized under one heading. As so often in such *suttas* some light exploration of the image has practical implications. It was on the issue of food that the Buddha departed from the ascetics, for his choice to rebuild his strength and vitality as a necessary preliminary for the practice of meditation was an essential step in his finding the 'middle way' between two extremes of self-mortification and over indulgence. For the person reading this text as an aid to meditation, there is implicit advice: the mind needs careful care and nourishment and risks lie in over-asceticism or rigidity.[36] It suggests also that if the practitioner is too harsh or peremptory with his or her own mind, or even if he just does not notice what happens to bring it benefit or harm, the corruptions will not be overcome. Imagery concerning food is constantly employed in the canon to describe the balance of meditation states. One text for instance describes the nature of each *jhāna* by comparing the first four to different supplies of nourishment and fuel for those in a citadel (see A IV 111). As with so many other Buddhist concepts, food acquires various intellectual, emotional and spiritual connotations as well as the literal and physical.[37]

This *sutta* also gives us evidence for the flexibility of the Buddha's teaching method: in another more famous context, the *Satipaṭṭhāna-Sutta*, the four foundations of mindfulness are described as sufficient to eradicate defilements, whereas here it is suggested that in practice something else might be needed too.[38] Such apparent anomalies recur throughout the *suttas*, which, addressed to different people at different times, sometimes supply simple modifications to meditation practices described elsewhere. The second section of the *sutta* is quoted in full by Buddhaghosa, to explain the way a meditator may know the readiness of his own mind to enter into *jhāna* and adjust it accordingly.[39]

The bad cook

Suppose, monks, a foolish, inexperienced, bad cook for kings or king's ministers were put in charge of various kinds of soups, that is, soups that are sour, bitter, pungent, sweet, sharp, mild, salty and unsalty.

That foolish, inexperienced, bad cook does not pick up signs of his employer's taste: 'Today my employer likes this soup', or, 'he reaches out for that one', or, 'he takes a good helping of this one', or, 'he praises this one', or, the bitter... the pungent... the sweet... the sharp... the mild... the salty... the unsalty.' In each case he does not pick up on the sign of his employer's taste.[40]

That foolish, inexperienced, bad cook does not earn clothing, wages or extras. For what reason? Because that foolish, inexperienced, bad cook does not pick up on the sign of his employer's taste.

In the same way, monks, here some foolish, inexperienced, bad monk abides contemplating the body in the body, ardent, clearly comprehending, mindful, having removed longing and discontent with regard to the world. But, although he abides contemplating the body in the body, his mind does not become concentrated, the corruptions of the mind are not abandoned, and he does not notice the sign. So he abides contemplating feeling in feelings... the mind in the mind... *dhamma* in *dhammas*... Although he abides contemplating *dhamma* in *dhammas* his mind is not concentrated, the corruptions of the mind are not abandoned, and he does not pick up on the sign.

That foolish, inexperienced, bad monk does not receive comfortable dwellings in this very life, nor does he get mindfulness and clear comprehension. For what reason? That foolish, inexperienced, bad monk does not pick up on the sign of his consciousness.

The good cook

Suppose, monks, a wise, experienced, good cook for kings or king's ministers were put in charge of various kinds of soups, that is, soups that are sour, bitter, pungent, sweet, sharp, mild, salty and unsalty.

That wise, experienced, good cook does notice the signs of his employer's taste: 'Today my employer likes this soup', or, 'he reaches out for that one', or, 'he takes a good helping of this one', or 'he praises this one', or, the bitter... the pungent... the sweet... the sharp... the mild... the salty... the unsalty. In each case he does pick up on the sign of his employer's taste.

That wise, experienced, good cook does earn clothing, wages and extras. For what reason? Because that wise, experienced, good cook does pick up on the sign of his employer's taste.

In the same way, monks, here some wise, experienced, good monk abides contemplating the body in the body, ardent, clearly comprehending, mindful, having removed longing and discontent with regard to the world. While he abides contemplating the body in the body, his mind does become concentrated, the corruptions of the mind are abandoned and he does notice the sign. So he abides contemplating the feeling in feelings...the mind in the mind...*dhamma* in *dhammas*.... As he dwells contemplating *dhamma* in *dhammas* his mind becomes concentrated, the corruptions of the mind are abandoned and he does pick up on the sign.

That wise, experienced, good monk does receive comfortable dwellings in this very life, he does get mindfulness and clear comprehension. For what reason? That wise, experienced, good monk does pick up on the sign of his consciousness.

(S V 149–52)

Particular hindrances

Specific hindrances are dealt with in the canon, but the means of treating them are manifold and not necessarily confined to instructions regarding any one meditation practice. From a practical point of view, elliptic and poetic material that is not overtly directed as meditative instruction can sometimes be more helpful and inspiring than the more specific direction of attention suggested in a *sutta* whose subject is meditation; for instance, a few lines on the effects of ill-will from the *Dhammapada*, such as Dhp 221–34, read in the right frame of mind, can be very effective. Here two texts show the Buddha dealing with the same hindrance, of sloth and torpor, in different ways.

Sloth and torpor (1)

This is one of the few *suttas* devoted entirely to one hindrance. It concerns Tissa, the Buddha's cousin, who trod a troubled if eventually successful path on his way to arahatship. On first entering the order he was irritable and too proud of his high rank.[41] According to the commentary, his age, fatness and liking for rich robes on first becoming a monk meant that he was at first mistaken for a senior Mahāthera: eventually his poor level of attainment becomes obvious.[42] It becomes clear if we pick our way through the material concerning Tissa that he found the spiritual life far from easy, so providing the modern reader a reassuring instance of a canonical figure experiencing just about all the hindrances and difficulties on separate occasions. One story recounts him visiting the Buddha in tears because his peers were all speaking harshly to him (see S II 282). The Buddha responds, plausibly, by pointing out that he speaks harshly to them himself and does not listen to anyone. At that time he is instructed to work on training his anger, conceit and guile.

In this *sutta* Tissa complains about the hindrance of sloth and torpor, which is making his body listless, as if drugged, and inducing doubt. The Buddha, rather than offering advice, rouses him by a series of questions: if there is still desire present in the body, do sorrow and grief arise? Tissa, answering in the affirmative, responds in the same way to questions about the presence of desire in the other five *khandhas*, of feeling, perception, formations and consciousness. Questions concerning the nature of the *khandhas* without desire follow, and the permanence and impermanence of each one in turn: the extensive repetitions for each question have been omitted. Tissa is forced to acknowledge their lack of permanence. Caroline Rhys Davids notes: 'it is a rare and precious glimpse surviving of the strong radiant magnetic personality imparting will to the weaker brother.'[43] It also shows us that the Buddha sometimes preferred unremitting cross-examination as a method of challenging this particular hindrance!

The story of Tissa serves as one of many illustrations that the Buddha's method of teaching is not one of a mechanical response to a particular set of problems. In another case where 'symptoms' are described in precisely the same terms, the Buddha does not resort to rigorous questioning, a tactic presumably particularly suited to rouse Tissa. Instead he gives positive advice: the meditator is told to guard the sense doors, practise moderation in eating, be vigilant, alert to skilful *dhammas* (*vipassaka*) and develop the factors of enlightenment (A III 69–70). This meditator is also described within the *sutta* as attaining arahatship. All goes well for Tissa in the end. Having clearly mastered economy of speech as well as the defilements he delivers, as an arahat, a single verse concerning yet another of the hindrances:

As if pierced by the sword, or as if his head were on fire,
In order to put away desire for the senses a monk should go forth, mindful (Th 39).

At Sāvatthī

Now at that time, Tissa, the Exalted One's cousin, was telling a large number of monks, 'Oh, friends! My body seems as if drugged, the directions are dim to me, the teachings are no longer clear to me. Sloth and torpor has set in, having overpowered my mind. I take no delight in the holy life and I have doubt about the teachings.'

And then the monks went to the Exalted One, paid respects to him and sat down to one side. They told him about this. At that the Exalted One addressed a certain monk in this way: 'Go, monk, and tell Tissa that I am asking for him.' 'Yes, sir,' the monk agreed, and he approached Tissa. Having gone up to him he said, 'The teacher, friend Tissa, has called for you.' 'Yes, sir,' Tissa replied. He went to the Exalted One, paid homage and sat down to one side. The Exalted One then said to him, 'Is it true, Tissa, that you were telling a large number of monks that your body seems as if drugged . . . that you take no delight in the holy life and have doubt about the teachings?'

'Yes, sir.'

'What do you think, Tissa? In a bodily form that is not free of lust, free of desire, of affection, of thirst, of passion and craving – when states of reverse and alteration arise in such a bodily form, do sorrow, lamentation, pain, discomfort and despair arise?'

'Yes, sir.'

'Excellent. And as with bodily form, so with feeling?'[44]

'Yes, sir.'

'Excellent. And as with feeling, so with perception?'

'Yes, sir.'

'Excellent. And as with perception, so with formations?'

'Yes, sir.'

'Excellent. And as with formations, so with consciousness?'

'Yes, sir.'

'Excellent. What do you think, Tissa, that in a bodily form that is free of lust, free of desire, of affection, of thirst, of passion and craving – when states of reverse and alteration arise in such a bodily form, do sorrow, lamentation, pain, discomfort and despair arise?'

'No, sir, they do not.'

'Excellent. And with feeling?... perception?... formations?... consciousness?... do sorrow, lamentation, pain, discomfort and despair arise?'

'No, sir, they do not.'

'Excellent. What do you think, Tissa, that bodily form is permanent or impermanent?'

'Impermanent, sir.'

'Excellent. And is feeling... perception... formations... consciousness permanent or impermanent?'

'Impermanent, sir.'

'Therefore... seeing this... he knows that there is no more existence in this form.'

'Suppose, Tissa, there were two men. One is not skilled in the path and one is skilled in the path. The man who was unskilled in the path might ask someone who was skilled in that path, and that one would reply, "Come, good sir, this is the path. Go on for a while and the path divides into two. Avoid the left-hand path and take the right-hand path. Go on for a while and you will see a forest thicket. Go on for a while and you will see a great swampy marsh. Go on for a while and you will see a steep precipice. Go on for a little and you will see a delightful stretch of even ground."

I have made this simile, Tissa, in order to communicate a meaning. Here is the meaning. "The man who is not skilled in the path" is a description for an ordinary man. "The man who is skilled in the path" is a description for the Tathāgata, an arahat, a Fully Awakened One. "The path dividing into two" is doubt. The "left-hand path" the wrong eightfold path. The "right-hand path" the noble eightfold path, that is, right view, right resolve, right speech, right action, right livelihood, right energy, right mindfulness and right concentration. The "forest thicket" is ignorance. The "great swampy marsh" is sense desires; the "steep precipice", anger and despair. The "delightful stretch of even ground" is a way of describing *nibbāna*.

So cheer up, Tissa, cheer up! I am here to speak to, I am here to help out, I am here to teach!'

The Exalted One spoke in this way. Delighted, Tissa rejoiced in what he had said.

(S III 106–9)

Sloth and torpor (2)

The most famous sufferer from the hindrance of sloth and torpor is one of the Buddha's chief disciples, Moggallāna.[45] Moggallāna, with his mastery of all the *jhānas*, psychic powers and ability to visit other realms is in some ways an exemplar of the tradition of *samatha* practice. He is not a crude personification, but the problems he experiences are to a certain degree representative of this approach. He encounters obstructions at each stage in the development of *jhāna* practice, before attaining arahatship (see S IV 263–9). The hindrance of sloth and torpor is associated elsewhere with the development of concentration to the exclusion of other factors (see A I 257).

Nodding Off

Thus have I heard. Once, when the Exalted One was staying among the Bhaggis on Crocodile Hill in the deer park at Bhesakaḷā Grove, Moggallāna sat nodding off near the village of Kallvāḷamutta, among the Magadhans.

And the Exalted One, with his purified divine eye surpassing that of men, saw him sitting nodding off. Just as a strong man might bend his arm backwards and forwards, the Exalted One vanished from the deer park and appeared before Moggallāna. And the Exalted One sat down at the appointed seat. And when he was sitting down, he said to Moggallāna, 'Are you nodding off, Moggallāna, are you having a snooze?'

'Yes, sir, I am.'

'Then, Moggallāna, at such time as the thought that sluggishness has descended on you, you should not pay attention to that thought, you should not make a major issue out of it.[46] It may be, that by abiding this way, your sluggishness will disappear.

If, abiding so, that sluggishness does not disappear, then, Moggallāna, you should reflect on and explore the *dhamma* in your mind, again and again, just as you have heard it, just as you have learned it by heart: you should consider it continually in the mind.[47] It may be, that by abiding this way, your sluggishness will disappear.

If, abiding so . . . you should repeat the *dhamma* in detail, just as you have heard it, just as you have learned it by heart.

. . . . you should pull both earlobes and massage your limbs with your hand . . .

....you should rise from your sitting practice, splash your eyes with water, look around in all directions and look upwards, at the stars and constellations...

....you should keep in mind the thought of light, resolve your mind upon the thought of day. As by day, so by night; as by night, so by day. So with the heart that is open and unencumbered you should cultivate a radiant mind...

....with senses withdrawn and the mind not going outwards, you should resolve your mind upon walking up and down, perceiving what is in front and behind...

If, abiding so, that sluggishness does not disappear, then, Moggallāna, you should lie down, on your right side, in the lion posture, placing one foot over the other, mindful, clearly comprehending, keeping in mind the thought of rising. And on awakening, you should get up quickly, thinking, "I'll not live yoked to the comfort of lying down, of reclining and sluggishness!" This is how you should train yourself.

Furthermore, Moggallāna, you should train yourself in this way, by thinking, "When visiting families I won't be puffed up with pride". In this way you should train yourself. For in families it may be that people are busy with work and do not notice when a monk has arrived. Then a monk might think, "Who, I wonder, has divided me from this family? These people do not seem to like me". And so, because he has not got anything, he is troubled, and from being troubled comes restlessness. From restlessness comes lack of control and through lack of control the mind is far from concentration.

Furthermore, Moggallāna, you should train yourself in this way, by thinking, "I won't engage in irritable talk". In this way you should train yourself. When there is irritable talk a great deal of wordiness is to be expected. From a great deal of wordiness comes restlessness. From restlessness comes lack of control and from lack of control the mind is far from concentration. I do not praise all association. I do not blame all companionship. But I do not praise companionship with householders and recluses [of itself]. Houses where there are few sounds and little noise, apart from the breath of people, secluded from men: companionship in such houses I do praise.'

When he had said this Moggallāna replied to the Exalted One. 'In what way can it be explained in brief, sir, how a monk can be delivered by the elimination of craving, and reach constant perfection, constant peace from exertion, constant holy life, and a final conclusion, foremost amongst gods and men?'[48]

'Here, Moggallāna, a monk has heard this; "It is not fitting that things in the world should be attached to". If a monk has heard this, he knows each state, knowing each state he understands each state. Understanding each state, whatever the feeling he is experiencing, whether pleasant, painful or neither, he abides with regard to those feelings observing impermanence, observing dispassion, observing cessation. When, with regard to those feelings, he abides observing impermanence, abides observing dispassion, abides observing cessation, seeing them as something to be renounced, he does not adhere to anything in the world. Without attaching to things, he does not crave them and without craving he attains, for himself, *nibbāna*. And he knows, "Birth is exhausted, the holy life has been lived, what has to be done has been done and there is no more of this world."

Such are the things in brief, Moggallāna, whereby a monk can be delivered by the elimination of craving, and reach constant perfection, constant peace from exertion, constant holy life, and a final conclusion, foremost amongst gods and men.'

(A IV 84–8)

4

LONGER TEXTS

I. Concentration and the fruits of recluseship – the *Sāmaññaphala-Sutta*

The very long *suttas* of the Pāli canon effect a slow chemical reaction in the listener that is like a meditation practice in itself. They take hours to chant in complete form: on a special blessing ceremony such as an all-night *Mahāpirit*, one long chant follows another, listeners look around, drop in and out to get a cup of tea, meditate, listen attentively or even doze off. The sense of leisurely exploration through narrative, action, dialogue, bardic lists of names, along with the repetitive rhythms of the chant, can make the listener feel as if aeons are passing in the manner of some Buddhist heavenly realm. It is difficult to communicate in an anthology this sense of ease, considered so important for meditation and listening to long texts, but some extracts are included here from the most comprehensive longer text on the subject of meditation, the *Sāmaññaphala-Sutta*.[1] An intensely dramatic and sophisticated work, it places the Buddha's teaching in a poignantly evoked narrative context. Not only does it include the classical description of the hindrances and the four *jhānas* – found with much the same formula, of which this is possibly the first example, elsewhere in the canon – but also it provides in the treatment of the six ascetics the most notable Buddhist criticism of his contemporaries, and vindication of the *saṅgha*, or order of monks, as the exemplars of the meditative life. Whatever author or authors constructed the final text, it is a dramatic *tour de force*, embodying both within the frame story and the explication of the doctrine a carefully constructed enactment of the Buddha's message. Only the sections directly pertaining to meditation are included, but some sort of background should be given first.[2]

The background story

It starts with the quietly electrifying introductory which provides the dramatic setting from which the teaching can be given. 'Frames' in the *suttas* can seem little more than cursory settings in a time and place, providing a means of distinguishing one from others. Some, however, particularly those in the *Dīghanikāya*, are highly particularized. As Manné demonstrates, it is not possible to appreciate the pertinence or the roundedness of the advice being given unless we know a bit about the people involved, why they are asking particular questions and the views that are being challenged.[3] Gombrich also notes, 'summaries of the Buddha's teaching rarely convey how much use he made of simile and metaphor' (Gombrich 1996: 65). It is difficult to read this *sutta* without sensing the metaphoric power of the extended preamble, which juxtaposes the kingly court and its pleasures, with a journey to the 'court' of the Buddha, where a different kind of leadership, and an entirely different kind of wealth and authority are described.

The text is addressed to Ajātasattu, whose story would have been familiar to those of the time.[4] Ajātasattu of Magadha, the son of King Bimibisāra, fell under the influence of Devadatta, the Buddha's envious cousin, who encouraged him to kill his father, a follower of his rival, the Buddha. Although the old man, hearing of this, abdicated his throne to his son, Ajātasattu imprisons his father and subjects him to a series of tortures. When he finally relents on the birth of his own son and attempts to free the king, the old man has died, without allowing resentment to cloud his mind. Although this tale would be widely known, within the text the fact of Ajātasattu's parricide is withheld until the end, presumably to intensify the low-key yet highly dramatic conclusion. To the Westerner there are echoes of the Oedipus story: and just as the familiarity of the story in a tragedy would not detract from the unfolding of the action, within the *sutta* itself the stain on Ajātasattu's kingship is suggested, but only gradually disclosed.

The apparent serenity of the opening, crafted with the theatrical skill one associates now with grand opera, opens on King Ajātasattu seated on the upper terrace of his palace, surrounded by his retinue, admiring the serenity of the night. The beauty of the full moon inspires the king to speculate as to what teacher they might visit. One by one the attendants suggest the different names of the leading teachers of the day, but at each the king remains silent. The king then asks the silent Jīvaka, who replies that the Buddha is now staying at his own mango grove nearby. It may well be, he adds, that a visit to him could bring the king peace, though we do not know at this stage why this should be needed. Moments of dramatic tension highlight the splendid journey of the entourage. The party has to alight from the elephants to reach the recluse; Ajātasattu is gripped by a curious horror at the silence of an assembly; his encounter with the Buddha himself, is, in epic style, delayed. In dramatic contrast to the pomp of the king the Buddha's leadership of five hundred monks, in his almost inaccessible assembly, 'calm as a lake', is so unobtrusive that he needs to be pointed out to Ajātasattu as 'leaning against a pillar'.[5] Whatever the reason for this detail, comparison is made between the magnificent, but troubled, leadership of the king and that of the teacher: the Buddha needs no throne. The preamble is a testimony to the power of the 'fruits of recluseship' even before the main discourse has even begun.

The next part of the *sutta* involves the king's account of the six other ascetics whom the king has consulted before and asked the same, plausible question: 'What are the benefits of the life of the recluse?' The six represent views current at the time of the Buddha, all rejected by him, which include, for instance, the idea that *kamma* has no effect, that there is no merit from paying respects to teachers, or that a particular ritual observance will bring enlightenment.[6] The main symptom of the teachers' inadequacy lies not just in their doctrines, however: none of them actually answers the question, offering instead their party line 'as if a man when asked what a mango was, should explain what a bread-fruit is': the king, making no response, had quietly taken his leave (D I 53).

The fruits of the recluse

The Buddha does answer the question, in terms Bodhi describes as 'reverberating down the centuries' (Bodhi 1989: 4). The first two fruits have shown easily discernible benefits: if one has been a slave or a householder before, one now has higher status than a king. These are sometimes perceived as worldly advantages, but they are clear answers to the question and would inevitably have interested a king: considerable play is made throughout the *sutta* upon the nature of status and leadership. The Buddha, in asserting the authority of the *saṅgha* in the royal presence, was not wanting to score points against the office of king, which he never does, but rather affirms that the realm of the recluse is of a higher order. To day the king of Thailand will, if spending time in a temple, formally relinquish the trappings of his position in a specially designated room; he then re-emerges in the white of any other lay person who is keeping extra precepts, paying respects to the monks accordingly. Precedence is always given to monks on buses and trains in the East and within the *saṅgha* hierarchy depends simply on seniority of ordination. There is something straightforward and even impersonal about this in practice: the monk receives this deference on behalf of the *saṅgha*. According to the rules of his training, a monk should not teach the *dhamma* unless those he is teaching have paid him the marks of respect of taking off shoes and sandals, sitting on a lower seat than him.[7] As Ariyesako points out, this not only ensures respect for the monk, but for the teaching too.[8]

After this the fruits and benefits are *sandiṭṭhikaṃ*, or visible, in the sense that the *dhamma* is described, as available to a practitioner:[9] they are stages and skills of the meditative life. The extract quoted below is from the section concerned with the third fruit, the first *jhāna* and its preparatory stages, to the end of the *sutta*. The extensive section on the *sīlas*, found in all the first *suttas* of the *Dīghanikāya*, is probably a later, if significant, interpolation and has also been omitted. These stress careful preparation before meditation and include all the wrong forms of livelihood for a monk.

The passage in this anthology starts with the contentment and happiness of the monk, that has just been compared, with perhaps ironic intent, to that of a secure, crowned king, who has defeated his enemies (D I 69). These paragraphs describe features of basic meditative practice we find throughout the Buddhist tradition: the confidence that arises from keeping *sīla*, the guarding of the senses, mindfulness and clear comprehension in daily life and contentment with little.

The hindrances

Only with the third fruit, the first *jhāna*, does the text move to meditation. The hindrances are described, with images that have now become one of the most popular ways of defining them. Their effect is likened to: (i) Being in debt (ii) Suffering from illness (iii) An imprisonment (iv) An enslavement (v) Being lost in a wilderness.

Specific comparison with the hindrances in their usual order is not made in the text, but the placing of the images immediately before the list suggests this intention: the commentary reads them in this way. The abandonment of sense desire is related to a man relieved at being able to clear a debt, just as a monk is relieved not to be plagued by the desire for sense pleasures. Abandoning ill-will is compared to a man who has suffered from a bilious disease regaining his taste for honey and sugar, just as a monk appreciates the value of his rules of training. Abandoning sloth and torpor is compared to someone enjoying a festival and remembering that on a previous occasion he was in prison during the festival and so could not enjoy it. Abandoning restlessness and worry is compared to the state of a slave who, through the help of a friend, is able to pay off his master and is now free, like a monk walking in happiness. The abandoning of doubt is compared to a strong man who, with his luggage in hand and well-armed, travels through a wilderness in company, so reaching a place of safety.[10]

However we assign each of the images, their depiction of a stark impingement of personal liberty and happiness is self-evident. For the inhabitant of ancient India, where illness and debt was a constant threat, punishment vicious in the extreme, enslavement a real possibility and travel through wildernesses notoriously dangerous, they would have represented the most pressing and recognizable fears for personal safety that life at that time could threaten.[11] They also, of course, appear frequently in modern usage to describe situations where one does feel metaphorically entrapped, enslaved, imprisoned, lost in wilderness or even in a phase of life where a problem troubles like a kind of sickness. The perspective here though is important: the images used describe states that the meditator should fear and dread internally, as in the end he or she is the agent responsible for them. Within the terms of meditation practice, the means by which these hindrances are transcended is by the exercise of mindfulness and concentration: their abandonment is always an essential element in the cultivation of *jhāna*.[12]

The *jhānas*

The section that follows describes the states that occur when the hindrances are overcome: the *jhānas*.[13] They are outlined in what is called a pericope, a piece of text that may be transported from one context to another and which is often introduced whenever a particular section of teaching is described.[14] This gives the full, classical description of the *jhānas* as the most important feature of Buddhist meditation practice. It also shows us the extent to the Buddha was anxious to ensure that attention was paid to description of elements of meditative practice in terms of body, feelings and intellect. Although the text does not make this association explicit, the pericope appeals to the first three foundations of mindfulness: it seems designed to ensure not only that the effects of *jhāna* on the body, feelings and mind are described, but that they are all, to a certain extent, awakened as well.

This is important for someone who wants to practice meditation, or who would like to understand the subject, because the descriptive elements which form the bulk of the text are often overlooked or glossed over in allusions to these states, thus producing a one-sided picture. The full version, complete with images, is frequent.[15] The mark of this version is its emphasis on the experiential effects of each state, first in a description of its effects on the entire body, and then, through the elaboration of a single image, to something with which it may be compared.[16] Given the context of great attentiveness with which *suttas* are heard this is presumably designed to arouse a sense of this in the hearer – or in our case the reader. In the events of the Buddha's early life as described in the *Mahāsaccaka-Sutta*, the experience of the first *jhāna* is described as comprehensive and far-reaching: it has profound effects on the perception of the body, the emotions and the intellect (see M I 246–7). It is also in that *sutta* juxtaposed as an alternative to practises that involve some form of torment to either the body or the mind. The pericopes, with their leisurely appeal to the entire person, describe these changes to the body and mind, and those of subsequent *jhānas*, with a memorable and lyrical precision.

The method can be seen in the similes associated with each. The first *jhāna* is described as a state of joy and happiness born of detachment, accompanied by initial thought (*vitakka*) and sustained thought (*vicāra*). The description is extended by an account of the physical effects of this state, in which the body is entirely pervaded with joy and happiness, and then by a simile, that of a bath attendant kneading soap powders into a ball of lather. The ball is made of powders strewn in a metal basin which are then gradually moistened together to form a whole. It is a pleasingly earthy image that, after the bare account of factors, provides a more three-dimensional sense of the meditation's effects: elements not naturally found together become rounded as one; the process is a skilled, gradual undertaking and the product works in a practical and cleansing way. Upatissa examines the simile in some detail: he compares the copper bowl to the earth *kasiṇa*; the hard bits of soap are like the properties of a mind not softened by joy and happiness, which are compared to the action of the water, while the rounding of the ball with moisture is like initial and sustained thought (PF 95–6). As so often in the *suttas*, the practice of meditation is associated with cleansing and a pleasant purificatory process. Much of its effectiveness depends upon its placing here after the analogies for the hindrances: the disease, the debt, the enslavement, the imprisonment and the desolation of being lost in a wilderness.

The movement on to further *jhānas* is a standard progression. I do not know of any place in the *nikāyas* or elsewhere which challenges this numerical order. It is difficult, however, to see the stages from the first to the fourth *jhāna* as entirely hierarchical. Another *sutta*, for instance, compares each to different kinds of food and fuel in a citadel: the first to provisions of grass, wood and water, the second to rice and corn, the third to sesame beans and cereals, the fourth to honey, oil, sugar and salt (A IV 111). Clearly all are useful, and the most choice elements are found in the last: but all, from the basic provisions with which the first *jhāna* is compared, serve different, vitally important functions to maintain the well-being and health of a city. As in the *sutta* discussed here, some sort of refinement from one *jhāna* to the next is undoubtedly intended, yet each has a heterogenous identity characterized by distinctive factors.

There are particularities in the account of each: in the second *jhāna*, the first two *jhāna* factors of initial and sustained thought are abandoned. Other features, not in themselves *jhāna* factors, come into play. The state is now described as possessing unification (*ekodibhāva*); in the absence of the factors associated with speech, it is calmed inwardly (*vūpasamā ajjhattaṃ*) and is the one *jhāna* associated with tranquil confidence (*sampasādanam*). The bodily effects are described with the comparison of a deep pool fed by cool springs that permeate and pervade it. Images of water and currents within flow of water are constantly employed throughout Buddhist literature, in both a negative and positive context: unrestrained water, as in flood, tends to be used for the corruptions and defilements. Such imagery is particularly effective in India, where clear water is a necessity that may be extremely hard to find in drought; in a monsoon river waters may be threatening and overwhelming.[17] The idea of a natural pool of water is particularly attractive and reassuring. It is active, yet contained; there is plenty of fresh water, streams are feeding this supply constantly, so within there is flow and no stagnancy. Upatissa writes of this image that the body should be considered like the pool, the absence of the streams to the absence of initial and sustained thought, the waves of water and their coolness are like the joy and happiness that pervades and cools the mind and body (PF 103–4).

In the third *jhāna* the meditator abandons the factor of joy and the meditator becomes equable (*upekkhako*), mindful and clearly comprehending. From other contexts we know that mindfulness is present in all *jhāna* – it is not possible to attain any meditation without the working together of the five faculties of faith, energy, mindfulness, concentration and wisdom. In this text mindfulness is also described as 'set up' when the meditator first sits cross-legged in an empty place. This is the first *jhāna*, however, in which it is specifically evoked. This is presumably because it becomes particularly strong, though in another commentary Buddhaghosa says that it is rather being enjoined, to prevent attachment (see Asl 219). At any rate, the relinquishment of the power of joy seems to lead to an increase in alertness, definition and even colour.[18] The explanatory image, of brightly coloured lotuses in clear water, suggests at once clarity and great depth of feeling. The lotus is endowed with a great diversity and richness of associations in Indian literature that encompass pleasures both of a spiritual and sensual kind.[19] In Indian literature the flower is associated not only with spiritual awakening, but with sexual beauty: a beautiful woman is described as 'lotus-faced', while lotus feet and lotus hands are also common epithets. The universal monarch, as an expression of his love and generosity towards his subjects, gives lotus tanks to them in the city, also filled with blossoms of different colours.[20] The lotus constantly recurs in early Buddhism as a symbol of awakening and purity. In this instance, the image is given an unusual slant, for the flowers are submerged so that they are completely covered in water, a detail that conveys the sense of complete immersion in the experience of *sukha*: Upatissa relates the body to the lotus.[21] The water here is no longer active, as in the *jhāna* in which joy is strong, but is, from the point of the view of the lotuses, present everywhere all around.

The description and the image of the fourth *jhāna* suggests once more a shift in ground and emphasis. Here the meditator relinquishes pleasure and pain, and enters a state of mindfulness and equanimity, without discomfort or ease. He is, it is said, like a man sitting covered in a clean white cloth, from head to foot. The whiteness of the cloth – a colour associated with royalty and leisure, as it can only be worn on occasions when it would not become dirty – reintroduces a human agent, whose body is entirely covered. Upatissa says that the man is 'protected from extremes of heat and cold, experiences an even temperature and is undisturbed in body and mind' (PF 112). The man in the simile, unlike the bathman of the first *jhāna*, is not active, but is enjoying benefits which have reached a natural conclusion, and which are felt throughout the entire body. This is the first of the images that does not use water as an important element, for it moistens in the first *jhāna*, is constantly feeding in the second, and is still and all-surrounding in the third: in the first two cases Upatissa compares the water involved to joy and happiness; in the third, where joy is abandoned, to happiness alone.[22] Here, where equanimity is strong, there is a movement to a different basis or level. The word clean (*parisuddha*) suggests that purification and immersion in water have already occurred: equanimity (*upekkhā*) is not presented as a rejection of feeling, but an emergence, as if water has been entered and fulfilled its purpose.[23] The man with the white cloth brings the images to a new ground.

Traditionally the fourth *jhāna* is seen to occupy a special position: it is the starting point for the formless realms, not mentioned in this *sutta*, and also for the higher knowledges (*abhiññā*), powers described in this *sutta*. From this state, the Buddha enters his *parinibbāna*.[24]

Samatha practice concerns the purification of feeling (*vedanā*). Exploration of the analogies aids an intuitive understanding of the nature of each meditation, to balance or complement analytic description. The ancient Indian mind, from the Vedic period onwards, loved to think through simile or metaphor, and it is through such an appeal that the whole description works. The *jhānas*, the text stresses, affect the mind, the body and feeling; these pericopes, found in so many *suttas*, seem specially designed to ensure that the awareness of the listener includes them all too.[25]

The higher knowledges **(abhiññā)**

The description of the *jhānas* is a turning point in the list. The following eight fruits, skills which are directly dependent on the fourth *jhāna*, are each preceded by the formula, 'With his mind thus composed, purified, translucent, unblemished, free from stains, softened, malleable and imperturbable, he directs and inclines his mind towards knowledge and vision'. Elsewhere the last six are termed the higher knowledges (*abhiññā*). Each of these knowledges is also accompanied by a simple image to which it is compared.

1 Insight into the four elements. Compared to a Veḷuriyan gem.
2 Mind-made body, compared to pulling a reed from its sheath.
3 The eightfold *iddhi* of (i) from being one to being many, and from many becoming one again (ii) unhindered, he becomes visible or invisible (iii) he passes through mountain walls, through city walls and through mountains as if through space (iv) he swims up and down through the earth as if through water (v) he goes through water as if over the earth (vi) he travels through the sky cross-legged (vii) he touches and strokes with his hand the sun and moon (viii) he holds mastery with his body as far as the world of Brahma. Compared to skilled potter or goldsmith or his apprentice making any shape he wants.
4 Divine ear, compared to hearing drums.
5 Knowing the minds of others, compared to looking in a clear pool or mirror.
6 Recollecting past lives, as if remembering another village.
7 Seeing rebirths of others, like watching a busy thoroughfare and people leaving and entering it.
8 Knowledge of the corruptions, like seeing the bottom of a pool.

These further fruits, each supposedly better than the one before, can be developed by the meditator when he has trained his mind thoroughly in the *sīlas* and the four *jhānas*. Approached only when the meditator is well established in the imperturbability of the fourth *jhāna*, they are considered to represent the highest powers of the mind. The presence of such powers are a contained and even an integral part of Buddhist understanding, though are often underplayed in a monastic and teaching context. This reticence is supported by some texts, which acknowledge but do not promulgate such phenomena. On one occasion, in his remonstrance towards the egoistic brahmin youth Kevaddha on their use for no purpose, the Buddha actively discourages their use. This does not mean he rejected them.[26] It is certainly an offence within the monastic code (*Vinaya*) to display these powers beyond the capacity of ordinary men; false claims to such powers constitute an immediate defeat, or expulsion from the order. Conscious false claims of any kind concerning meditation, however, also fall under the same offence.[27] The Buddha treats them with caution, but does not reject them: at the time of the Buddha the display of psychic powers appears to have been *de rigeur* as a means of proving a teacher's mettle, as seen at the spectacular psychic challenge at the beginning of the *Vinaya* between a nāga and the Buddha.[28] The word *iddhi* is derived from the Sanskrit *ardh*, or Pāli *ijjhati*, meaning to prosper or flourish: within the terms of ancient Indian understanding, they represent proof of success, the flowerings of the successful and skilful mind.[29] A hunter, able to catch game, displays his *iddhis*, just as the birds that outwit him possess theirs; a king possesses *iddhis* if he has personal beauty, long life, health and popularity.[30] People would expect a monk to have his too: Bodhi points out the term soon acquired overtones of spiritual success, or spiritual power, and so came to converge with success in attaining arahatship as well.[31]

The whole area, however, raises questions about which the modern mind is deeply uneasy: psychic powers and the recollection of past lives are not skills that we are encouraged to accredit, far less cultivate. In Asian countries, at a popular and folk level, this is not the case, and magazines and anecdotes are often concerned with the recounting of a past life experience or some strange psychic event. Brought up in England, I can only say that even before the 'new age', it seems to me there has always existed a kind of subterranean acceptance of many, if not all, of such phenomena. Strange coincidences, meeting people in extraordinary circumstances and the sensing of supernatural presences are all the stuff of anecdotes and experience, acceptable to many Christians as happy intimations that the universe is ordered in ways beyond our present understanding. The events themselves are not regarded as odd or unusual. Whether these faculties are spontaneous *iddhis* or have some other cause is beyond the scope of this study: they do not, however, accord with the modern tenets of rationalism and conventional Christian belief. What seems important, from the human point of view, is the effect on the person involved. My impression is that where it is accompanied by good sense it is not only not harmful but very beneficial. In Buddhist cultures, where such powers have been accredited for centuries, the understanding of the world they imply provides all kinds of psychological escape valves. Until recently in Sri Lanka, for instance, a child's difficulties or nightmares were felt to stem from a past life, and so ways are found of dealing with that, that seem to work whatever the 'truth' of the recollection.[32] It is also helpful for relatives to chant blessings for a dead person to help them in their next life. Chants politely send away unhappy beings born as 'ghosts' and welcome the presence of happy and benign deities.[33] In these cases, doctrines associated with *iddhis* are used in a way that is intended to promote health of mind: such ceremonies provide a focus for familial and societal support at times of psychological trauma and major life events.

Clearly, however, such powers, if they are possible, could be misused or arouse fear and superstition. Saddhatissa makes the point that Christ is never described as misappropriating power in performing miracles and, like the Bodhisatta when tormented in his nāga rebirths, refrains from using them to escape persecution.[34] As a benefit from meditative practice they are all described as the product of the mind that has been trained to the level of the fourth *jhāna*, after which they are thought worthy of cultivation. Consideration of the facilities that are suggested by each power gives an understandable reason for this. Equanimity, and its attendant mastery of the area of feeling, would ensure that partiality or dislike should not feature in their use, so providing an inbuilt antidote to abuse or misappropriation. As Gethin points out, this list, with the same formula found in the *Sāmaññaphala-Sutta*, is so constantly associated with the last fruit, the destruction of the corruptions (*āsavas*), as to suggest that the development of these powers, once the mind has attained the fourth *jhāna*, is in some sense salvific.[35]

The Buddha himself did not support displays of psychic powers to 'show off', but practised them himself as a teaching means. He uses the 'divine eye', which can see what is far away, to find out those meditators who are suffering or experiencing difficulties. He then conjures up a 'mind-made body' to go and visit them and deliver advice.[36] Moggallāna uses psychic powers to teach in the heavens.[37] Modern Buddhists might explain a visit from the Buddha at a time of need as some kind of manifestation of a guide or teacher from the unconscious mind that comes to one's aid when one needs it. At any rate, whether the world suggested by these last powers does genuinely describe, for instance, the ability to see the troubles of another being with the divine eye, or to visit another realm, or whether we read them now as metaphoric descriptions, the teaching administered on the basis of that tends to be pragmatic and straightforward. When the Buddha 'sees' a struggling meditator and then visits him in a mind-made form, it is not the *iddhis* that strike us: it is the sensible advice, which is thoroughly practical and carefully geared to the practitioner's needs.

In this text the fruits of the recluse do not transport the meditator to a heaven realm or a palatial dwelling. The last and most significant fruit pertains to insight into the corruptions that bind all existence, which confers no special power other than that of complete freedom for the mind. This is communicated through the simile of looking to the base of a clear pool, a pleasant and natural experience that is in accordance with the spirit of all the analogies used to describe the other fruits. Like the memory of life in another village, the pulling of a reed from a sheath, or the activity of watching people moving around in the streets below it is a simile recognizable to everyone: the highest fruit of the meditator, the recluse, is not that the world changes for him but that, having practised the stages in turn, he sees the world that is already there with different eyes.

The *sutta* ends with masterly understatement. King Ajātasattu, profoundly moved by the discourse, confesses his great crime. The Buddha does not admonish him, but gives him the one consolation that having acknowledged his fault he will at some time in the future attain restraint. The listeners would also be aware of a further irony: King Ajātasattu was also subsequently murdered by his own son. After the king departs the Buddha notes that the king, apart from this terrible crime, was a just man, and that had he not been stained by his actions he would have attained the *dhamma* eye, stream-entry.

Sāmaññaphala-Sutta

'And how, great king, is a monk a gatekeeper for the faculties of sense?

Here, a monk, seeing a visible object with the eye, does not grasp at the appearance nor does he grasp at its various details. Because harmful, unskilful states such as longing and discontent would assail him if he were to abide without restraint with regard to the eye faculty, he practises restraint, guards the eye faculty and achieves restraint over the eye faculty. Here, hearing a sound with the ear ... smelling an odour with the nose ... tasting a flavour with the tongue ... touching a physical object with the body ... apprehending an object with the mind, the monk does not grasp at the appearance nor does he grasp at the various details. Because harmful, unskilful states such as longing and discontent would assail him if he were to abide without restraint with regard to the faculty of mind, he practises restraint, guards the faculty of the mind and achieves restraint over the faculty of the mind. Endowed with this noble restraint over the faculties of sense he experiences within himself an untainted happiness.

'In this way, great king, a monk is a gatekeeper for the faculties of sense.

'And how, great king, is a monk endowed with mindfulness and clear comprehension? Here, a monk acts with mindfulness and clear comprehension when walking backwards and forwards, in looking ahead or behind, when bending and stretching, in wearing his outer and inner robe and carrying his bowl, when eating and drinking, chewing and swallowing, when defecating and urinating, when walking, standing, sitting, falling asleep, waking up, talking and keeping silent. In this way, a monk is endowed with mindfulness and clear comprehension.

'And how, great king, is a monk content? Here, a monk is content with his robe to cover his body and his almsfood to fill his stomach. Wherever he goes he takes just these with him, just as a bird carries his wings as his only burden when he goes into flight. In this way, wherever a monk goes, he is content with his robe to cover his body and his almsfood to fill his stomach and takes just these with him.

'In this way, great king, a monk is content.

'Then he, endowed with this noble heap of virtues, this noble restraint of the sense faculties, this noble mindfulness and clear comprehension and this noble contentment, finds for himself a place of seclusion, the roots of a forest tree, a mountain cave or a mountain cleft, a charnel ground, a jungle thicket, or a heap of straw in the open air. After he has returned from the almsround and eaten his food he sits, folding his legs in a cross-legged position, makes his body straight and sets up mindfulness before him.

'Abandoning longing for the senses, he abides, with a heart free from longing, and purifies his mind of longing.

'Abandoning ill-will and hatred, he abides with his mind purified of ill-will and hatred, and, compassionate, wishing for the welfare of all sentient beings, he purifies his mind of ill-will and hatred.

'Abandoning sloth and torpor, he abides free from sloth and torpor, and, perceiving light, mindful and clearly comprehending, he purifies his mind of sloth and torpor.

'Abandoning restlessness and worry, he abides in calm, and, with a mind made inwardly peaceful, purifies his mind of restlessness and worry.

'Abandoning doubt he abides having crossed over doubt, and, without being troubled about what is or is not wholesome, he purifies his mind of doubt.

'Suppose a man were to incur a debt to start up a business, whose business prospered: he would then pay off his old debts and with what was remaining could support a wife. Then he would think, "Before this I got into debt to start up a business, but now it has prospered and with what is remaining I can support a wife". And on that account he would be glad and rejoice.

'Suppose a man were to become ill, in pain, terribly sick, so that he could not enjoy his food and had no strength in his body. After some time, he would be free of that illness, enjoy his food and recover his bodily strength. Then he would think, "Before this I was ill…". And on that account he would be glad and rejoice.

'Suppose a man were to be bound in a prison. After some time, he would be released from his imprisonment, safe and without any loss, and with no diminishment of his property. Then he would think, "Before this I was in prison…". And on that account he would be glad and rejoice.

'Suppose a man were a slave, without independence, subject to another, unable to go where he wished. After some time he would be released from slavery and gain his independence, he would no longer be subject to another, able to go where he wished. Then he would think, "Before this I was a slave…". And on that account he would be glad and rejoice.

'Suppose a man, with wealth and possession, were to undertake a journey on a road through a wilderness, where food was scarce and there were many dangers. After some time, he would get through the wilderness and, safe and secure, reach the outskirts of a village. Then he would think, "Before this I was undertaking a journey…".

'And on that account he would be glad and rejoice.

'In this way, great king, a monk sees that when these five hindrances have not been abandoned in him, it is like a debt, a sickness, an imprisonment, enslavement and a road in a wilderness. But when he sees that these five hindrances have been abandoned in him, it is like freedom from debt, good health, release from prison, freedom from slavery and a place of safety. When he sees these five hindrances have been abandoned in him, gladness arises. In the one who is glad, joy arises. The body of the one who is joyful becomes tranquil. The one who is happy concentrates the mind.

'This monk, quite secluded from sense desires, from unskilful states, enters and abides in the first *jhāna*, which is accompanied by initial thought and sustained thought, filled with the joy and happiness born of seclusion. He pervades, drenches, saturates and suffuses this very body with the joy and happiness born of seclusion, and there is no place in his entire body that is not suffused with this joy and happiness. Suppose a skilled bathman, or his assistant, were to sprinkle powdered soap into a metal dish, splash water all around it and knead it into a soap ball, so that the ball of soap would be taken up, permeated and steeped in moisture, inside and outside, yet would not trickle. In the same way, a monk pervades, drenches, saturates and suffuses this very body with the joy and happiness born of seclusion, and there is no place in his entire body that is not suffused with joy and happiness.

'This, great king, is a visible fruit of recluseship more excellent and choice than the ones before.[38]

'Furthermore, with the subsiding of initial thought and sustained thought, a monk enters into and abides in the second *jhāna*, which is accompanied by internal peace, confidence and unification of the mind, is free from initial thought and sustained thought, and is filled with the joy and happiness born of concentration.

He pervades, drenches, saturates and suffuses this very body with the joy and happiness born of concentration so that there is no place in his entire body that is not suffused with joy and happiness.

'Suppose, there were a deep lake whose waters well up from below. It would have no inlet for water from the east, from the west, from the north or from the south, nor would it be replenished from time to time with showers of rain. Yet a current of cool water does well up from the depths of the lake and pervades, drenches, saturates and suffuses the whole lake, so that there is no place in the entire lake that is not suffused with cool water. In the same way, the monk pervades, drenches, saturates and suffuses this very body with the joy and happiness born of concentration, so that there is no part of his entire body that is not suffused with joy and happiness.

'This, great king, is a visible fruit of recluseship yet more excellent and choice than the ones before.

'Furthermore, with the fading away[39] of joy, the monk, equanimous, mindful and clearly comprehending, experiences that happiness in the body about which the noble ones declare, "The one who is equanimous and mindful abides in happiness", and enters and abides in the third *jhāna*. He pervades, drenches, saturates and suffuses this very body with the happiness that is free from joy, so that there is no part of his entire body that is not suffused with happiness.

'Suppose, there were in a lotus pond blue, white and red lotuses that have been born in the water, grow in the water, never rise above the water but are nourished immersed in water. From the tips to the roots they are pervaded, drenched, saturated and suffused with water so that there is no part of the lotus that is not suffused with cool water. In this way a monk pervades, drenches, saturates and suffuses this very body with the happiness that is free from joy, so that there is no place in his entire body that is not suffused with happiness.

'This, great king, is a visible fruit of recluseship yet more excellent and choice than the ones before.

'Furthermore, great king, with the abandoning of happiness and pain and the disappearance of the earlier pleasant and unpleasant feeling, the monk enters into and abides in the fourth *jhāna*, that is beyond pleasure or pain, and is purified by equanimity and mindfulness. And he sits suffusing this very body with a purified and translucent mind so that there is no place in his body that is not suffused with a purified and translucent mind.

'Suppose a man were to sit enveloped from the head down with a white cloth, so that there would be no place in his body that was not enveloped with the white cloth. In this way, a monk sits suffusing his body with a purified and translucent mind, so that there is no place in his body that is not suffused with a purified and translucent mind.

'This, great king, is a visible fruit of recluseship yet more excellent and choice than the ones before.

'With his mind thus composed, purified, translucent, unblemished, free from stains, softened, malleable and imperturbable, he directs and inclines his mind towards knowledge and vision. And he knows, "This body of mine is material, made up of the four elements, born of mother and father, nourished by rice and gruel, its nature is impermanence, subject to rubbing, pummelling, break up and destruction. And this is my consciousness, bound and tied up with it".

'Suppose, there were a Veḷuriyan gem of the finest water, eight faceted, skilfully cut, clear, translucent, flawless and excellent in every way. And through it is threaded a string that is blue, or yellow, or red, or white, or orange. In just this way, a monk with his mind composed, purified, translucent, unblemished, free from stains, softened, manageable and unperturbed, directs and inclines it to knowledge and vision. A man with good eyes holds it in his hand and reviews it, "This is a Veḷuriyan gem of the finest water . . . ". In the same way, a monk with his mind thus composed, purified, translucent . . . directs and inclines it to knowledge and vision. And in this way he knows, "This body of mine is material, made up of the four elements. . . . And this is my consciousness, bound and tied up with it".

'This, great king, is a visible fruit of recluseship yet more excellent and choice than the ones before.

'With his mind thus composed . . . he directs and inclines it towards magically creating a mind-made body. From this body, he creates another body, of mind-made form, with all parts and limbs complete, with special powers.[40]

'Suppose a man were to pull out a reed from its sheath. He would think, "This is the reed, this is the sheath. The reed is one thing, the sheath another. It is from the sheath that the reed has been drawn". And, similarly, were he to take a snake from its slough or a sword from its scabbard. In the same way with his mind thus composed, purified, translucent, unblemished, free from stains, softened, malleable and imperturbable, he directs and inclines it towards magically creating a mind-made body.

'This, great king, is a visible fruit of recluseship yet more excellent and choice than the ones before.

'With his mind thus composed . . . he inclines it to the supernormal powers. He then exercises the various manifestations of supernatural power: from being one, he becomes many, and having been many he becomes one; he appears and disappears; he goes without obstruction through a wall, a rampart, a mountain as if through space; he swims in and out of the earth as if it were water; he walks on water, without sinking, as if it were earth; sitting cross-legged he travels through space like a bird on the wing; with his hand he touches and strokes the sun and the moon, powerful and mighty as they are; he reaches in the body even up to the Brahma heaven.

'Suppose a skilled potter or his apprentice were to make and mould from well-prepared clay whatever shaped vessel he might wish. Or suppose a skilled ivory worker or his apprentice or a skilled goldsmith or his apprentice were to make and fashion whatever shaped vessel he might wish. In the same way, with his mind thus composed, purified . . . he directs and inclines it to the supernormal powers.

'This, great king, is a visible fruit of recluseship yet more excellent and choice than the ones before.

'With his mind thus composed . . . he directs and inclines it to the divine ear. With his divine ear, purified and surpassing that of human beings, he hears sounds both divine and human, near and far.

'Suppose a man travelling on a major road were to hear the sound of a kettle drum, of a tabor, of a conch horn, cymbal, drum and would think, "That is the sound of a kettle drum, of a tabor, of a conch horn, cymbal, drum". In this way, with his mind thus composed, purified... he directs and inclines it to the divine ear. With his divine ear, purified and surpassing that of human beings, he hears sounds both divine and human, near and far.

'This, great king, is a visible fruit of recluseship yet more excellent and choice than the ones before.

'With his mind thus composed... he directs and inclines it to the knowledge that encompasses the minds of others. Encircling the minds of other beings and other individuals with his own mind, he knows them.

He knows a mind that is with desire as with desire, and a mind free from desire as free from desire.

He knows a mind with hate... a mind free from hate.

He knows... a deluded mind... an undeluded mind.

He knows... a constricted mind... a scattered mind.[41]

He knows... a mind grown great... a mind that has not grown great.[42]

He knows... a surpassable mind... surpassing mind.[43]

He knows... a composed mind... a discomposed mind.

He knows... a liberated mind... an unliberated mind.

'Suppose a woman, man, youth or girl, fond of ornaments, were to review his or her own facial reflection in a mirror or bowl of water, that is purified, pellucid and clear, he or she would know if there were a mole, "there is a mole here, there is one there"; or he or she would know, if there were none, "there is no mole here and no mole there". In this way with his mind thus composed... he knows a liberated mind as liberated and an unliberated mind as unliberated.

'This, great king, is a visible fruit of recluseship yet more excellent and choice than the ones before.

'With his mind thus composed... he directs and inclines it to the knowledge of the recollection of past lives. He recollects his numerous past lives, that is, one birth, two births, three, four, five, ten births; twenty, thirty, forty, fifty births, a hundred, a thousand, a hundred thousand births, many aeons of world contraction, of world expansion and of world expansion and contraction. "There, my name was such and such, my family was such and such, my caste was such and such, my food was such and such, I experienced such and such pleasant and painful circumstances, I lived for so long a time. Falling away from there I arose there." He remembers his various past births, their circumstances and their details.

'Suppose a man were to go from his village to another, and from that to yet another, and then from there return to his own village. He would think, "I went from my own village to that village. There, I stood in such and such a way, sat in such a such a way, spoke in such and such a way and remained silent in such and such a way. From that village I went to another. In that village, I stood in such and such a way, sat in such a such a way, spoke in such and such a way and remained silent in such and such a way. From that village I returned to my own village." In the same way with his mind thus composed, purified... he remembers his various past births, their circumstances and their details.

'This, great king, is a visible fruit of recluseship yet more excellent and choice than the ones before.

'With his mind thus composed... he directs and inclines it to the knowledge of the arising and falling away of other beings. He with the purified divine eye that surpasses that of men sees beings falling away and arising; he recognises the inferior and the superior, beautiful and ugly, fortunate and unfortunate, and he knows how beings fare according to their *kamma*, in this way, "Certainly, these beings, who were endowed with bad conduct in their body, speech and mind, who reviled noble ones, who had wrong view, and acquired for themselves the *kamma* that is the result of wrong view, they, on the break up of the body after death go to an unhappy state, a bad destiny, a lower realm, a hell. These beings, however, who were endowed with good conduct in their body, speech and mind, who did not speak against noble ones, who had right view, and acquired for themselves the *kamma* that is the result of right view, they, on the break up of the body after death go to a happy state, a heavenly world." In this way he, with the purified divine eye that surpasses that of men, sees beings falling away and arising; he recognizes the inferior and the superior, beautiful and ugly, fortunate and unfortunate, and he knows how beings fare according to their *kamma*.

'Suppose there were a tall house in the middle of a square courtyard. There a man with good eyes might stand and see people going into a house and leaving it, walking in the street or sitting in the middle of the courtyard. And he would think, "These people are going into a house and leaving it, these are walking in the street and these are sitting in the middle of the courtyard". In this way, with his mind thus composed, purified, translucent,... he, with the purified divine eye that surpasses that of men, sees beings falling away and arising; he recognises the inferior and the superior, beautiful and ugly, fortunate and unfortunate, and he knows how beings fare according to their *kamma*.

'This, great king, is a visible fruit of recluseship yet more excellent and choice than the ones before.

'With his mind thus composed... he directs and inclines it to the knowledge of the elimination of the corruptions. He knows, "this is suffering", just as it really is. He knows, "this is the origin of suffering", just as it really is. He knows, "this is the cessation of suffering", just as it really is. He knows, "this is the way to the cessation of suffering", just as it really is. He knows, "these are the corruptions", just as they really are. He knows, "this is the origin of the corruptions", just as it really is. He knows, "this is the cessation of the corruptions", just as it really is. He knows, "this is the way leading to the cessation of the corruptions", just as it really is. Knowing in this way and seeing in this way, his mind is delivered from the corruption of sense desire, from the corruption of becoming, from the corruption of ignorance and the knowledge arises in him, "this is deliverance!" He knows, "Birth is exhausted, the holy life has been fulfilled, what has to be done has been done, and there is no more beyond this".

'Suppose there were in a mountain glen a lake whose water is clear, limpid and unruffled. A man with good eyes, standing on the bank, would see oyster-shells, sands and pebbles, and shoals of fish, darting around and keeping still. He would think, "This a lake whose water is clear, limpid and unruffled and within it there are oyster-shells, sands and pebbles, and shoals of fish, darting around and keeping still".

'In the same way, with his mind thus composed, purified . . . he knows, "Birth is exhausted, the holy life has been fulfilled, I have done what has to be done, and there is no more beyond this".

'This, great king, is a visible fruit of recluseship yet more excellent and choice than the ones before. And there is not, great king, another fruit of recluseship yet more excellent and choice than this one'.

'When the Exalted One had finished speaking, King Ajātasattu said to him, 'Excellent, sir, excellent! It is just as if someone had set something straight which had fallen down, revealed what had been hidden, showed the way to someone who had been lost, and held up a lamp in the dark, so that those with eyes to see could discern shapes. Just so has the Exalted One illuminated the *dhamma* in various ways. And I, sir, go to the Exalted One for my refuge, I go to the *dhamma* for my refuge and I go to the *saṅgha* for my refuge. May the Exalted One accept me as a lay disciple from this day forth, as long as I shall live! An offence overcame me, sir, who was so stupid, so lost and so bad, that just for the sake of power I deprived my father, a just man and a just king, of his life. May the Exalted One acknowledge my confession of an offence as an offence for the sake of my restraint in the future.'

'Indeed, great king, an offence overcame you, who was so stupid, so lost and so bad, that, just for the sake of power, you deprived your father, a just man and a just king, of his life. But since you have confessed your offence as an offence and are practising the *dhamma*, I acknowledge it. There will be growth in the noble discipline, for the one who sees his offence as an offence and confesses it for his future restraint.'

When this had been said, the Māgadhan Ajātasattu, son of the Vedehans, said this to the Exalted One, 'But now, sir, I must go, I have a great deal of business and work to be done'. 'Do now, great king, as you see fit.' The Māgadhan Ājatasattu, son of the Vedehans, rejoiced in what the Exalted One had said and expressed his gratitude. Rising from his seat, he paid homage, and keeping his right side towards him, departed.

And soon after the Māgadhan Ajātasattu, son of the Vedehans, had left, the Exalted One addressed the monks. 'This great king, monks, has ruined himself; he has damaged himself. But if, monks, this great king had not deprived his father, a just man and a just king, of life, in that very seat the pure and stainless eye of *dhamma* would have arisen for him.'

Thus spoke the Exalted One. Delighted, the monks rejoiced in what the Exalted One had said.

(D I 71–85)

5

LONGER TEXTS

II. The four foundations of mindfulness – the *Satipaṭṭhāna-Sutta*

It is sometimes said that it is in those words least susceptible to translation that the life of any tradition may be found. This is certainly true of the word *sati*, now always translated as mindfulness. The word derives from the root for 'memory' (Skst *smṛti*) though this does not quite accommodate all its shades of meaning, which is more an 'attentiveness directed towards the present'.[1] Mindfulness is that quality that characterizes the mind that is alert, awake and free from befuddlement. Rightly applied it becomes a path factor, the first of the factors of enlightenment, considered to be the basis of all Buddhist meditation teaching.[2] According to the *Abhidhamma*, it is present and a distinguishing mark of all skilful consciousness. To be mindful is to be steady and awake: one *sutta* compares *sati* to the gatekeeper of a citadel who 'refuses entrance to those unknown, but admits those he knows, for the protection of those inside' (A IV 110). There are many accounts and books written about the subject of this all-important quality.[3] It is not being confused or shallow, so that the mind does not 'wobble'.[4] It is likened to a good minister, who carries out each job that is needed at the right time; or salt in food: just as this brings out the quality of each taste in a dish, so mindfulness, which is aware of each sensory impression as it occurs, brings out the particular nature of each experience (see Asl 121–2). It is described as the opposite of superficiality and forgetfulness (Dhs 14). The Buddha said it is the one faculty that can never be unbalanced and is useful at all times (S V 115).

This *sutta*, one of the major texts of the canon, describes how to arouse and apply this faculty in a number of different situations. From this, in the longer version (*Mahāsatipaṭṭhāna-Sutta*), there is more extended exploration of the nature of the four noble truths, the teaching given by the Buddha to those most near to an understanding of the nature of things as they are, and the eight path factors.[5] This may be found in the *Dīghanikāya* (D II 290–315). The *Satipaṭṭhāna-Sutta* has been so influential in the Buddhist tradition that some modern works should be mentioned which have explored it more fully than is possible here, both from an academic and a practical point of view. In this context, where a close precision to detail is needed, there is sometimes an interesting and helpful overlap between the two approaches.[6] Probably the most important work is Soma Thera, *The Way of Mindfulness*, which includes the commentary and sub-commentary on the *sutta*. For the practitioner Nyanaponika Thera's *The Heart of Buddhist Meditation* (1969) is still a classic, with an emphasis on the *vipassanā* approach represented by the Burmese *satipaṭṭhāna* method. Much of the material included in the *sutta* forms the basis of Bhikkhu Buddhadāsa's *Mindfulness of Breathing* (1998) and Saddhatissa's *The Buddha's Way* (1971). Notes to the *sutta* by Bhikkhus Ñāṇamoli and Bodhi in the *Middle Length Discourses of the Buddha*, along with Bodhi's extensive notes on the closely related *saṃyuttavagga*, provide a perspective with an academic emphasis.[7] More generally, we find in the *sutta* the instructions for practices, which, developed in various ways, are taught throughout the Buddhist tradition: in particular the recommendations for activities during daily life as well as in meditation practice.[8] Some conform closely to the injunctions given in the *sutta*, to the extent that it constitutes their chief text. Nearly all, *samatha* and *vipassanā* alike, employ some of the methods described in the *sutta*: in order to help a reading of the text in a practical context, this very brief introduction will include some explanatory quotes from modern teachers.

The text is structured around the four foundations of mindfulness, a list whose importance cannot be overemphasized.[9] Two translations have been taken for the word *satipaṭṭhāna:* either that of an establishing in the sense of a sphere (Skst *upasṭhāna*), or a range or domain of mindfulness (*paṭṭhāna*). The former is etymologically most likely though the commentaries tend to favour the latter.[10] They form the first four of the constituents of enlightenment, and are perceived as a kind of foundation stone of any meditative practice. These are the body, the feelings, the mind and *dhammas*. The practice of body mindfulness incorporates a number of meditations classified by Buddhaghosa under separate categories. It is here defined not only according to the method suggested by Buddhaghosa, in terms of the thirty-one (or two) parts of the body (28), but also as the first four stages of breathing mindfulness (29), the defining of the four elements (40) and the basic instructions for *asubha* objects (11–20), here divided into nine rather than ten.[11] These are considered in this book under each topic. Practices are assigned to one of the foundations of mindfulness, in the following way:

1 Body: (a) the first four of the sixteen stages of mindfulness of breathing, (b) mindfulness and clear comprehension in the four postures, (c) mindfulness and clear comprehension in all bodily activities, (d) the thirty-one parts of the body, (e) the four elements, (f) the *asubha* contemplations.
2 Feeling (*vedanā*).
3 Mind (*citta*).
4 *Dhammas*: (a) the five hindrances, (b) five groups of clinging (*khandhas*), (c) the six sense bases, internal and external,[12] (d) the seven factors of enlightenment, (e) the four noble truths (not elaborated in the shorter version reproduced here), (f) the eightfold path (not included in shorter version).

If we look at the ways mindfulness is being described in this *sutta* it becomes clear that it is not simply a matter of the identifying or labelling mind, a function of what is termed in the Buddhist tradition perception or identification (*saññā*), but a way of developing awareness in all spheres of life and in various activities during the day. Much of the *sutta* is devoted to body mindfulness and includes a number of practices involving being aware of what the body is doing at any moment: the contact of the feet on the ground, the air on the face, the manner in which one is walking and all the impressions that meet the senses all come under this. The movement of the breath in and out of the body is also a subject for mindfulness. The *sutta* lists each of these foundations as applying both internally, to one's own bodily experience, externally, in the awareness of what is happening in others and in the world around, and both internally and externally, in an awareness that moves between and encompasses both what is going on inside and outside. This threefold application is repeated for each practice and for each of the foundations of mindfulness.

A short extract from a modern *vipassanā* meditation school, expressed in modern colloquial speech, translates the directness of much of the Buddha's own instructions on the practice of body mindfulness into modern idiom: it demonstrates the way that bodily mindfulness is taught now, in this case with a slight emphasis towards the cultivation of insight.

> You have to be aware of what state your body is in. Is it upright, balanced, relaxed and tranquil? Or is it falling about, unbalanced, slack and loose? Perhaps it is as taut as an over-tightened violin string; rigid and stiff, full of tension and feeling as though it may break apart at any minute.
>
> Is the breathing smooth, quiet and gentle? Or is it noisy, ragged and harsh? . . . To be aware of these things is to be mindful of body.
>
> To be aware of your own bodily state is to be mindful of body, internally. To be aware of another's bodily state is to be mindful of body, externally. To be aware that you are being affected as a result of getting caught up in your perception of someone else's bodily discomfort, is to be aware of the body both internally and externally.
>
> To know that the body is calm and quiet is to be mindful of body. To restrain the urge to tense muscles in an attempt to concentrate is to be mindful of body.
>
> As you observe, you become aware that all of the bodily things you attend to are transient: they do not last; they cannot last. You become aware of the 'rise and fall' of bodily phenomena. You come to experience the mark of transience (*anicca*) for yourself.
>
> (James 1986: 57)

The second foundation of mindfulness is what is being felt – whether pleasant, neutral or unpleasant. The third foundation of mindfulness is awareness of the tenor of the mind – knowing whether the mind is, for instance, confused, full of hatred, or constricted. The *sutta* lists sixteen of these states as being the object of mindfulness. The fourth foundation of mindfulness is that of *dhamma* or *dhammas*. Also one of the most difficult words in the canon to translate, this term is found as a recollection practice where, in the singular, it refers specifically to the teaching. As the fourth foundation of mindfulness here it applies to 'things as they are', or 'phenomena'.[13] It could certainly be argued that within a Buddhist understanding there is only a fine distinction between phenomena, or things as they are, and an awareness of the teaching. If one knows things as they are, one knows the nature of suffering, or disease, its cause, that there is freedom from that and the path that leads to freedom in any given situation. This large question, subtle and important both from an academic and from a practitioner's point of view, cannot be discussed fully here. At any rate this area of mindfulness appears to be of a different order from the first three, that includes and transcends them in its understanding of the applicability of what is path at any given moment or in any situation: this translation puts '*dhamma* in *dhammas*'. This emphasis on process, of being aware how things come to the mind and pass away, informs this foundation, alongside a directing of the attention to a perception of all our experiences, of whatsoever kind, in terms of their arising, enduring and ceasing. Saddhatissa describes the application of mindfulness at this stage as 'the most difficult but the most fruitful': an opportunity to see events and the mind that observes them in a completely different way (Saddhatissa 1971: 56).

Each practice is discussed under its own heading in this book. Particular mention, however, should be made of mindful walking practice, based upon this *sutta*, the usual way of complementing and balancing the sitting practice, particularly on extended meditation courses. This is mentioned elsewhere in the canon and is recommended, for instance, to Moggallāna as a means of combating sleepiness. A walking place (*caṅkamana*) is often specially designated outside Buddhist temples. The canon itself does not give advice as to how to undertake the practice.[14] It is normally now undertaken within a specified area, walking very slowly backwards and forwards. Various instructions are given as to how to observe this process, and different stages of the movement of the foot and body may be defined by the meditator: for instance he may divide the process into three stages of raising, lifting and lowering each foot onto the ground. Other stages or refinements of the practice can be developed according to the balance of concentration and mindfulness present at the time. A sense of peace is found in the exploration of a rhythmic bodily activity, with alertness, for instance, to the moment of letting go at the shift between one foot to the other. Such fine attention is not possible or encouraged in normal activities. Dhammasami writes after discussion of walking practice as a meditation to be practised in seclusion: 'Just have one awareness when you are crossing the road. Develop the awareness that you are crossing the road' (Dhammasami 1999: 98). This stress on knowing what one is doing in all areas of life, in all postures, is the feature of the companion quality to mindfulness, clear comprehension, which Buddhadāsa terms 'wisdom-in-action, ready comprehension, clear comprehension: the specific application of wisdom (*paññā*) as required in a given situation' (Buddhadāsa 1988: 154). The commentary describes four kinds of clear comprehension, explained also by Nyanaponika.[15] Where mindfulness is seen as awareness of what is occurring, knowing the purpose and application of any activity is the province of clear comprehension.[16]

The *sutta* is of a completely different genre from the one before. There is almost no narrative context and so nothing kin to the tragic irony that animates the quest of King Ajātasattu and underlies the description of each fruit of the recluse's life. Ornament, dialogue and incidental description are minimal, while the style seems deliberately pared down.[17] The presence of the *jhānas* and the *iddhis* is implied by the inclusion of practices that arouse them, but no direct mention is made of them. The main area of concern in this *sutta* is not on benefits but on practice: it is a portmanteau of instructions for what the meditator should do simply if he wants to try and master the basics of the meditative life. The *sutta* certainly did travel in different forms; this version, at any rate, is crafted with unusual care. The movement from the individual experience of the breath, to the experience of the postures, the activities of the body, then its parts, and then finally the stages of decomposition of a body that culminate in the pile of bone powder, demonstrate an increasing emphasis on the mark of not-self (*anattā*). Through feelings, mind and finally *dhammas*, this, accompanied by a sense of mindfulness and clear comprehension at all times, opens up a path ahead, which can be lived and experienced in every event through the fourth foundation. The methods described still provide the basis of most Buddhist meditation systems, particularly, but not exclusively, those with an emphasis on *vipassanā*. The *sutta* uses pieces of text and advice found in many other parts of the canon: their arrangement here as a series is seminal, with the movement from one section to the next a continuous reflection of its purpose.

Satipaṭṭhāna-Sutta

Thus have I heard. Once the Exalted One was staying amongst the Kurus, in their market town, Kammāsadhamma. There he addressed the monks in this way: 'Monks'. 'Venerable Sir', they replied.

'This, monks, is the direct path for the purification of beings, for the surmounting of grief and lamentation, for the disappearance of suffering and pain, for the attainment of the way, for the realization of *nibbāna*: that is, the four foundations of mindfulness.

'What four? Here, monks, a monk practises contemplating the body in the body, ardent, mindful and clearly comprehending, having put away longing and discontent with the world. He practises contemplating feeling in feelings, ardent, mindful and clearly comprehending, having put away longing and discontent with the world. He contemplates mind in the mind, ardent, mindful and clearly comprehending, having put away longing and discontent with the world. He contemplates *dhamma* in *dhammas*, ardent, mindful and clearly comprehending, having put away longing and discontent with the world.

'And how, monks, does a monk practise contemplating the body in the body?[18] Here, monks, a monk goes to a forest, or the roots of a tree or an empty place and sits, folding his legs in a cross-legged position, making his body straight and sets up mindfulness in front of him. Mindful, he breathes in; mindful, he breathes out. As he breathes in a long breath, he knows, "I am breathing in a long breath", or, as he breathes out a long breath, he knows, "I am breathing out a long breath". As he breathes in a short breath, he knows, "I am breathing in a short breath"; or, as he breathes out a short breath, he knows, "I am breathing out a short breath". He trains thus: "Experiencing the whole body, I will breathe in"; he trains thus, "Experiencing the whole body I will breathe out". He trains thus: "Tranquillizing the bodily formation, I shall breathe in", he trains thus, "Tranquillizing the bodily formation I shall breathe out". Just as a skilled turner or his apprentice, when making a long turn, knows, "I am making a long turn", or, when making a short turn, knows, "I am making a short turn", so, breathing in a long breath a monk knows, "I am breathing in a long breath", and, breathing out a long breath he knows, "I am breathing out a long breath". He knows . . . short breath . . . conscious of the whole body . . . he trains thus, "Tranquillizing the bodily formation I shall breathe out."

'In this way, he practises, contemplating the body in the body, internally; or he practises, contemplating the body in the body, externally; or he practises contemplating the body in the body both internally and externally. He practises contemplating the arising of *dhammas* in the body, the ceasing of *dhammas* in the body or he practises contemplating the arising and ceasing of *dhammas* in the body. Or else mindfulness that "there is a body" is established in him, just to the extent necessary for knowledge and mindfulness. And he practises independent, clinging at nothing in the world. In this way, monks, a monk practises contemplating the body in the body.

'And again, monks, a monk, when walking, knows, "I am walking"; when standing he knows, "I am standing"; when sitting he knows, "I am sitting"; when lying down he knows, "I am lying down"; or, however his body is disposed, he knows it.

'In this way he practises, contemplating the body in the body internally, externally and both internally and externally . . . In this way too, monks, a monk practises contemplating the body in the body.

'And again, monks, a monk acts with clear comprehension when going backwards and forwards. He acts with clear comprehension when looking ahead or behind, when bending and stretching, in wearing his robes and carrying his bowl, when eating and drinking, chewing and swallowing, when defecating and urinating, when walking, standing, sitting, falling asleep, waking up, talking and keeping silent.

'In this way he practises contemplating the body in the body internally, externally and both internally and externally . . . .In this way too, monks, a monk practises contemplating the body in the body.

'And again, monks, a monk takes stock of the body upwards, from the soles of the feet and downwards, from the tips of the hair, bounded by skin, as full of many kinds of impurity, in this way: "In this body there are hairs of the head, hairs on the body, nails, teeth, skin, flesh, sinews, bones, bone-marrow, kidneys, heart, liver, diaphragm, spleen, lungs, large intestines, small intestines, the contents of the stomach, excrement, bile, phlegm, pus, blood, sweat, fat, tears, grease, saliva, mucus, oil in the joints and urine". It is just as if, monks, there was a bag, open at both ends, filled with various kinds of grain, such as hill rice, husked rice, beans, peas, millet and white rice, and a man with good eyes were to open it and take stock of it in this way: "This is hill rice, this is husked rice, this is beans, this peas, this millet and this white rice"; so, too, monks, a monk reviews the body . . . as full of many different kinds of impurity in this way: "In this body there are hairs of the head . . . oil in the joints and urine" '.

'In this way, he practises contemplating the body in the body internally, externally and both internally and externally . . . . In this way too, monks, a monk practises contemplating the body in the body.

'And again, monks, a monk takes stock of this same body, however placed or disposed, in terms of the four elements of earth, water, fire and air: "In this body there is the element of earth, the element of water, the element of fire and the element of air". It is just as if, monks, a skilled butcher or his apprentice had slaughtered a cow and was sitting at a crossroads with it cut into pieces. In just this way a monk reviews this same body, however placed or disposed, in terms of the four elements of earth, water, fire and air: "In this body there is the element of earth, the element of water, the element of fire and the element of air".

'In this way he practises contemplating the body in the body internally, externally and both internally and externally . . . . In this way too, monks, a monk practises contemplating the body in the body.

'And again, monks, it is as if a monk sees a body dead for one day, dead for two days, dead for three days, bloated, blue-black and festering, discarded in the charnel ground. He then makes a comparison with his own body, reflecting, "Truly, this body of mind is also of the same nature, it will become like that and will not escape from it". In this way he practises contemplating the body in the body internally, externally and both internally and externally . . . . In this way too, monks, a monk practises contemplating the body in the body.

'And again, monks, it is as if a monk sees a body discarded in the charnel ground, being devoured by crows, vultures, hawks, dogs, jackals or by various kinds of worms . . . a body discarded in the charnel ground, a skeleton with flesh and blood, bound together by sinews . . . a skeleton, without flesh, smeared with blood, bound together by sinews . . . a skeleton, without flesh and blood, bound together by sinews . . . a body with loose bones scattered in all directions, here a bone of the hand, there a bone of the foot, a shin bone, a breast bone, a hip bone, a back bone and a skull . . . a body with bones bleached white, the colour of shells, he then makes a comparison with his own body . . . a body that is bones in heaps, more than a year old . . . a body that is bones rotted and crumbled to powder . . .

'In this way too, monks, a monk practises contemplating the body in the body.

'And how, monks, does a monk practise contemplating feeling in feelings? Here, monks, when feeling a pleasant feeling, a monk knows, "I feel a pleasant feeling"; when feeling a painful feeling he knows, "I feel a painful feeling"; when feeling a feeling that is neither pleasant nor painful he knows, "I feel a feeling that is neither pleasant nor painful. When feeling a pleasant physical feeling he knows, "I feel a pleasant physical feeling"[19]; when feeling a pleasant non-physical feeling he knows, "I feel a pleasant non-physical feeling". When feeling a painful physical feeling he knows, "I feel a painful physical feeling"; when feeling a painful non-physical feeling he knows, "I feel a painful non-physical feeling". When feeling a physical feeling that is neither pleasant nor painful he knows, "I feel a physical feeling that is neither pleasant nor painful". When feeling a non-physical feeling that is neither pleasant nor painful he knows, "I feel a non-physical feeling that is neither pleasant nor painful".

'In this way he practises contemplating feeling among feelings internally, externally and both internally and externally. He practises contemplating the arising of *dhammas* in feelings, the ceasing of *dhammas* in feelings or he practises contemplating the arising and ceasing of *dhammas* in feelings. Or else mindfulness that "there is a feeling" is established in him, just to the extent necessary for knowledge and mindfulness. And he practises independent, clinging at nothing in the world. In this way, monks, a monk practises contemplating feeling among feelings.

'And how, monks, does a monk practise contemplating the mind in the mind?[20]

Here, monks, a monk knows a mind that is with desire as with desire, and a mind that is free from desire as free from desire. He knows a mind with hate as with hate, and one free from hate as free from hate. He knows . . . a deluded mind . . . an undeluded mind. He knows . . . a constricted mind . . . a scattered mind.[21] He knows . . . a mind grown great . . . a mind that has not grown great.[22] He knows . . . a surpassable mind . . . surpassing mind.[23] He knows . . . a composed mind . . . a discomposed mind. He knows . . . a liberated mind . . . an unliberated mind.

'In this way he practises contemplating mind in the mind internally, externally and both internally and externally. He practises contemplating the arising of *dhammas* in the mind, the ceasing of *dhammas* in the mind or he practises contemplating the arising and ceasing of *dhammas* in the mind. Or else mindfulness that "there is mind" is established in him, just to the extent necessary for knowledge and mindfulness. And he practises independent, clinging at nothing in the world. In this way, monks, a monk practises contemplating the mind in the mind.

'And how, monks, does a monk practise contemplating *dhamma* in *dhammas*?

'Here, monks, a monk practises contemplating *dhamma* in *dhammas* in terms of the five hindrances. And how does a monk practise contemplating *dhamma* in *dhammas* in terms of the five hindrances? If sense desire is present in him, he knows that sense desire is present in him. If sense desire is not present in him, he knows that sense desire is not present in him. He knows how sense desire that was not present came to arise in him; he knows how sense desire that has arisen in him is abandoned and how sense desire that has been abandoned will not arise again in the future.

'If ill-will is present in him... sloth and torpor... restlessness and worry... if doubt is present in him, he knows that doubt is present in him. If doubt is not present in him, he knows that doubt is not present in him. He knows how doubt that was not present came to arise in him; he knows how doubt that has arisen in him is abandoned and how doubt that has been abandoned will not arise in the future.

'In this way he practises contemplating *dhamma* in *dhammas* internally, externally and both internally and externally. He practises contemplating the arising of *dhamma* in *dhammas*, the ceasing of *dhamma* in *dhammas* or he practises contemplating the arising and ceasing of *dhamma* in *dhammas*. Or else mindfulness that "there are *dhammas*" is established in him, just to the extent necessary for knowledge and mindfulness. And he practises independent, clinging at nothing in the world. In this way, monks, a monk practises contemplating *dhamma* in *dhammas* in terms of the five hindrances.

'And again, monks, a monk practises contemplating *dhamma* in *dhammas* in terms of the five aggregates of grasping. And how, monks, does a monk practise contemplating *dhamma* in *dhammas* in terms of the five aggregates of grasping? Here a monk reflects: such is material form, such is the arising of material form, such is the ceasing of material form; such is feeling, such is the arising of feeling, such is the ceasing of feeling; such is perception... such are formations... such is consciousness, such is the arising of consciousness, such is the ceasing of consciousness.

'In this way he practises contemplating *dhamma* in *dhammas* internally, externally and both internally and externally....In this way, monks, a monk practises contemplating *dhamma* in *dhammas* in terms of the five aggregates of grasping.

And again, monks, a monk practises contemplating *dhamma* in *dhammas* in terms of the six internal and external sense spheres. And how?.... Here, monks, a monk knows the eye, he knows visual objects, and he knows whatever fetter arises dependent on the two. And he knows a fetter that has not yet arisen comes to arise, and he knows how a fetter that has arisen is abandoned, and he knows how a fetter that has been abandoned will not arise in the future. He knows the ear, he knows sounds... he knows the nose, he knows smells... he knows the tongue, he knows tastes... he knows the body, he knows sensory objects... he knows the mind and he knows mental objects and he knows whatever fetter arises dependent on the two. And he knows a fetter that has not yet arisen comes to arise, and he knows how a fetter that has arisen is abandoned, and he knows how a fetter that has been abandoned will not arise in the future.

'In this way he practises contemplating *dhamma* in *dhammas* internally, externally and both internally and externally.... In this way, monks, a monk practises contemplating *dhammas* in *dhammas* in terms of the six internal and external sense spheres.

'And again, monks, a monk practises contemplating *dhamma* in *dhammas* in terms of the seven factors of enlightenment. And how . . . ?

'Here, monks, if mindfulness is present in him a monk knows that the factor of awakening that is mindfulness is present in him; if mindfulness is not present in him he knows that the enlightenment factor that is mindfulness is not present in him. He knows how the unarisen enlightenment factor that is mindfulness came to arise in him; he knows how the enlightenment factor that is mindfulness comes to perfection through cultivation.

Here, if investigation of *dhamma* is present in him . . . if effort . . . joy . . . tranquillity . . . concentration . . . if equanimity is present in him a monk knows that the enlightenment factor that is equanimity is present in him . . . he knows how the enlightenment factor that is equanimity comes to perfection through cultivation.

In this way he practises contemplating *dhamma* in *dhammas* internally, externally and both internally and externally . . . In this way, monks, a monk practises contemplating *dhammas* in *dhammas* in terms of the seven factors of enlightenment.

And again, monks, a monk practises contemplating *dhamma* in *dhammas* in terms of the four noble truths. And how does a monk practise contemplating *dhamma* in *dhammas* in terms of the four noble truths? Here, monks, a monk knows suffering as it really is, he knows the origin of suffering as it really is, he knows the cessation of suffering as it really is and he knows the way that leads to the cessation of suffering as it really is. In this way he practises contemplating *dhamma* in *dhammas* internally, externally and both internally and externally. . . . In this way, monks, a monk practises contemplating *dhamma* in *dhammas* in terms of the four noble truths.

And indeed, monks, whoever cultivates these four foundations of mindfulness in this way for seven years, one of two results may be expected for him. Either final knowledge, here and now, or, if there is a trace of grasping left, the state of non-return. Let alone seven years, monks. Whoever cultivates these four foundations of mindfulness in this way for six . . . five . . . four . . . three . . . two years . . . one year . . . seven months . . . six . . . five . . . four . . . three . . . two months . . . one month . . . two weeks. . . . Let alone two weeks, monks. Whoever cultivates these four foundations of mindfulness in this way for seven days, one of two results may be expected for him. Either final knowledge, here and now, or, if there is a trace of grasping left, the state of non-return.

Because of this it was said: "This leads only one way, monks, to the purification of beings, to the surmounting of grief and lamentation, to the disappearance of suffering and pain, to the attainment of the way, to the realization of *nibbāna*: that is, the four foundations of mindfulness".

Thus spoke the Exalted One. Glad in heart, the monks delighted in what the Exalted One had said.'

(M 1 55–63)

6

1–10. THE TEN *KASIṆA* PRACTICES

It is natural for the eye to rest upon an object of beauty or simplicity. When the mind relaxes, attention sometimes goes to a view – the sea or the sky for instance – or a simple object in front of the sphere of vision, like a flower, or a stone, a piece of glass. The nature of the attention is affected by the nature of the object: a tiny object, such as a jewel, has a different effect from a vast one, such as the sea. One of the most specialized and mysterious practices for the attainment of *jhāna* is that of the *kasiṇa*, which develops and purifies this propensity of the mind to settle on and find gladness in a single object. An association with the Vedic word for entire or whole (*kṛtsna*) is likely: the object occupies the whole of the attention in such a manner that all other kinds of thought or disturbance simply drop away (see DP I 661).[1]

An object in the external world is taken representing, usually, one of the four elements or the four colours of white, red, yellow and blue. Attention rests upon the device, while mindfulness is sustained by the internal repetition of a word that describes that element or colour. If the earth *kasiṇa* is taken the word earth is repeated while contemplating a disc made of earth itself, if water the word water over a disc of water, and so on. The hindrances are gradually purified so that *jhāna* is attained. It is the 'purest' form of *samatha* meditation, in that even breathing mindfulness, which, like *kasiṇa* practice, also said to lead to all four *jhānas*, includes an element of *vipassanā*: the breath is moving and changing, so impermanence is easily discerned. The object of the *kasiṇa* practice may have flaws of various kinds, and in the case of the air element involve some movement. The three marks of impermanence (*anicca*), suffering or dis-ease (*dukkha*) and not-self (*anattā*) are, however, less evident, so that it is said to lead naturally, with mindfulness, to the cultivation of *samatha*. From the four *jhānas* it leads to formless meditation. It is also said to provide a basis for the development of the psychic powers (*iddhis*).[2]

The ten *kasiṇas* are mentioned as a list repeatedly in the *Suttapiṭaka*.[3] The first eight are the four elements, earth, water, fire and air, and the four colours, of blue, yellow, red and white; the last two space and consciousness. The list was soon modified: the *Dhammasaṅgaṇi* omits the last two as means of producing *jhāna* in the form sphere, as does the *Paṭisambhidāmagga*.[4] The grounds for this, explained by Buddhaghosa, are that the two, as described in the *suttas*, are more suited to the first two formless *jhānas*, that of infinite space and infinite consciousness (in Asl 186). The ten *kasiṇas* as they appear in Buddhaghosa's list are of earth, water, fire, air, blue, red, yellow and white, light (*āloka*) and limited space (*paricchinna-ākāsa*). Upatissa's list is, in practice, the same as that of Buddhaghosa, for although he lists space and consciousness for 9 and 10, he describes, in the text itself, light and limited space: the formless realms are discussed after the earth *kasiṇa*.[5] Although the meditation on light is sometimes thought to be non-canonical, it is cited in the list in the *Jhānavagga* and there is at least one *sutta* which seems to describe it as a separate practice, as we shall see in this chapter.[6] As Buddhaghosa notes, *kasiṇas* do not arouse complexity of thought, as do such objects as the Triple Gem or the related recollections (21–6), regarded as arousing a more discursive attention, also considered important for the healthy development of meditation. At the end of his discussion of the devices Buddhaghosa says that the practice will not work well unless the practitioner feels the confidence and steadiness that can be produced by the recollections (see Vism V 41).

Instructions concerning the device

According to the *Vimuttimagga* and the *Visuddhimagga* the practitioner takes a contained and limited external form embodying or representing one of the four elements, the four colours, light or confined space, and uses it as an object for concentration: size, colour and the limiting of the edges of the object are subject to specific recommendations.[7] The *Visuddhimagga* outlines first the way in which the device, or circle (*maṇḍala*), should be constructed and then the procedures for using this as a meditation. Setting up the *kasiṇa* device for use is described as if it were part of the meditative process itself. As Buddhaghosa notes, advice on its construction should be given by the teacher and followed with great care: for the earth device, for instance, clay of the right colour, like that in the Ganges 'which is the colour of dawn', should be chosen, so as not to confuse the object with one of the colour meditations (see Vism IV 24). It should be kept somewhere away from general view, though it can be portable or fixed. It should be a specified size, for, as Buddhaghosa notes, quoting an apparently older commentary, 'it should be the size of a bushel (*suppa*) or a saucer (*sarava*)'.[8] It should also have clear edges, so that it is limited in some way, to avoid confusion in the mind as to where it begins and where it ends.

The other *kasiṇa* objects are also described (see Vism V). For water, a bowl of clear water should be taken. Only, according to Buddhaghosa, if one has had prior experience should one take the ocean itself, or a natural occurrence of this element, such as a pool or a lagoon, as an object. For fire, a fire should be made up in a tree root or a shed, and then viewed through a hole. Again, only if one has had previous experience should one take flames without a clear border to distinguish the object from others occupying the visual field. For air, the motion of growing sugar cane or the tops of trees or the ends of hair is taken. For colours, blue, yellow, white or red flowers should be arranged in a tray, with set limits, or a cloth of the appropriate colour should be cut to size. Only the experienced meditator should take the object as it appears naturally as a bush of flowers, a cloth or a gem, or, in the case of the white *kasiṇa*, as the disc of the moon (see Vism V 26). For light, a circle of light thrown on the ground is taken, or a lamp inside a pot, perceived through a hole. For space, a hole should be made in a hut, or a piece of leather or in a rush mat, as the object. Again for both these two, 'natural' occurrence of light, as in moonlight or, for space, a keyhole or any hole in the wall, should only be taken by an experienced meditator.

The practice is conducted, according to Buddhaghosa, after careful preparations. The meditator washes, reviews the dangers of sense pleasures, and practises the recollection of the Triple Gem (21–3). He regards the disc, keeping the eyes relaxed and not too widely open, repeating the word, such as 'water' or 'fire', which describes his subject. Care is taken throughout that the mind does not become sleepy or strained. When mindfulness and concentration become balanced a mental image (*nimitta*) arises. Such a sign, which forms the basis for all *samatha* practice leading to *jhāna*, is developed through a series of stages so that it becomes stable and the mind becomes one-pointed.[9] After considering the constructed device, the 'acquired image' (*uggahanimitta*) is visualized in the mind's eye, which is then in time replaced by the 'counterpart image' (*paṭibhāganimitta*), compared to a mirror, the full moon emerging from clouds, a washed mother-of-pearl dish or cranes seen against a thundercloud (Vism IV 30–1). This image is associated with a refreshing sense of joy, happiness and one-pointedness. Buddhaghosa gives detailed descriptions of the qualities of each one of the *jhāna* factors, which become balanced through the image (see Vism IV 88–109).[10] The meditator needs to guard carefully against activity that might make him or her lose the sign, such as careless talk or excessive sensory indulgence (see Vism IV 34–41). As the mind is purified temporarily of the hindrances, first access concentration (*upacāra*), and then, after the faculties are developed, absorption (*appanā*) is reached.[11] Upatissa's description of the practice is less detailed. He does note, however, that the initial device may be of different shapes, 'of the size of a round rice-sifter, a metal gong and may be circular, rectangular, triangular or square . . . according to the principal teacher's instructions, a circle is best' (PF 73). He says that the meditator should treat the image 'as if it were a precious jewel' (PF 79).

Kasiṇa ***practice in the canon***

We need the commentators for this information as little about the construction of the device is given in the canon. The *Cuḷasuññatā-Sutta* provides a description of what appears to be an earth *kasiṇa*, though does not refer to it as such by name.

> Again Ānanda, a monk, not attending to the perception of humans, not attending to the perception of forest, attends to the oneness dependent on the perception of earth. His mind enters into that perception of earth and becomes confident, settled and set upon it. Just as a bull's hide becomes free from folds when fully stretched with a hundred pegs; so too, a

> monk, not attending to any of the highs and lows of this earth, to the rivers and marshes, stakes and thorns, mountains and plateaus, attends to the singleness dependent on the perception of earth.
>
> (M III 105)[12]

This passage suggests that either a device, in the form of a bull's hide, or a large area of earth, or both, may have been taken as the preliminary object.[13] We could make any number of inferences about the lack of information given in the canon. Buddhaghosa may have been making recommendations based on an oral tradition dating back to the time of the Buddha; he cites earlier commentators. He also mentions 'secret texts' (*gūḷhagantahaṃ*) which will not be received from the teacher if he does not pay proper respects.[14] He may have been providing a written record of traditions that could predate the Buddha. It has been argued, for instance, that the devices derive from the Vedic practices or from Śaṅkhya philosophy. Given the atmosphere of experimentation of the time it would be very difficult to draw definite conclusions about this.[15] The canon may not describe how to make the devices because that sort of information was so *readily* available that it was not considered necessary for inclusion: we do not find much about posture in the canon, presumably because there were so many people around to ask or observe. In the case of the *kasiṇa* there were, perhaps, plenty of practitioners around to demonstrate its construction. Buddhaghosa's careful instructions perhaps suggest that he is making a judgement on the best method from a number of different or rival schools. He says he is aiming his recommendations for beginners who need clearly established limits such as the size of the object. Buddhaghosa and Upatissa are cautious, in not recommending accidental or 'natural' occurrences of each object, though this could simply be an expression of a concern that the object should be clearly defined and the practice treated with care.

Certainly, Buddhaghosa's frequent references to the need for consultation about this practice suggest that it has always been considered one that should be taught by a practitioner. The purified image that is developed by the *kasiṇa* practice is regarded as beautiful, *sobhana ārammaṇa*. Just as the objects of the foul meditations are considered suitable for those prone to desire, the characteristic of this meditation is that the purity of the object is considered for its beauty, and so is suitable for those prone to ill-will.[16]

The beautiful object

This brings us more generally to the treatment of the natural world in the Buddhist tradition. It is essential to consider this, for some objects, such as the perception of loathsomeness in food (39) and the *asubhas* (11–20), are chosen for their repugnance, which can and often does give a misleading and negative impression of objects suitable for meditation. The texts treat the beautiful object with understandable care, which may be seen by comparison with the meditation on the foul: this is used both as the cause of unskilfulness, in the case of ill-will, and the means of its removal, in the case of desire. There is a more complex attitude towards the beautiful object. Desire can very easily be aroused in the sense sphere and is, according to the *Abhidhamma*, accompanied by many of the factors of joy, spontaneity and delight that are present in skilful consciousness. The only time where an object that arouses sexual desire is employed by the Buddha is in the famous case of Nanda, a homesick monk who misses a girl he wants from his village. The Buddha shows him the 'dove-footed' *deva* women that can be his if he continues to practise: Nanda stays in the order, becomes an arahat and turns his back on the motives that had induced him to stay (Ud 21–4)![17] This, however, is exceptional. In some texts the object for correcting ill-will is understood as the image derived from considering many beings in the practice of loving kindness (31); this, rather than a sense-sphere object, is sometimes taken as the beauty that is regarded as the antidote for a predisposition to hatred.[18]

Such caution does not mean that Buddhist meditation avoids a beautiful external object or that it fails to acknowledge beauty in the natural world. Appreciation of nature in its various manifestations is taken for granted in Buddhist practice and is so deeply imbued in popular understanding of the factors likely to give rise to skilful consciousness (*kusala citta*) that it is rarely stated. This needs emphasizing as there is now a widespread belief, a perhaps unintentional by-product of recent trends within the tradition that have begun to invade Buddhist countries themselves, that Buddhism and meditation can and should create a hard 'detachment' that rejects natural beauty or denies feeling.[19] For this reason 'non-attachment' is a better description of the state of mind of equanimity than detachment, which is easily confused with a subtle hatred (*dosa*) or indifference.[20] Buddhist meditation, involving factors such as joy (*pīti*) and happiness (*sukha*), can hardly be described as cold, for mindfulness of feeling requires sensitivity to what those feelings are: as human beings our emotions are stirred by what is seen and the texts reflect this. As we saw in one or two texts at the beginning of this anthology arahats utter lyrical paeans involving the natural world when they attain enlightenment.[21] Places such as forest groves and lakes are often described in the *suttas* as delightful (*ramanīya*), while pages of poetry are devoted to the description of the forest hermitage in the *Vessantara Jātaka*.[22] This accords with the ancient and modern Indian assumption that the forest hermitage, the *aśrama*, should be located in a beautiful and tranquil place.[23] In Thailand and Sri Lanka forests are chosen as sites for meditation centres not just for their privacy, but because they give a chance for practitioners to experience nature and the elements away from the bustle of cities.[24] Walks that involve awareness of natural surroundings, particularly in the countryside, are constantly encouraged for meditators in all traditions to ensure that attention does not become inward or strained. As Buddhism becomes established in other countries meditation centres are often sited in rural settings, such as the Samatha Centre in Wales and Viveka monastery at Chithurst. This attitude towards objects perceived in the external world may be seen in all sorts of other aspects of modern Buddhist practice: shrines covered with banks of frangipani, lotus and butter lamps awaken great depth of feeling precisely because they are so beautiful and capable of communicating serenity by visual means. Buddhist meditation does not teach rejection of the natural world, rather the freedom that arises from being able to appreciate it, without attachment.

Such an understanding, felt to be self-evident, is translated only occasionally into doctrinal analysis but can be seen in the assumption that the human birth is a fortunate destination (*sugāti*). It is also evident in the *Abhidhamma* understanding that the beautiful or skilful *citta* that forms the basis of the human mind would normally be elicited in an active sense by objects in the natural world, and remain so if mindfulness is sustained.[25] The *citta* is regarded as beautiful (*sobhana*), because of its nature and object. When attention rests without attachment and in peace its nature is moved and steadied by the object itself: rather as the mind that regards the sea or the sky is changed by the vastness and the simplicity of what is seen. This in turn affects the body and emotions, bringing them to a sense of unification and calm. When the object is seen again after some time, it allows a return to the earlier state: just as a glimpse of the sea or blue sky can reawaken a sense of being on a holiday when there was a great deal of joy and happiness present. In another commentary, Buddhaghosa says that it is a beautiful external object, rather than the practice on loving kindness, which is 'beautiful' (see Asl 189).[26]

Two other lists suggest some variety in method for the *kasiṇa* practice at the time of the Buddha.[27] They are the deliverances (*vimokkhā*) and the spheres of transcendence (*abhibhāyatanāni*), both of which seem associated with the use of the *kasiṇa*. The three lists are often positioned together in the *suttas* though the order is shuffled in different contexts.[28] The *kasiṇa* practice, with an object that is so refined it takes the mind to the form sphere, should, say the manuals, be taken up under appropriate conditions and the practice guarded. These canonical lists, discussed later, suggest that from the beginning measures were taken to ensure that attachment or craving should not develop, either to the mental state that arises, or to the object. There was possibly felt to be a risk of defiled *jhāna*, or wrong concentration.[29]

The commentaries also teach the exercise of great technical skill in dealing with the object and the mental states produced by it. The manifold permutations in the way the *kasiṇa* object is discussed in the *Dhammasaṅgaṇi*, where the object and consequent consciousness may be limited (*parittaṃ*) or immeasurable (*appamāṇaṃ*), suggest that from the earliest times flexibility was encouraged (see DhS 160–247). This is perhaps to prevent fixed views about the universe developing through meditative experience.[30] Just as little has been said about the *kasiṇas* in writing, even less has been said about one of the most important aspects of *samatha* practice, the ability to emerge from states of great happiness and peace.[31] The texts point out, both by implication and by overt instruction, that skill in leaving behind meditation states is as important as skill in attaining them.[32] So one list is included later on the importance of what are called the *samatha* masteries.[33]

In the present day in monasteries throughout the East *kasiṇa* discs may still be seen of the kind described by Buddhaghosa near or around the meditation hall and his specifications for construction are closely followed.[34] As one of the pure *samatha* practices, it is practised to this day under conditions of seclusion and confidentiality. Stone insets for the practice have been found at Anurādhapura, suggesting that it was from the earliest times a popular meditation, but the dates of these are uncertain.[35]

Mahāsakuludāyi-Sutta

This section is taken from a very long discourse delivered by the Buddha to Sakuludāyi, a member of the *paribbājakas*, whose adherence to a life of right action, right speech and right livelihood aligned them to a certain extent with Buddhism.[36] This *sutta* is of particular importance because it lists in full the seventy-five meditation objects in much the same form as in the *Jhānavagga*.[37] A large section describes five things which disciples revere, and which, it is suggested, are exemplified by the Buddha's behaviour: eating little, contentment with any given robe, almsfood, lodging etc. The Buddha describes a further five qualities: his virtue, knowledge and vision, wisdom, the fact that he answers questions about the four noble truths and, under the fifth heading, that he teaches the *bodhipakkhiyādhammā*, the eight deliverances, the eight spheres of transcendence, the ten spheres of the *kasiṇa*, the first four *jhānas*, insight knowledge and the six higher knowledges.

The very length of the *sutta* presents an apparent problem characteristic of much of the Buddha's teaching method: it is often difficult to isolate any one teaching on meditation from other aspects of the eightfold path. Few long *suttas* only teach meditation. In this *sutta* much of the text is devoted to careful description of bodily activity and aspects of monastic daily life such as the almsround and the wearing of robes, all of which fall under the general umbrella of Buddhist practice. Teaching about spiritual practice comes only in the last section. This placing must be significant: pre-eminence in this text is given to the practice of meditation, but in a context where other aspects of the holy life are explored.

The eight deliverances (vimokkhā)

This list is one of a few in the *Jhānavagga* where some elements overlap with features often found in other lists: here the formless attainments (35–8) are included. Deliverance here refers to temporary release from opposing states and release by delighting in the object, usually the beautiful colour of the *kasiṇa* image.[38] The liberation in this context is not permanent, but pertains to the freedom with which the mind can rest upon an object without hindrances or strain and without being pulled by desire or hatred: an *Abhidhamma* commentary compares this to the relaxation and confidence that a child feels letting his limbs dangle on his father's lap.[39] The list also shows the way that the practice of the formless realms, discussed later in the anthology, was felt to be supported and related to the perception of forms, here both internal and external.

Eight spheres of transcendence (abhibhāyatanāni)

An *abhibhāyatana* is a sphere of mastery or transcendence.[40] Not much is known about the list, in which examples of colour found in the natural world are taken as the basis for meditation. The 'internal forms' are the pure colours derived from within the body, such as red for blood, white for bone or teeth. The 'external forms' perhaps denote another way of practising with external manifestations of colour as well as the devices described by Buddhaghosa: he says they are advantages that come from *kasiṇa* practice though does not describe them in detail.[41] It suggests that there were possibly other, rather more free ways of deriving the practice of *jhāna* through means of a colour, in this case through the kinds of subjects which, as we have just seen, Buddhaghosa recommends for someone with prior experience.

In the *Dhammasaṅgaṇi* the spheres of transcendence are linked to the *rūpa jhānas*, and, according to the commentary, are considered another way of entering form *jhāna*.[42] The list implies variations on the *kasiṇa* involving use of the visual or eidetic part of the mind. Some *Dhammapada* stories include descriptions of the attainment of *jhāna* taking a colour or one of the elements. The objects are derived both from the imagination and from the external world. In one story, a golden lotus is created by the Buddha for a meditator as an object; when the meditator has attained *jhāna*, the Buddha causes the lotus to wither so that he might see impermanence. The practitioner then sees genuine lotuses, some flourishing and some withered, and gains a further stage of insight (BL 3: 162–3). Although such stories are post-canonical, they perhaps indicate the nature of some of the imaginative exercises practised at the time of the Buddha. The *Yogalehrbuch*, a fifth-century meditation text found at Turfan, also suggests that visualization was sometimes used for *kasiṇa* practice.[43] In this manual even an external object is considered unnecessary: the imagination is used to conjure up an image of, for instance, fields of different coloured lotuses, which are then transformed in the mind's eye to another object, and then to something else again.[44]

Whether or not any of these methods were practised at the time of the Buddha, the list of the spheres of transcendence stresses the importance of learning control over one's response to the appearance of an object, whether the colour is perceived internally or externally. Both the appearance of beauty and ugliness are regarded as something from which the mind needs to be free.[45]

The list also indicates the importance within the tradition accorded to learning skill in the use of *kasiṇa*.[46] The frequent presence of all three lists together suggests that they act to support one to another and are associated with allowing the mind to move with greater ease and flexibility from one state to another on the basis of *kasiṇa* practice.[47] This is the way they are discussed by Upatissa: he treats the three lists as working in slightly different ways to develop facility in entering *jhāna*, in practising different states in ascending or descending order, and even, according to him, missing out states in between.[48]

Kasiṇa ***practice***

The chief feature of this list is the presence of elements 9 and 10, which differ from Buddhaghosa's treatment. As explained earlier, he substitutes light and limited space for the *kasiṇas* of immeasurable space and consciousness.[49]

Extract from Mahāsakuludāyi-Sutta
'Again, Udāyi, I have pointed out a course of action for my disciples, practising which, disciples of mine cultivate the eight deliverances.

- Possessed of material form, he sees forms: this is the first deliverance.
- Not perceiving material forms internally, he sees material forms externally: this is the second deliverance.[50]
- He releases his mind onto the beautiful: this is the third deliverance.[51]
- By completely surmounting the perception of material forms, by leaving behind perceptions of sensory impact and by not paying attention to perceptions of diversity, he enters upon and abides in the sphere of infinite space, reflecting , "space is infinite": this is the fourth deliverance.
- By completely surmounting the sphere of infinite space, reflecting, "consciousness is infinite", he enters upon and abides in the sphere of infinite consciousness: this is the fifth deliverance.
- By completely surmounting the sphere of infinite consciousness, reflecting that "there is nothing", he enters upon and abides in the sphere of nothingness: this is the sixth deliverance.
- By completely surmounting the sphere of nothingness he enters upon and abides in the sphere of neither perception nor non-perception: this is the seventh deliverance.
- By completely surmounting the sphere of neither perception nor non-perception he enters upon and abides in the cessation of perception and feeling: this is the eighth deliverance.

And as to this, many of my disciples abide, having reached the accomplishment and perfection of higher knowledge.

Again, Udāyi, I have pointed out a course of action for my disciples, practising which, disciples of mine cultivate the eight spheres of transcendence.

- Perceiving forms internally, he sees forms externally, limited, of beautiful and ugly appearance. "Transcending these, I know them, I see them": he perceives in this way. This is the first sphere of transcendence.

- Perceiving forms externally, he sees forms externally, immeasurable, of beautiful and ugly appearance. "Transcending these, I know them, I see them": he perceives in this way. This is the second sphere of transcendence.
- Not perceiving forms internally, he sees forms externally, limited , of beautiful and ugly appearance. "Transcending these, I know them, I see them": he perceives in this way. This is the third sphere of transcendence.
- Not perceiving forms internally, he sees forms externally, immeasurable, of beautiful and ugly appearance. "Transcending these, I know them, I see them": he perceives in this way. This is the fourth sphere of transcendence.
- Not perceiving forms internally, he sees forms externally, blue, of blue colour, characterized by blue and of blue luminosity.[52] As the flax flower is blue, of blue colour, characterized by blue and of blue luminosity, or again as fine Benares muslin, smoothly finished on both sides, is blue, of blue colour, characterized by blue and of blue luminosity, even so, not perceiving forms internally, he sees forms externally, blue, of blue colour, characterized by blue and of blue luminosity. "Transcending these, I know them, I see them": he perceives in this way. This is the fifth sphere of transcendence.
- Not perceiving forms internally, he sees forms externally, yellow, of yellow colour, characterized by yellow and of yellow luminosity. As the kaṇṇikāra[53] flower is yellow . . . or again as fine Benares muslin . . . he sees forms externally, yellow, of yellow colour, characterized by yellow and of yellow luminosity. "Transcending these, I know them, I see them": he perceives in this way. This is the sixth sphere of transcendence.
- Not perceiving forms internally, he sees forms externally, red, of red colour, characterized by red and of red luminosity. As the bandhujīvaka flower is red . . . or again as fine Benares muslin . . .[54] he sees forms externally, red, of red colour, characterized by red and of red luminosity. "Transcending these, I know them, I see them": he perceives in this way. This is the seventh sphere of transcendence.
- Not perceiving forms internally, he sees forms externally, white, of white colour, characterized by white and of white luminosity. As the morning star is white, of white colour, characterized by white and of white luminosity . . . or as fine Benares muslin . . . he sees forms externally, white, of white colour, characterized by white and of white luminosity. "Transcending these, I know them, I see them": he perceives in this way. This is the eighth sphere of transcendence.

And as to this, many of my disciples abide, having reached the accomplishment and perfection of higher knowledge.

Again, Udāyi, I have pointed out a course for disciples, practising which, my disciples cultivate the ten spheres of the *kasiṇa*.

- One is aware of the earth *kasiṇa*, above, below, across, undivided, immeasurable.
- Another is aware of the water *kasiṇa*, above, below, across, undivided, immeasurable.
- Another is aware of the fire *kasiṇa*, above, below, across, undivided, immeasurable.
- Another is aware of the air *kasiṇa*, above, below, across, undivided, immeasurable.
- Another is aware of the blue *kasiṇa*, above, below, across, undivided, immeasurable.
- Another is aware of the yellow *kasiṇa*, above, below, across, undivided, immeasurable.
- Another is aware of the red *kasiṇa*, above, below, across, undivided, immeasurable.
- Another is aware of the white *kasiṇa*, above, below, across, undivided, immeasurable.
- Another is aware of the space *kasiṇa*, above, below, across, undivided, immeasurable.
- Another is aware of the consciousness *kasiṇa*, above, below, across, undivided, immeasurable.

And as to this, many of my disciples abide, having reached the accomplishment and perfection of higher knowledge.'

(M II 12–15)

The five masteries (vasiyo)

Although this list does not refer to the *kasiṇas* by name, it is included here for its importance for all *samatha* practice, of which the *kasiṇa* is taken as the paradigm. It is a description of the skills often taught at the outset of learning meditation, although they might not be described in such a specialized way. They are the ability to advert or bring to mind the meditation practice, to enter into a meditation, to keep it going for a set period of time, to emerge from it and, lastly, to remember it and reflect upon it. They are described by Buddhaghosa and, by implication, Upatissa.[55] Although these commentators describe the techniques as pertaining to *jhāna*, the principles are regarded as generally applicable. As Cousins points out, the techniques are ancient.[56] References to each are found in the *suttas*, but they are not collected together in quite the same way as in the *Abhidhamma*.[57]

Adverting (āvajjanavasī)[58]

This describes the ability to advert to or turn to different states. Buddhaghosa says that the perfection of this quality may be found in the twin miracle performed by the Buddha, in which the elements of fire and water coexist together. This post-canonical story describes the miracle that, it is said, only Buddhas can perform.[59] In day-to-day practice it means that the five *jhāna* factors of initial thought (*vitakka*), examination or sustained thought (*vicāra*), joy (*pīti*), happiness (*sukha*) and one-pointedness (*ekaggatā*) are so developed that the meditator can bring them to mind when needed.

Entering (samāpattivasī)

This is the ability to enter into and attain meditational states. Buddhaghosa takes as an example of this the ease with which the arahat Moggallāna enters into *jhāna* very quickly, as in the case of his taming of the nāga Nandopananda.[60] While the commentaries apply this only in the specialized sense to *jhāna*, when beginning practice it is taken as the ability to put aside daily distractions and enter into meditation wholeheartedly.

Resolving, remaining (adhiṭṭhānavasī)[61]

This is the ability to enter into a state and remain there for a predetermined period. The word is the same used in the *Jātaka* stories for the perfection of resolve (Ja I 23). Such undertakings are common as part of Buddhist practice, as, for instance, on full moon days when they are undertaken in the decision to keep extra precepts for the whole twenty four hours. This is not unlike the application here: a determination is made and kept to sit in meditation for, say, half an hour. It is sometimes compared to the resolve made on going to sleep to wake up at a certain time, which many people seem to be able to do at will.[62]

Emergence (vuṭṭhānavasī)

This is the ability to leave a meditation state at the end of the meditation practice: it is the word commonly used as a verb to describe the completion of a meditation in the *suttas*. It is sometimes described in the *suttas* as skill in being able to emerge from meditation with clear comprehension.[63] The *Anupadasutta*, in which the arahat Sāriputta defines in close detail all the *jhānas* and the emergence from them, is particularly noteworthy as an example of this and the next mastery (see M III 25).

Reviewing (paccavekkhaṇavasī)

This describes a feature of meditation much stressed by both Buddhaghosa and Upatissa, the reviewing of the practice which has just been conducted, noting states which have arisen and detecting any flaws and defects in the object and in mental state. It is considered an important aspect of all stages of *samatha* practice to avoid attachment and as part of the preparatory process for the next stage. One sutta in the *Aṅguttaranikaya* describes the *paccavekkha nimitta*:

> Monks, just as someone might consider another, and when standing might consider another sitting, or sitting might consider another lying down; even so the review image (*paccavekkhānimitta*) is rightly grasped by the monk, rightly held by the attention, rightly reflected upon, rightly penetrated by insight.
>
> (A III 25)[64]

Like much of the meditation advice in the *Aṅguttaranikāya*, it is not found elsewhere in the canon. It does, however, feature in Chinese versions of the *Satipaṭṭhāna-Sutta*, under body mindfulness, suggesting that it was considered a useful simile for teaching meditation as Buddhism spread.[65]

A number of *suttas* enjoin various skills in meditation, of which these masteries are just a few. Their presence suggests that meditation was taught from the time of the Buddha as a skilled craft with techniques to protect nascent skills and to prevent attachment. One list delineates a group of seven, in which, the *sutta* says, the arahat Sāriputta is said to be proficient: skill in concentration, skill in its attainment, its maintenance, in emerging, in the well-being (*kallita-)* of it, in its range and in its application.[66] Such emphasis on flexibility and clear-headedness does not support the notion of meditation as a passive or quiescent activity, an impression sometimes given by translations such as 'trance' or 'hypnotic trance' for *jhāna*. According to the *Abhidhamma*, the mind in the first *jhāna* has all the same factors that it does during skilful daily life: the other four faculties of wisdom, effort, mindfulness and faith are present as well as that of concentration (see DhS 160). These methods seem designed to ensure that the practitioner feels he has some control and genuine freedom of movement. They are 'things by which a meditator can make the mind turn according to his wish and not turn according to the mind's wish' (A IV 34). The meditation based on the *kasiṇa* practice appears to be *kusala*, with all the connotations of a word that suggests skill as well as goodness and health.

> *Mastery*
>
> There are five kinds of mastery: adverting, entering, resolving, emerging and reviewing.
>
> He adverts to the first *jhāna*, where, when and for as long as, he wishes; there is no difficulty in adverting; so it is mastery of adverting. He attains to the first *jhāna*, where, when and for as long as, he wishes; there is no difficulty in attaining; so it is mastery of attaining. He remains in the first *jhāna*, where, when and for as long as, he wishes; there is no difficulty in remaining, so it is mastery of remaining.

He emerges from the first *jhāna*, where, when and for as long as, he wishes; there is no difficulty in emerging; so it is mastery of emerging. He reviews the first *jhāna*, where, when and for as long as, he wishes; there is no difficulty in reviewing; so it is mastery of reviewing.

He adverts to the second *jhāna*... the third *jhāna*... the fourth *jhāna*... the sphere of boundless space... the sphere of boundless consciousness... the sphere of nothingness... the sphere of neither perception nor non-perception... [so for all masteries] where he has no difficulty in reviewing: in this way it is mastery of reviewing.

These are the five kinds of mastery.

(Patis I 99–100)

Elements

This text refers to the light element (*ābhādhātu*), apparently as a basis for *jhāna*. The perception of light is often associated with abandoning the third hindrance, sloth and torpor.[67] The second element described, of beauty (*subhadhātu*), refers to the object of the *kasiṇa* practice and the *jhāna* associated with it.[68] Here, just as light is contrasted with darkness, so the beautiful object is contrasted with the foul. The formless realms (35–8) are then described, developed on the basis of the 'form', the object that is taken for the first four *jhānas*. The unusual slant of the text demonstrates the flexibility with which the canon classifies objects for meditation.

At Sāvatthī

'There are, monks, these seven elements. What seven? The element of light, of beauty, of the sphere of infinite space, of the sphere of infinite consciousness, of the sphere of nothingness, of the sphere of neither perception nor non-perception, of the cessation of perception and feeling. These, monks, are the seven elements.'

When this was said, a certain monk said to the Exalted One, 'Dependent on what, sir, are these seven elements discerned?'

'The element of light, monks: this is discerned dependent upon darkness. The element of beauty: this is discerned dependent upon foulness. The element of the sphere of infinite space: this is discerned dependent upon form. The element of the sphere of infinite consciousness: this is discerned dependent upon the sphere of infinite space. The element of the sphere of nothingness: this is discerned dependent upon the sphere of infinite consciousness. The element of the sphere of neither perception nor non-perception: this is discerned dependent upon the sphere of nothingness. The element of the cessation of perception and feeling: this is discerned dependent upon cessation.'

'But how, sir, is the attainment of each of these elements to be reached?'

'As for the element of light, of beauty, of the sphere of infinite space, of the sphere of infinite consciousness, of the sphere of nothingness: the attainment of each of these elements is reached through perception. As for the element of the sphere of neither perception nor non-perception: the attainment of this element is reached through the remainder of the formations. As for the element of the cessation of perception and feeling: this is reached by the attainment of cessation.'

(S II 149–51)

7

11–20. THE TEN FOULNESS (*ASUBHA*)

The meditation on foulness (*asubha*) introduces a very different kind of object. In the canon, its treatment is comparable to the meditation on the thirty-one parts of the body, with one important difference: the body for consideration is a corpse. This meditation is also said to lead to *jhāna*, from where it can be taken as an object for insight. The practitioner is encouraged to visit a charnel ground and see the various stages of decomposition of the body after death. In practice, the two meditations are sometimes presented together, as in the *Satipaṭṭhāna-Sutta.*[1] Awareness of the foul is particularly recommended for those temperaments prone to desire: the Buddha for instance suggests it to his son, renowned for conceit concerning the beauty of his body.[2] It is, however, usually taught in a monastic framework. The object of the tenth foulness meditation, that of a skeleton, can be seen in the shrine rooms of many monasteries throughout the East and is the most obvious reminder of the future destiny and underlying structure of all our bodies: the photograph of its original owner is also often displayed. Indeed in one or two *suttas* the skeleton is mentioned as the first meditation object to be taken based on the body. In this it is closer to the Western monastic practices of Mediaeval and Renaissance times, where the skull, the *momento mori*, has often been associated with the process of contemplation: in Rome one monastery displays the bones of past monks, presumably for this purpose.[3] Elements of this practice are inevitably suggested at Buddhist funerals in the East where a public cremation occurs: sometimes the body is placed in the local temple for everyone to see before the funeral.

Before we move on to discussion of the technicalities of the practice, we should consider first the highly charged nature of this object, and how it would have appeared at the time of the Buddha. A dead body is not thought of as a wholesome source of interest in our society: we are wary of the sight of a corpse as if it is in some sense dangerous or sinister, and might lead to morbid fears. Everything we know about ancient Indian culture suggests that this was the case then too, though physical evidence of death would not seem as strange at the time of the composition of the *suttas* as it does now. The stench and sight of recently deceased corpses would be a common sight. Bodies were, if possible, burnt on the day of death, but if no relatives were around, or if there was insufficient money to buy wood, they would be consigned to charnel grounds, inauspicious sites where corpses would be heaped one upon another, visible in varying degrees of decomposition. This would have made the physical evidence of death fairly obvious.[4] Given the high risk of premature death in ancient India, most would presumably have thought about the ways that it can and will occur; most families would have lost children.

Despite this familiarity, the meditation must have seemed unusual at the time: dead bodies were certainly regarded as inauspicious, and to this day a death in India is regarded as polluting. A.L. Basham notes, 'As a man was born in impurity so he died in impurity. Nearly all ancient peoples had a horror of contact with a corpse, and India was no exception.'[5] Buddhist practice, however, sidestepped and even ignored this taboo. For instance Buddhist monks traditionally procured their robes from shrouds taken from corpses: the rags were washed, dyed and sewn together. Ven. Vajirañāṅa says that the meditation is exclusively Buddhist; as it is mentioned in the *Vinaya* in connection with the third *parājika* offence it seems to date from the earliest stratum of the tradition.[6] It does not seem to occur in other traditions, though the parts of the body in their loathsome aspect are mentioned in the *Maitrī Upaniṣad* in a passage that probably betrays some Buddhist influence.[7]

In order to embark on the meditation as described in the canon, one needs to find a body in one of the stages of decomposition. Because each of these stages share one characteristic, that of foulness, Buddhaghosa says that this practice may be undertaken on the foul aspects of another human's living body, though because of health and beauty the signs may be less evident. Khantipālo, a modern teacher, comments, however, that this could produce unhealthy aversion to that person too (see Khantipālo 1981: 98). The body of a member of the opposite sex is not suitable as it might arouse lust (Vism VI 42). The best-known *suttanta* source for this practice is the contemplation described in the *Satipaṭṭhāna-Sutta*, in which the monk compares his own body to that of a corpse.[8] In this sequence the corpse undergoes successive stages of degeneration:

1 Bloated corpse (*uddhumātaka*), blue–black (*vinīlaka*), festering (*vipubbaka*)
2 Corpse gnawed at by wild beasts (*khajjamāna*)
3 A skeleton (*aṭṭhikasaṅkhalika*) with flesh, blood and sinews
4 Skeleton stripped of flesh but bloodied and with sinews
5 Skeleton without flesh or blood but with sinews
6 Scattered bones
7 Bones white like sea shells
8 A heap of bones
9 Powdered bones.

In one *sutta*, five stages are listed with the process of decay reversed from skeleton, to the worm infested, the bloody, with cracked skin, to the bloated: this is also the order used in the *Jhānavagga* (see A I 38–42). Buddhaghosa and Upatissa, however, describe the foul meditations and level of attainment made possible by the meditation in the same way as the *Dhammasaṅgaṇi*. Under the states that are good (*kusala*), the text says that the practice leads to the first *jhāna* and describes the object in ten different forms:

1 Bloated corpse
2 Blue-black corpse
3 Festering corpse
4 Corpse with cracked skin (*vicchiddaka*)
5 Corpse gnawn and mangled (*vikkhāyitaka*)
6 Corpse cut to pieces (*vikkhittaka*)
7 Corpse mutilated and cut in pieces (*hatavikkhittaka*)
8 Bloody corpse (*lohitaka*)
9 Corpse infested with worms (*puḷavaka*)
10 Skeleton (*aṭṭhika*).[9]

Within the canon, meditation on a dead body is associated with *samatha* practice. A mental image (*nimitta*) arises from a generalized sense of the body, which may then be used as an object for release from the sense-sphere and for the attainment of *jhāna*. In the *Satipaṭṭhāna-Sutta* an element of insight is introduced as well: 'Truly, this body of mine is also of the same nature, it will become like that and will not escape from it'.[10] The *sutta* that describes five *asubha* contemplations gives a slightly different emphasis: it says that it is of great fruit, leads to arahatship or the state of non-returner, and that security from bondage (*yogakkhema*), urgency (*saṃvega*) and dwelling in great comfort (*phāsuvihāra*) are aroused (S V 129–34). The stages by which it may be used as a formal practice leading to first *jhāna* are outlined in the *Visuddhimagga* and the *Vimuttimagga*, where the image that arises on the basis of each one is described (see Vism VI and PF 132–8).

Significantly, Buddhaghosa devotes scrupulous attention to the procedures that should act as a preliminary to this meditation: one should check with one's teacher that it is a suitable practice, tell people that one is going to the charnel ground, memorize the route carefully, remember landmarks along the way and know the way back home (see Vism VI 52–65). This is, he claims, to ensure that should fear of spirits, grave-robbers, the dead rising or any other kind of terror beset the meditator he has recourse to set procedures that will allow him to return to where he is staying in safety. Bearing these preliminaries in mind carefully, the practitioner 'as happy and joyful as a warrior' should go to find his meditation subject: the bloated corpse, which only lasts for two days, is the rarest of all these meditation subjects and he may have needed to wait for it. Despite this, the commentary, interestingly, insists that should anyone ask him the day, he answers them even if he does not know, and might risk losing the mental image by replying (see Vism VI 60). This and the other preliminaries to the undertaking serve as a reminder that even though, or perhaps because, this is such a specialized practice one should not neglect completely routine interchanges with others, and should be careful that if the practice does prove alarming, one has some basic guidelines to follow to find one's way back to familiar surroundings.

As we can see from this summary, differences in emphasis and method must have always been part of this meditation. For instance Ñāṇamoli and Bodhi note that it is possible to undertake this practice by going through each stage of the degeneration of the corpse in turn in one's mind and suggest, on the basis of the words with which the practice is introduced, 'as though (*seyyathāpi*) a monk might see a body…' that it may not have needed an actual corpse in the first instance but might have been performed as an imaginative exercise.[11] Indeed this is how it is described in fragments of the imperfectly preserved *Yogalehrbuch*, a later meditative treatise found on the Silk Road, which makes extensive use of visualization for all meditation practises.[12] Although Buddhaghosa and Upatissa describe it as leading only to the first *jhāna* it is possible that it was developed to higher *jhānas* through the exploration of one feature, such as colour. In later texts this basis is used as a means of developing skill in handling and controlling images. Buddhasena's *Yogācārabhūmi* describes visualization of the 'white bones emitting a flux of light which grows into a blue jewel tree and so on'.[13] Given the use of colour in *kasiṇa* practice it is not impossible that this was sometimes used after the practice on the form of the body.

So where to find the objects of this meditation? As we have noted, most monasteries where meditation is practised to this day keep a skeleton or selection of bones for this practice: bones are also often used as an example of the element of earth. It hardly needs stating that the steps needed to procure the object for most of the later stages of this practice would be illegal in many countries, including Britain. When Maurice Walshe died (1998), however, his body was at his request and by a special dispensation displayed at Amaravati in Hemel Hempstead in England for several weeks, and it was possible to see it undergo a number of the stages of putrefaction described among the foulness meditations. Those who visited found the process of examining the body surprisingly peaceful. Children, however, seemed more cheerful about examining the blackened fingers and nails and touching them than their squeamish parents. Perhaps we have lost a perspective that comes from seeing many human bodies, routinely. The agitation or sense of urgency (*saṃvega*) intended by one of the *suttas* later is the rush of energy that arises from viewing the object, but as we have seen in the commentaries the meditator is instructed to take steps before embarking on the meditation to prevent this becoming prurient or unwholesome. There is, one suspects, a knife-edge of balance between whether this remains a suitable object for the practice of meditation or a means of eliciting unhealthy excitement (*vipphandana*).[14]

In later forms of Buddhism the meditation becomes associated with tantric practises and with the accumulation of power: a visit to a cemetery requires a certain nerve, which, trained and tested, becomes a means of breaking free from social conventions.[15] As we have seen from the preparations advised by the commentaries, and the way the practice is so often associated with other meditations in the canon, this is not being encouraged in early Buddhism. Indeed one *sutta*, based upon the *Vinaya* story which gave rise to the ruling concerning the taking of life, seems specially designed to warn against unwise attention with regard to this practice: we have included it here. In Thailand and Burma the practice is conducted in the monastic community under supervision, in trips to a hospital morgue.[16]

So is there potential for harm in this practice? One Christian nun with whom I discussed the exercise said it was the one Buddhist meditation which caused her real concern as it could lead to disrespect for one's own body. The tradition of course stresses that meditation objects should be assigned with great care, but perhaps some words should be said about the general attitude to one's own body in Buddhist meditative practice. In the canon the middle way in one's attitude to one's body is often stressed, and certainly self-mortification is actively discouraged, the intent of the practice being simply to be free from the body, not to hate oneself for having one.[17] All forms of hatred (*dosa*) are unskilful. The Meghiya story, quoted earlier, stresses that we are not the best judges of our own practices; I know of no school of meditation that suggests this practice to newcomers, or that it be undertaken without supervision. As Khantipālo notes: '... *a word of warning*: meditation on the unattractiveness of the body can be very potent and should only be practised with moderation and care if one has no personal contact with a teacher of Buddhist meditation' (Khantipālo 1980: intro. unpaginated).

Ugliness

These verses, given to the monk Kappa, give a strikingly vivid description of ugliness in the human body. According to the life story given by the commentary, he was the son of a governor and was inclined to great sensory overindulgence. The Buddha perceives him with divine vision, visits him and delivers a discourse larded with similes and metaphors of the most repellent kind.[18] The ancient Indian equivalent of 'yuk' seems to be the intended effect! Kappa subsequently became an arahat. Only one nun, appropriately named Abhayā, 'Fearless', is described as attaining arahatship on the basis of examination of a corpse. Nuns were excluded from visiting cemeteries: it was felt then, as to a certain extent now, dangerous for women to travel anywhere alone, so her attainment presumably occurred before the rule was formulated.[19] Buddhaghosa's warning against a woman considering a male dead body, however, suggests that it was sometimes undertaken by women (Vism VI 42).

567. Full of varied stains, a great dung producer,
Like a mildewed pool, a great boil, a great wound,
568. Full of pus and blood, smeared in a cesspit:
The body trickles water and always oozes, foully.
569. Coated with a coat of flesh, dressed in a jacket of skin:
Putrid, the body is worthless.

570. A string of bones joined together, with ties of sinew threads,
A meeting together of this and that, it makes its posturing.
571. Set on a course for death, it hangs around with the king of death.
Only when he abandons it, right here, does a man go where he wishes.
572. The body is covered in ignorance, tied up in a fourfold knot;
The body is sinking in the flood, caught in a net of sticky inclinations.
573. Yoked up to the five hindrances, afflicted with thought,
Pursued by craving, the very root, covered with the covering of delusion,
574. So this body rolls on, set in motion through the machinery of *kamma*.
Success ends in failure; diverse in nature, the body fails.
575. Silly, blind, ordinary men, who cherish this body:
They fill up the fearful cemetery; they go once more to becoming.
576. Those who steer clear of this body, as if it were a dung-smeared snake,
Vomiting up the root of it all: they will become cooled, without corruptions.

(Th 567–76)

Kulla

This group of verses is ascribed to the arahat Kulla, in which he describes seeing the body of a woman cast away, eaten and full of worms.[20] Kulla was born at Sāvatthī in a wealthy family and was often seized by fits of lustful passion, and so was frequently sent to charnel grounds to meditate. According to the commentaries he attained the first *jhāna* and then arahatship.

393. I, Kulla, going to a burial ground, saw a woman cast away,
Abandoned in the cemetery, being eaten, permeated by worms.
394. Diseased, impure, rotten: see the body, Kulla!
Oozing and trickling, it is the delight of fools.
395. Taking the teaching as a mirror for the attainment of knowledge and vision,
I reflected upon this body, empty inside and out.
396. As this, so that; as that, so this.
As below, so above; as above, so below.
397. As by day, so by night; as by night, so by day.
As before, so it is after; as after, so it is before.
398. There is not such delight in the five kinds of musical instruments
As there is for he who is one-pointed, who sees things truly.

(Th 393–8)

An emergency

This *sutta* gives us one of the strangest stories of the canon, a shortened version of the *Vinaya* account of the circumstances leading to the declaration of the third *parājika* offence, against the taking of life (see Vin III 68–70). The Buddha teaches the foulness meditation and then decides to spend some time in solitude.

The monks, left to themselves, devote themselves to consideration of the diverse aspects of the foulness of the body. Such is the shame engendered by this exercise however that the order assembled there embark on a series of mass suicides, with as many as thirty monks killing themselves on one day.

It is difficult to know whether to include this *sutta*, in which a number of monks the Buddha's instructions have such extreme consequences, as a cautionary tale under this heading or under that of breathing mindfulness (29), as the provider of an emergency antidote for a practice which has in some sense gone awry. The former is chosen on the grounds that it gives an example – admittedly extreme – of how a strong meditation practice, inappropriately pursued and in the absence of a teacher, can be like taking powerful medicine out of turn. The antidote is *ānāpānasati samādhi*, breathing mindfulness meditation as a *samatha* practice.

Did the Buddha make some kind of mistake in his initial recommendations? Or did he perceive that such an extreme measure was the only medicine that would work on this group of people, knowing there would be some successes, but a high and spectacular rate of failure? The commentary gives an account of the incident: a number of men who had been hunters in a past life are all reborn together and become monks. The Buddha, seeing their unfortunate *kamma*, realizes that they are to reach violent ends, either killing themselves or others. He gives the instructions for the practice and then goes on retreat knowing there is nothing he can do to prevent the result: those who are stream-enterers or higher cannot of course take a lower rebirth, and do not try to kill themselves or others; the others do.[21]

Whatever the background, the Buddha's recourse to breathing mindfulness as an immediately efficacious antidote suggests its particular suitability for dealing with imbalances in meditation. The fact that no *kasiṇa* needs to be constructed, and that no person is taken as an object, for whom violent disgust or attraction may also be conceived, such as might be the case for the *brahmavihāras*, would render it particularly suitable as an emergency measure. Certainly the simile of the rain cloud that bursts after all the dust and dirt have been unsettled by the dry season must have spoken with refreshing directness. There can be few images so expressive of emotional relief for someone used to the unbearable tension preceding the rains in an Indian climate, and few that can make a particular meditation practice seem so attractive after one which can lead to self-disgust. Interestingly the analogy implies no criticism of the practice on the foul: it suggests that while it is in the natural order of things for dirt and dust to be unsettled, the rain cloud that dispels this is always welcome. Once again the *sutta* reminds the reader why advice from a teacher may be timely and necessary.[22]

At Vesālī

Thus have I heard. At one time the Exalted One was staying at Vesālī in the Great Wood in the Peaked Gable Hall.

Now at that time the Exalted One was giving a varied talk to the monks on the subject of foulness: he was speaking in praise of foulness, and in praise of the cultivation of meditation on the foul.

Then the Exalted One addressed the monks, 'I wish to go into retreat, monks, for about two weeks. I should not be approached by anyone except the person who brings food.'

'Yes, sir', the monks replied and no one approached the Exalted One except the person who brought food to him.

Now the monks said, 'The Exalted One has given a varied talk on the subject of foulness; he has been speaking in praise of foulness, and in praise of the cultivation of meditation on the foul'. And they spent their time practising meditation on the foul in its various applications. Worried about the body, ashamed and disgusted, they looked for a weapon; in one day ten monks used the knife against themselves, in one day twenty or thirty monks did so.[23]

Now at the end of the two weeks the Exalted One returned from retreat and addressed Ānanda: 'Why, Ānanda, does the order of monks seem so depleted?'

'That is because the Exalted One gave a varied talk on the subject of foulness; he spoke in praise of foulness, and in praise of the cultivation of meditation on the foul. And the monks spent their time practising meditation on the foul in its various applications. Worried about the body, ashamed and disgusted, they looked for an executioner; in one day ten monks used the knife against themselves, in one day twenty or thirty monks did so. It would be good, sir, if the Exalted One, would explain some other method so that the order of monks might become established in knowledge.'

'Very well, Ānanda: call together in the assembly hall as many monks as are staying dependent on Vesālī.' 'Yes, sir', Ānanda agreed and, when he had got together as many monks as were staying dependent on Vesālī he approached the Exalted One and said, 'The order of monks, sir, have assembled. Let the Exalted One come when he sees fit'.

Then the Exalted One went to the assembly hall, sat down on the appointed seat and addressed the monks in this way:

'It is just as if, monks, in the last month of the hot season, when the dust and dirt fly up, a great rain cloud out of season were to disperse and settle them. In just this way, monks, concentration by means of breathing mindfulness, when cultivated and made much of, is peaceful and choice: it is a sublime and happy abiding too, that disperses and settles harmful, unskilful states whenever they arise. And how is this so?

Here, monks, a monk goes to a forest, or the roots of a tree or an empty place and sits, folding his legs in a cross-legged position, making his body straight and sets up mindfulness in front of him . . . [as for breathing mindfulness (29)] . . .

Cultivated in this way, monks, concentration by means of breathing mindfulness, is peaceful and choice: it is a sublime and happy abiding too, that disperses and settles harmful, unskilful states whenever they arise.'

(S V 320–2)

8

THE RECOLLECTIONS

The first six

The recollections (*Anussati*): (21–26) The six recollections

The word *anussati* is derived from the Sanskrit word *anusmṛti*, a remembrance or recollection. Its root word, *sati*, is usually employed in the sense of mindfulness; the prefix *anu* suggests an action performed repeatedly. So the first six recollections are things to be thought about or brought to mind again and again: they are known as *anussatiṭṭhānā*, the establishments of recollection. They first appear as a list of six, but also as a list of ten, with the inclusion of what are known as four mindfulnesses: breathing mindfulness (*ānāpānasati*), mindfulness of death (*maraṇasati*), mindfulness of body (*kāyagatāsati*) and the recollection of peace (*upasamānussati*). In the text that follows, it is said that any one of these ten leads to *nibbāna*. We probably should not take this too literally, for in the canon and in modern practice they are usually taught alongside other meditations, which they complement and support. Texts such as these, however, are worth bearing in mind as reminders about the canonical treatment and discussion of effective meditation practices. Few limits are placed within the canon itself upon their potential as means of obtaining various meditative states.

Buddhaghosa says that none of the recollections, with the exception of breathing mindfulness (29) and body mindfulness (28) lead to *jhāna*, but to a state known as *upacāra*, or access concentration.[1] At this stage, not mentioned in the canon, the hindrances are suppressed but the five faculties of faith, effort, mindfulness, concentration and wisdom have not been developed to a sufficient extent for the mental image to become settled so the meditator can enter full meditation. Reasons for this limitation vary for each object: by and large, the objects are considered too complex or too encompassing.[2] Some objects are considered not to lead to *jhāna* for their very profundity – implying that they encourage other reflective or investigative qualities that are necessary or helpful in the stages to enlightenment. Buddhaghosa says that the *samatha* practices on the loathsomeness of food (39), the determining of the four elements (40), mindfulness of death (27) and mindfulness of peace (30) do not lead to *jhāna* but are suitable for the intelligence type (see Vism III 121–2). As we shall see, the canon and the commentaries regard these recollections as important and even essential to ensure that development in meditation is balanced. The canonical *Mahāniddesa* recommends that for the one who has faith the sign that inspires confidence (*pasādanīyaṃ nimittaṃ*) should be cultivated: the Buddha, the *dhamma* and the *saṅgha* (21–3) and virtue, *sīla* (24) (Nidd 1 360).

The first six, on the Buddha, the *dhamma*, the *saṅgha*, virtue (*sīla*), *cāga*, the letting go or release that may arise through generosity, and *devas* tend to be assigned in groups. The most common arrangement is a whole list, or a cluster with the first three and one or more from the next three. The first three (21, 22, 23) are usually placed together with the same formula for each. The recollections also occur as a five: in one case they occur without *cāga* (21, 22, 23, 24, 26: A I 30). In another, where some emphasis has also been placed on the practice of *sīla*, its recollection is omitted (21, 21, 23*, 25, 26).[3] As this tendency suggests, the six involve elements which are difficult to disentangle, as daily practice, the whole atmosphere of Buddhist devotion and the underlying perception of the world as involving constant rebirth in different realms are all inextricably knitted into any understanding of each as a formal recollection.

Each recollection is treated singly in these two chapters.[4] After a short text describing the importance of all ten the section begins though, as does so much Buddhist practice, with the first three as a group.

> *Ten recollections*
> 'Monks, there is one thing, which, if cultivated and made much of, conduces to complete turning away and dispassion, to cessation, to peace, to higher knowledge, to awakening, to *Nibbāna*.
>
> What is that one thing? It is the recollection of the Buddha. Monks, this is one thing, which if cultivated and made much of, conduces to complete turning away and dispassion, to cessation, to peace, to higher knowledge, to awakening, to *Nibbāna*.
>
> Monks, there is one thing, which, if cultivated and made much of, conduces to complete turning away and dispassion, to cessation, to peace, to higher knowledge, to awakening, to *Nibbāna*. What is that one thing? It is the recollection of the *dhamma*... the recollection of the *saṅgha*... the recollection of virtue... the recollection of generosity... the recollection of *devas*... mindfulness of breathing... mindfulness of death... mindfulness of body... the recollection of peace.
>
> Monks, this is the one thing, which if cultivated and made much of, conduces to complete turning away and dispassion, to cessation, to peace, to higher knowledge, to awakening, to *Nibbāna*.'
>
> (A I 30)

21–23. The Triple Gem

Even if they never practise meditation, many Buddhists regard paying homage to a shrine, a Bodhi tree or a *stūpa*, lighting incense and candles and chanting to the Triple Gem, as an important part of their devotional practice. The precepts, undertakings not to kill, steal, indulge in harmful sexual behaviour, to lie or to become intoxicated, are seen as a way of freeing the individual from unhappy or self-destructive ties. Although many Westerners learn meditation without taking refuge, in the East it is felt to help prevent problems of over-attachment or projection and so is considered as important as any one of the other *kammaṭṭhānas* as the first step in meditation. Richard Randall, who became the monk Kapilavaddho in the fifties, recalled this sense of priority:

> He then told me that he would see that I first became ordained a *samanera* and that later he would arrange and be responsible for my final higher ordination as a *monk*. But to begin with he wanted me to undertake meditational instruction as a layman. It would be necessary therefore that I officially take upon myself the precepts and rules of training of a lay Buddhist and this we would do immediately.
>
> (Randall 1990: 26)[5]

Ven. Suvaḍḍhano writes of the recollections on the Triple Gem, 'Just as the earth receives and supports our footsteps, so it is necessary right from the beginning in developing these work places (*kammaṭṭhānas*) to have a shelter and solid foundation for the mind' (Suvaḍḍhano 1961: 2). For some, taking refuge helps to settle the mind before meditation, sets a helpful separation between every day activities and meditation, and imparts a sense of stability and direction. Richard Gombrich says of faith: 'The word most used is *pasāda*, which indicates emotion as much as belief, a calm and happy confidence that something is so…calm and happiness are themselves "profitable", "skilful" states of mind, little steps along the path to *nibbāna*' (Gombrich 1988: 119). A post-canonical commentary describes the refuges in this way:

> The Buddha is like one who passes down the inheritance of *dhamma*; *dhamma* true is like that inheritance; the *saṅgha*, which is like a group of children who are heirs to an inheritance, is heir to the inheritance of *dhamma* true.[6]

After the refuges and precepts a description of the attributes of the Buddha, the *dhamma* and the *saṅgha* often follows. These attributes, commonly chanted at most Buddhist festivals, form the basis of the three recollections as they are described in the canon. This text has been placed in the Pāli below the English as within the Theravāda tradition it is so often heard in this way and many Buddhists would recognize it, perhaps without knowing the meaning of each word or that it embodies the usual formulation of the recollection of the Triple Gem.[7] It gives the formula by which each of the first three recollections is conducted singly, as a practice on its own.

Chanting

Although the Buddha himself made no specific reference to the practice, for the sake of historical context and present custom a word should also be said here about different modes of chanting, regarded in most Buddhist countries as a living spiritual tradition in its own right.[8] Throughout Southeast Asia the *Iti pi so* chant, called after the first three words, which forms the basis of this recollection, is also chanted routinely as part of the lay life. In Southern Buddhism various 'schools' of chanting have flourished, occasionally in specialist centres, such as, in Thailand, in the royal monasteries. The way the enumeration of the qualities of the Triple Gem, the *iti pi so*, is repeated is itself regarded as a form of meditation, requiring alertness, awareness of the movement of the sound and flow of sound within the body and attentiveness to the presence of other chanters.[9] The method by which any chant is enunciated may vary according to occasion and locality: there is a great difference, for instance, between the slow, mellifluous 'waves' of alternations between chanters found in some Sri Lankan chanting, and the more astringent, vigorous chants of Thai daily practice. In all these traditions the act of chanting is regarded as a practice in itself, so the chants are preserved with meticulous care throughout Southeast Asia: many monks make their study and memorization – of which the *Iti pi so* is but one example – their main form of spiritual and daily practice. One monk told me that when chanting he felt he was developing all five factors of *jhāna*.[10]

Iti pi so

This chant is thought to have a particular enlivening and awakening effect within Buddhist tradition. It is difficult to communicate the effect these recollections have on those for whom the Buddha, the knower of all worlds, the *dhamma*, the understanding of the way things are and the *saṅgha*, the community of those who have practised the teaching, are regarded as present and active in the world: it can though be observed just by a visit to a Buddhist temple in the early evening, when many people drop by after work to light some candles and incense, offer flowers, and do some chanting before going home. The words in bold at the beginning denote the 'opening' chanted by a monk or lay practitioner before the rest join in.

By this reason the Exalted One is an arahat, fully awakened, perfect in knowledge and conduct, well gone, the knower of worlds, incomparable leader of people to be tamed, teacher of gods and men, a Buddha, the Exalted One.

Iti pi so bhagavā *arahaṃsammāsambuddho vijjācaraṇasampanno sugato lokāvidū anuttaro purisadamma–sārathi satthā devamanussānaṃ buddho bhagavā ti*

The *dhamma* is well taught by the Exalted One, visible here and now, immediate, inviting inspection, leading onwards, to be experienced by the wise for themselves.

Svākkhāto *bhagavatā dhammo sandiṭṭhiko akāliko ehipassiko opanayiko paccattam veditabbo viññūhī ti*

The *saṅgha* of the Exalted One's disciples is practising the good way, practising the straight way, practising the true way, practising the proper way, that is, the four pairs of people, the eight types of individuals; this *saṅgha* of the Exalted One's disciples is worthy of gifts, worthy of hospitality, worthy of offerings, worthy of añjalis, the unsurpassed field of merit for the world.

Supaṭipanno *bhagavato sāvakasaṅgho uju paṭipanno bhagavato sāvakasaṅgho ñāyapaṭipanno bhagavato sāvakasaṅgho sāmīci paṭipanno bhagavato sāvakasaṅgho yadidaṃ cattāri purisayugāni aṭṭha purisapuggalā esa bhagavato* *sāvakasaṅgho āhuneyyo pāhuneyyo dakkhiṇeyyo añjalikaraṇeyyo anuttaraṃ puññakkhettaṃ lokassā ti.*

The Triple Gem as practice

So how are these practices conducted as meditations? As described in the *Visuddhimagga*, they comprise complex exercises which list conceptual elements which are brought to the mind to encourage confidence and cheerfulness – that the Buddha is the 'knower of all worlds', for instance, and that he is the 'charioteer of men to be tamed' (see Vism VII 2–67). Although the later commentarial tradition says that this does not lead directly to *jhāna*, the introduction to the first story of the *Jātakas*, also traditionally attributed to Buddhaghosa, says that any of the first three recollections can lead to all stages of the path.[11] Given the popular appeal of the stories, this statement in the first tale of the collection suggests the practices were considered central for the laity. As it is taught in most Theravāda countries it is sometimes given as a walking practice, in which the qualities are brought to mind as a way of encouraging confidence and energy. The qualities of different aspects of the Buddha, the *dhamma* and the *saṅgha* are reflected upon and allowed to rest in the mind in a leisured way.

The canon does not explicitly state that these recollections do *not* lead to *jhāna*, but they do not appear to be regarded as a means of focusing the mind. They are not included in the *Dhammasaṅgaṇi* list of meditation objects.[12] This does not diminish their importance: the potential of the practice on the Triple Gem as a means of attaining stages in the path is particularly emphasized in the 'Simile of the Cloth', where one who practises in this way is said to be 'washed with an inner washing', just as cloth is washed before being dyed (M I 39). Imagery connested with washing or cleaning is constantly associated with all of the first six recollections.[13] The practices assigned to the laywoman Visākhā in one of the texts later are striking and do not occur elsewhere.[14] The *Mahāniddesa* describes the recollections as ensuring the arising of beautiful joy (*kalyāṇa pīti*), perhaps implying that they act as a protection against other less skilful forms of joy which might arise, based on desire or taint (Nidd 1 491–2). Another *sutta* states that just by any one of these practices some become pure.[15]

Other texts included here indicate that from canonical evidence, recollection on aspects of the Triple Gem is a practice suitable for times when sitting meditation is not possible. They are given to householders to develop in daily life, where circumstances make other forms of *samatha* meditation difficult. The practices seem designed both as a preparation for more formal sitting practice and for the return to daily business.

21. Recollection of the Buddha (*Buddhānussati*)

The first recollection is a bringing to mind of the qualities of the being who is fully awakened, the Buddha.[16] This recollection, in the formula given earlier, is said to induce a sense of confidence and happiness, so that something of the qualities associated with the Buddha may be found in the practitioner too. Ven Vajirañāṇa writes:

> In the mind of him who meditates on the recollection of the Buddha, the thoughts arise repeatedly with reference to the Buddha's virtue. With the consequent exaltation of mind, full of joy and gladness, he becomes increasingly strengthened in faith and devotion.
>
> (BMTP 185)

Upatissa claims that the practice does not lead to *jhāna* if one aspect of the Buddha is taken as an object; but says that from it the four *jhānas* may arise.[17]

The texts are filled with the presence of the Buddha himself as a teacher and communicator in all sorts of ways and it is worth considering briefly the extraordinary diversity of attributes with which he is said to be endowed.[18] He is the teacher of both gods and men, and in the *Lakkhaṇa-Sutta* thirty-two physical attributes of the Great Man (*mahāpurisa*) are ascribed to him, all associated with excellencies of character, by which the bearer is said to be destined to become a Buddha or a universal monarch (see D II 142–78). These marks have become part of the iconography of the Buddha in all traditions of Buddhism, and draw together some straightforward physical features with those that are idealized and heroic. Some of the attributes are god-like, suggestive of a being endowed with supernatural powers: his skin is said to shine like Sakka, lord of the Thirty-Three Gods, and his voice is soft as the Indian songbird, like that of Brahma.[19] The straightness of his frame is compared to that of Brahma. Other features attributed to him in this *sutta* are extraordinary in that they embody qualities expressed through symbolic means: features such as the thousand-spoked wheels that arise on the palms and soles of the feet, and the *anulom*, the light, cotton-like tuft of hair that arises between the eyebrows, are frequently found in later depictions in sculpture and painting. One or two are conventionally heroic, such as the unusually long arms, for instance, a feature of Indian epic and *kavya* poetry.[20] Other marks of a more mundane kind are described within the same list, such as evenly rounded shoulders and the lion-like upper part of the body. The first mark of all states that the Buddha walks literally like a very down-to-earth human, with a level tread, evenly raising his foot and evenly placing the whole of his foot on the ground. That such a mundane attribute is given as the first distinguishing feature of the teacher seems a deliberate assertion of his status as a human, for it differentiates him clearly from deities in Indian literature, whose feet are traditionally thought not to touch the surface of the ground.[21]

It is as a teacher that helps and gives guidance that the Buddha is described in the Pāli texts. There is ample evidence for instance that the Buddha himself was anxious to avoid hero worship of an unhealthy kind, and the texts placed together here show some hard-nosed reminders to avoid this pitfall. In one *sutta* that follows, included under the recollection of the *dhamma* (22), a meditator is warned not to bask in reflected glory. The Buddha saw himself as the hand that points to the moon, not the moon itself. He rebutted Sāriputta's praise of him as the greatest being who ever lived, reminding him of other Buddhas who have lived in the past, and that he is just one of a great lineage (see D II 82–3). The Buddha's anxiety to avoid excessive attachment to his person is seen in the *Mahāparanibbāna-Sutta* when the Buddha gives comfort to a grieving Ānanda – who, as the only non-enlightened being, provides us with a useful foil to the dramatic momentum of the text – by encouraging him to be a refuge to himself. Through the presence of Ānanda he is then able to deliver his teaching to the common man: the unenlightened man or woman who might be listening to the *sutta*, should have the confidence to stand on his or her own and not be disturbed by the absence of a living Buddha to teach him.[22] The frequency of *suttas* in the canon given by his disciples and approved by him also indicates that he had a careful eye for the long-term survival of the tradition and that the teachings of those that followed him were valued. He did give instructions as to what should be done with his body after death – presumably to prevent dispute over this. Certain sites are also recommended in this text as pilgrimage sites: this is the only place in the canon where such recommendations are given, and their presence here suggests that the Buddha, or the composers of the texts, wished to ensure that the devotional element should be acknowledged, but should not overwhelm other features of the teaching (D II 140–2).

The Buddha was also liable himself to old age, sickness and death. Like any other being in the sense sphere, he was made up of the five *khandhas* of body, feelings, identification, formations and consciousness. It is said that he could have extended his lifespan, but Ānanda fails to request him to do this, so preventing this extraordinary event occurring (see D II 118). None of these features however detracts from the extraordinary achievement of the Buddha or the way in which he is perceived amongst practising Buddhists. The Buddha is called *atideva*, one above the gods, the *devas* and those of the Brahma realms (Th 489). We do find in the canon the almost magical descriptions of the *Lakkhaṇa-Sutta* and description of his psychic abilities, the *iddhis*, as exhibited in the Twin Miracle, as well as more mundane observations of his power.[23] These powers, magnificent in themselves, are also usually exhibited with intent to help another (see A IV 87).

This is all far too large a study for this book: it suggests though that in the single figure of the Buddha we can see a creative integration of many diverse elements, including a number of very different ways of perceiving teachers and the possibilities of what it is to be fully human. A new perspective on the recollection of the Buddha is also given by the suggestion that it is one that he practised himself, in his visualization of earlier Buddhas in the *Apadāna*. In this text, he employs techniques we associate with Northern schools of Buddhism:

> 20. The pillars and posts and beautiful golden gateways made of special Jambu gold, choice wood and also silver shone (around the mansion).
>
> 21. (The entrances) had many junctions, were well-proportioned, made colourful by doors and crossbars (and had) many overflowing pots containing lotuses and water-lilies on either side.

22. I also (mentally) created all the Buddhas of the past, the Leaders of the World, together with their companies of monks and their disciples, in their natural colour and form.

23. All the Buddhas, together with their disciples, entered by that door and were seated, (each) on a chair made completely of gold, (arranging themselves) in a noble circle.

(Ap 20–3; Mellick Cutler trans.)[24]

A description by the Buddha of the six Buddhas that preceeded him may also be found in the *Mahāpadāna-Sutta*; another tradition gives twenty-four previous Buddhas.[25]

The importance of the recollection on the Buddha in other forms of Buddhism

Subsequent developments in Buddhism developed this kind of meditation further: many of the developments of the *Mahāyāna* devolve around the single practice of the recollection of the Buddha.[26] In these practices, there is a more explicit extension of the recollection to include all aspects of the eightfold path, and all possible meditative states. If the Buddha represents the *dhamma*, then his bodily form must be an embodiment of the teaching, and it should be possible to be aware of all aspects of the path through bringing him to mind. If the Buddha is the one who is 'Thus Gone' (*Tathāgata*) the experience of *nibbāna* must be possible simply from the recollection of his presence.[27] If the world systems are filled with potential Buddhas or bodhisattas, then the imaginative exercise that summons oceans upon oceans of them, in front, behind, above and below – each in their own Buddha-field – extends the visualization process even further. This development of the practice to encompass many other aspects of the meditative process also accompanies stress upon certain details which are described in a few texts within the canon, but which become central to much later iconographic description of the Buddha, particularly in the Mahāyāna. The thirty-two marks, discussed earlier, are integral to the development of both Theravāda and Mahāyāna practice as characteristics of the Buddha as an externally and internally visualized form.[28] Some of these, such as the wheels on the soles of the feet, the *anulom* between the eyebrows, the *sama*, or evenly rounded shoulders and the turban crown of the head feature in visual representations of the Buddha in all forms of Buddhism.[29] The various Buddhist traditions of the first centuries CE developed the recollection of the Buddha with extraordinary creativity: the stamp of this is felt in many Buddhist practices, in many different schools.

While the canon provides many correctives to prevent excessive sentimentality, many Buddhists feel a great emotional release in paying homage to the being who disclosed the path. The poem from the *Suttanipāta*, quoted here, is a canonical testament to the simplicity and grace of such faith.

An old man's practice

These devotional verses are uttered by an old man, Piṅgiya, as he brings to mind and extols the qualities of the Buddha. He is said by the commentaries to have been 120 years old and very feeble physically at the time. Although he did not apparently attain arahatship on this occasion, he does subsequently become an arahat.[30] This piece, taken from a longer poem composed of dialogue amongst disciples, suggests that the practice of the old man in keeping the Buddha in his mind's eye involves, even in this very early canonical work, visualization as an aid to devotion (see Gombrich 1997: 11ff.). The Buddha is described as 'Alone, dispelling darkness, seated in brilliance' (1136); the speaker 'cannot stay away from him even for a moment' (1140) and 'see [s] him with my mind as if with my eye, being attentive day and night' (1142). Throughout the poem, the Buddha is felt as an all-present, pervading power, protecting the old man and leading him onwards although his sight is failing and his body weak and near death.

From a historical as well as from the technical meditative point of view, the poem raises interesting questions. The description seems designed to create an image in the mind that aligns the text with the visualization practices of the Northern schools. In these highly structured and complex practices, the meditator, after requisite initiations, instructions and *pūjas*, imagines the Buddha seated on a throne as the basis of a practice that pays homage to him, and then allows a link to be made between that imaginative vision and with his own heart, mind and body.[31] The visual complexity of the more formal of these practices, and the way that they are linked with mantras, offerings and hand gestures (*mudrās*), means that considerable importance is attached to the practice being something apart from the usual activities of the day. The practitioner makes his preliminaries and gives the practice his full attention. It is therefore important to make a clear ending to any sitting and to put aside the object of the practice once it is completed. Visions are dissolved, any 'deities' that have been asked to attend are asked to leave and the meditator is instructed to be aware of the world of the physical senses and impressions.[32]

In this poem, however, the image is not of such a complex kind that it needs the kind of attention required for formal visualization. The text suggests merely the presence of the Buddha, described visually but also in more general terms for his wisdom and encouragement. One does not need to be a Buddhist to appreciate this poem's expressive power. It demonstrates an element of the teaching often found in Buddhist countries, particularly amongst the old, that confounds any impression that Buddhism is entirely 'rational' and non-emotional.[33]

Piṅgiya

1133. The one who dispels darkness is the Buddha, whose eyes see all around, who has gone to the end of the world. He has passed beyond all existences, is free from corruptions (*āsavas*) and has abandoned all misery. The one who has been named truly is served by me, brahmin.

1134. Just as a bird, leaving behind a scrubby wood, might go and live in a richly fruitful forest, so I too, leaving those of little vision, have arrived, as a goose reaches a great lake.

1135. Those who expounded to me earlier, before I heard Gotama's teaching, said, 'this is how it is; this is how it will be'. But all that was hearsay; all that was speculation.

1136. Alone, dispelling darkness, seated in brilliance: this is Gotama, the bringer of light, of abundant wisdom and abundant sagacity.

1137. He is the one who gave me the teaching that can be seen, that is immediate, the destruction of craving, free from distress, the likeness of which does not exist anywhere.'

1138. 'Can you keep away from him even for a moment, Piṅgiya, from Gotama, of abundant wisdom, from Gotama, of abundant sagacity?

1139. Who gave you the teaching that can be seen, that is immediate, the destruction of craving, free from distress, the likeness of which does not exist anywhere?'

1140. 'No, I cannot stay away from him even for a moment, brahmin, from Gotama, of abundant wisdom, from Gotama, of abundant sagacity.

1141. It was he who gave me the teaching that can be seen, that is immediate, the destruction of craving, free from distress, the likeness which does not exist anywhere.'

1142. I see him with my mind as if with my eye, being attentive day and night, brahmin. I pass the night revering him. For that reason I think there is no staying away from him.

1143. My faith and joy, my mind and mindfulness do not go away from the teaching of the Gotama. In whatever direction the one of abundant wisdom goes, in that direction I bow down.

1144. I am old and of feeble strength. For that very reason my body does not go there. So I go constantly on a mental journey for my mind, brahmin, is joined to him.

1145. I lay floundering in the mud; I floated from island to island. Then I saw the Fully Awakened one, the flood crosser, who is without corruptions.

1146. 'Just as Vakkali has announced that he has been freed by faith, and Bhadrāvudha and Āḷavi Gotama too, so you also should be freed by faith.[34] You, Piṅgiya, will go to the far shore of the realm of death.'

1147. 'My faith is all the greater for hearing the sage's words. He has removed the veil, the Fully Awakened One: he is without barrenness and brings illumination.

1148. He knows the higher gods. He knows everything, above and below. The Teacher makes an end to the questions, for those who are in doubt and have acknowledged it.

1149. Assuredly I shall go to that which cannot be moved, that which cannot be shaken, the likeness of which does not exist anywhere. There is no doubt in me about this. Remember me as one whose heart has been freed!'

(Sn 1133–49)

22. Recollection of the *dhamma* (*dhammānussati*)

The word *dhamma* has many associations, and whole treatises could be written on its translation and meaning.[35] Broadly speaking, it may be taken as the fourth foundation of mindfulness – how things are – which is found after and is to a certain extent a higher development of the foundations of mindfulness based on the body, feelings and mind. To act in accordance with how things are, which is in accordance of the four noble truths, is also *dhamma*, in which sense the term moves towards the sense of what is just or right. *Dhamma* in the sense meant here is the teaching that leads one to see how things are, and to provide encouragement at each stage of the path. It is described by the formula for the *iti pi so* chant.

Some distinction is made between the *dhamma* as it is passed down through the three baskets, of the *Suttas*, the *Vinaya* and the *Abhidhamma*, and the *dhamma* which leads to complete enlightenment. The first kind, the teachings that are recorded in the texts, is regarded as of utmost importance because it is the means which makes possible the second. Throughout history the preservation of texts orally, and later in physical form, has been one of the main pursuits of certain sections of the *saṅgha*. According to Buddhist tradition the *dhamma* in this sense is impermanent, and the word of the Buddha will in time be lost, just as it has been lost in the past: there have been Buddhas before, as we saw in the last extract. Various stories and legends are related to this: the Burmese say that they will be lost when the *Paṭṭhāna*, the last book of the *Abhidhamma*, is no longer chanted correctly, while other traditions say that when there are no more monks to practise the teaching it will be lost. Sri Lankan Buddhism is permeated with all kinds of stories about the end of the Buddha's teaching – perhaps such stories are intended to arouse greater purpose for those felt to be lucky in having the teaching now.

At any rate the *dhamma* that leads to freedom, in the sense of the texts themselves, may be lost, but its laws are an inevitable part of life in *saṃsāra*. These laws never cease to operate, making the *dhamma* a refuge in both senses certainly for the near future. As a refuge, it refers to that formulation which corresponds to and leads to an understanding of things as they really are: that is the teaching of the Buddha, wherever it is found. Buddhaghosa and Upatissa differ in their interpretation of this recollection. The *Visuddhimagga* analyses the formula given above in detail, displaying his great love of wordplay (*nirutti*) as a means of elucidation (see Vism VII 68–88). Upatissa says simply that the *dhamma* here 'means extinction, *nibbāna*, or the practice by which extinction, *nibbāna* is reached' and cites the thirty-seven constituents of enlightenment as subjects to be brought to mind (PF 149–50). He says that it should be recollected in the following way:

> It is the eye; it is knowledge; it is peace; it is the way leading to the immortal; it is renunciation; it is the expedience whereby cessation is

won; it is the way to the ambrosial; it is non-retrogression; it is the best; it is non-action, solitude, exquisiteness. It is not soothsaying. It is the most excellent object for the wise man's mind. It is to cross over to the other shore; it is the place of refuge.

(PF 150)

Practice according to dhamma

This was said by the Exalted One, spoken by the arahat: so I have heard.

'When referring to a monk who practises according to *dhamma*, this is the proper way of defining practice according to *dhamma*. When he is speaking, he speaks only in accordance with *dhamma*, not with what is not. When he applies his mind he applies it only to thoughts in accordance with *dhamma*, not thoughts that are not. By avoiding both speech and thought that are not in accordance with *dhamma* he abides with equanimity, mindful and clearly comprehending.

The one who takes pleasure in the *dhamma*, who delights in the *dhamma* and reflects over the *dhamma*:

As he recollects the *dhamma*, he does not fall away from it.
When walking or standing, sitting or lying down,
His heart is inwardly settled, and he attains to tranquillity.'
This is the meaning of what was said by Exalted One: so I have heard.

(It 81–2)

Avoiding blind faith: Vakkali

These two texts, involving the same person but taken from different collections, are juxtaposed to indicate the emphasis the Buddha placed on the practice of his teaching rather than personal adulation. According to the commentaries, the brahmin, Vakkali, was so devoted to the Buddha that he spent all his time in contemplating his appearance.[36] Because of this the Buddha delivers the rebuke in the first *sutta*. It did not apparently deter Vakkali from his adulation and, on the last day of the rains, the Buddha instructs him to depart. One version of the story says that, when dismissed, Vakkali went to practice meditation at Gijjhakūṭa, but was too temperamentally disposed to faith to be able to master insight: he also becomes gripped by stomach cramps. The Buddha appears to teach him and Vakkali attains arahatship. The verses, uttered by Vakkali himself, reveal his new independence: his faith has been translated from a limited kind of hero worship into a practical and useful support to meditation, capable of being tested by difficulty.

The hem of the robe

This was said by the Exalted One, said by the arahat, I have heard.

'Monks, even though a monk might take hold of the hem of my robe and follow right up behind me, step by step, if he is covetous for senses pleasures, darkly passionate, is malevolent of mind, corrupt in thought, of muddled mindfulness, lacking in clear comprehension, unconcentrated, of wandering mind and discomposed faculties, then he is far from me and I am far from him. What is the reason? That monk, monks, does not see *dhamma*. He who does not see *dhamma*, does not see me.

Monks, even though a monk might live a hundred leagues away, if he is not covetous for sense pleasures, not darkly passionate, not malevolent of mind, uncorrupt in thought, with mindfulness established, clearly comprehending, concentrated, of a one-pointed mind and composed faculties, he is near to me and I am near to him. What is the reason? That monk, monks, sees *dhamma*. He who sees *dhamma*, sees me.

Although he follows right behind, full of great longing and annoyance,
See how far away he is from him!
The one who desires from the one who is free from desire,
The one who is not quenched from the one who is quenched;
The greedy one, from the one without greed.
But whoever, with knowledge of *dhamma*, has fully understood the *dhamma*:
He becomes free from desire, like a peaceful, unruffled lake.
See how close he is to him!
The one who is free from desire to the one who is free from desire;
The one who is quenched to the one who is quenched;
The one without greed to the one without greed.'
This is the meaning of what was said by Exalted One: so I have heard.

(It 90–2)

Vakkali

350. 'You are laid low by stomach cramps, in the forest woodland,
And have come to a wretched place for food: how, monk, will you get on?'

351. 'Suffusing the body with an abundance of joy and happiness,
Enduring even a wretched living, I shall abide in the wood!

352. Cultivating the foundations of mindfulness, the faculties, and the powers,
Developing the factors of awakening, I shall abide in the wood!

353. I have seen men stirring up energy, resolute, constantly exercising effort,
Harmonious and united: I shall abide in the wood!

354. Recollecting the Fully Awakened One, the foremost, the tamed, the composed,
Not becoming weary, by day or by night, I shall abide in the wood.

(Th 350–4)

23. Recollection of the *saṅgha* (*saṅghānussati*)

This practice brings to mind the community of those that have followed the path. The object is best represented by the *saṅgha*, the community of monks (*bhikkhus*) and nuns (*bhikkhunīs*), exemplars of a way of life that aims to embody freedom. The *saṅgha* still collectively live by the guidelines established by the Buddha in the *Vinaya*: for this that they are regarded as worthy of veneration. According to the *Vimuttimagga*, awareness of the *bhikkhusaṅgha* is the salient characteristic of this recollection, and an appreciation of its virtues a near cause (see PF 150). The formula for this practice, however, given under the Triple Gem, describes a larger community in the *ariyasaṅgha*, all those that have attained to the four stages of enlightenment: stream-entry, once-return, never-return or arahatship. Each of these stages has a path, and a fruit of that path, a benefit that occurs as a result of it, so there are eight 'types' of individuals who have reached one of these stages. Buddhaghosa and Upatissa state that the recollection is specifically directed to these eight types: those who have experienced the paths or fruits of stream-entry, once-return, never-return, or arahatship include laymen, laywomen, as well as monks and nuns who have attained these states.[37] When any food and offerings are made to monks and nuns, they often emphasize that such gifts are not just personal, or just to the individual monk or nun involved: they are made to this matchless field of merit, known as the community of disciples (*sāvakasaṅgha*). Such gifts are considered one of the highest forms of giving, because they nourish and sustain those that embody the life of the Buddha's teaching.

A large gathering of monks, in their saffron, cinnamon and orange robes, is an impressive assembly. Perhaps the most effective evocation of the power of the *bhikkhusaṅgha* as a living, teaching community is the opening of the *Ānāpānasati-Sutta*, on breathing mindfulness (29), where, in the presence of the Buddha, groups of monks are described teaching others on the night of a full moon.[38]

A forest sutta

At Sāvatthī. Standing to one side, that *deva* recited this verse in the presence of the Exalted One.

'Those who live in the forest,
Peaceful, leading the holy life,
Eating just one meal a day:
Why is their complexion so serene?'

The Exalted One replied,
'They do not grieve over the past,
Nor do they yearn for the future.
They keep themselves with what is present:
Because of that their complexion is serene.

Through yearning for the future,
Through grieving over the past,
Fools dry up and wither
Like a green reed that has been cut.'

(S I 5)

24. Recollection of virtue (*sīlānussati*)

Some of the happiest occasions for laity and monks in Buddhist countries are *uposatha*, or *poya* days as they are sometimes known, on which the laity sometimes take additional precepts and keep what is known as *sīla*: a largely untranslatable term whose meaning is taken variously as good conduct, good behaviour or virtue.[39] *Uposatha* days are festive, with a lot of lights, offerings of flowers, good food, laughing, firecrackers as well as peaceful practice. The idea that it might be useful and restorative to remember one's own virtue, however, can seem pretty leaden to Westerners. The conscious practice of virtue has itself acquired cold associations; the idea of its recollection sounds positively alarming. For Asians who are practising Buddhists, however, keeping *sīla* is just regarded as very happy and auspicious: it ensures that you are strong, healthy, long-lived and extremely good looking (in the next lifetime at any rate if you feel there is not much hope for this one!). It also protects from harm. A modern Burmese teacher writes:

> In fact in this world there is no greater adornment than purity of conduct, no greater refuge, and no other basis for the flowering of insight and wisdom. *Sīla* brings a beauty that is not plastered onto the outside, but instead comes from the heart and is reflected in the entire person. Suitable for everyone, regardless of age, station or circumstance, truly it is the adornment for all seasons. So please be sure to keep your virtue fresh and alive.
>
> (Sayadaw U Pandita 1992: 13)

This recollection is conducted with the formula, 'The virtues are unbroken, and whole, unspotted, untarnished, purified, praised by the wise, untainted and leading to concentration of mind'. In the series of texts under the 'elevens' in the *Anguttaranikāya*, there seems to have been some interchangeability in the way the practice and its recollection are assigned.[40] Throughout the canon and the commentaries the practice of *sīla* is described as an essential preliminary to meditation practice: if the mind is reasonably free from guilt or confusion about daily activities, then it is easier to establish calm and insight. Buddhaghosa devotes the preliminary section of the *Visuddhimagga* to the practice of *sīla* (see Vism I 1–160). Just as the practice of the recollection of the qualities of the Triple Gem is, in the canon, often recommended to lay people, so bringing to mind the qualities of the five precepts, or the ten precepts of *uposatha* days, is considered a natural development of this that encourages the mind and dispels doubts about oneself or way of practice. The Buddha explicitly denounces boasting about one's own virtue.[41]

Keeping the five precepts is the base line of virtue. For festival times or meditation courses, when it is customary to wear white, eight or ten precepts may be taken. These include the undertakings not to carry money, wear adornments or jewellery, not to go to any shows, not to sleep in high and luxurious beds and, crucially, living for that day what is called the chaste life, of a brahma (*brahmacariya*). For traditional Asian society, as in many religious orders in Christianity, chastity, when actively chosen, is regarded as possessing a special potency: the one who practices it increases rather than diminishes his or her happiness and power. For a Thai, spending a day wearing white and ten precepts for the day is not seen as undermining masculinity or femininity. In fact rather the reverse applies: until recently a Thai woman would expect any man she marries to spend some time as a monk because he would not be a complete man, and able to control his bodily desires, until he had done so. The five precepts, which make the undertaking to refrain from behaviour that harms oneself and others, such as killing, stealing or cruel sexual practices are also felt to give protection in daily life. Many Thai women see the simple taking of refuge and the practice of *sīla* with the five precepts as the source of physical beauty and grace: remembering them brings a sense of confidence and freedom from fear.[42] In Buddhism the third precept of the laity (*kāmesumicchācāra*) does not mean abstention from sexual intercourse, but practising it in a way which does not involve excess or harm to oneself or others. In traditional Indian society health, wealth and sexual happiness are felt to be natural accompaniments to marriage, an attitude also associated with lay Buddhism. Happy couples are said to be like *devas* (see A II 58–61). For the *saṅgha* the 227 rules of the *Vinaya* constitute the basis of the practice of *sīla*

The exercise is recommended with those on the Triple Gem. For those brought up in the Buddhist tradition the practice and recollection of *sīla* is felt to be a great protection for the mind, and a safeguard against 'demons', both inner and outer.[43] Buddhaghosa writes that it ensures freedom from fear, nightmares and harm from others and that the practitioner lives in communion with his fellows (see Vism VII 105–6).

> *Heaven*
> This was said by the Exalted One, spoken by the arahat, I have heard. 'Endowed with two things, monks, a person is placed in heaven as if carried there. With what two things? Virtue and right view. Endowed with these two things, monks, a person is placed in heaven as if carried there.
>
> Virtue and right view –
> If a person is endowed with two things,
> at the break up of the body
> That wise man is reborn in heaven'.
> This is the meaning of what was said by Exalted One: so I have heard.
> (It 26)

Verse from the 'Thousands Chapter'
And anyone who lives for a hundred years, with bad behaviour and unconcentrated mind
It would be better for him to live for one day, practising virtue and meditating.
(Dhp 110)

25. Recollection of generosity (*cāgānussati*)

In the East the practice of giving (*dāna*) is considered an auspicious starting point for meditation: the one who gives to others will be more open to receive the states that meditation offers. Throughout Buddhist countries, one of the most popular forms of lay practice is for those who visit temples and monasteries to make donations of money and food. Hospitality is a basis of lay activity and giving to monks and teachers is considered the best form of this.[44] Advice and encouragement to those who give is a frequent motif throughout the canon. Precision and aptness are the keynotes that govern the way the giving of food, donations and, the highest gift of all, the teaching is recommended: all should be given only when the time, place and circumstances are correct (see A III 42). The *suttas* attach considerable importance to the worth of the recipient, the appropriateness of a gift to a particular occasion and the time when it is given: teachers, those that are wise and the *saṅgha* are considered to be the best recipients. The underlying perception is that the giving of food and support is always good, but to the *saṅgha* it creates a means of sustaining a whole way of life (see A III 50–3).

Again there is the assumption that it is not just giving which is thought to bring merit and good luck, it's recollection too. The practice is undertaken with the formula,

> It is a gain for me, a very good gain for me, that amongst those possessed with the stain of meanness, I live as a householder with the stain of meanness removed from my mind, freely generous, pure handed, delighting in letting go, giving what is asked, rejoicing in giving and sharing.

The distinction between two terms is slight but important for this meditation: while giving (*dāna*) denotes the act and the practice, generosity (*cāga*) is the state of release which is involved when anything is freely given up. The word may also refer to the giving up of unwholesome mental states such as hatred or desire.[45] The act of giving is considered to be itself transformatory: according to the *Abhidhamma*, for instance, it is not possible to experience hatred or desire at the moment an object or present is relinquished.[46]

Early examples of the spontaneous practice of the recollection may be found in the *Vimāna* stories and commentaries, post-canonical works that reflect lay practices and assumptions dating from the early days of the tradition. A number of tales describe one act of generosity, in particular to a monk, being efficacious at the moment of death, thus producing a fortunate rebirth in a heaven realm for the giver.[47] The practice of placing records of donors, who were thought to become beautiful, long-lived and destined for heavens, onto the walls of shrine halls and temples, dates from the earliest times.[48] The important aspect for this recollection is remembering the joy that in the first instance prompts and can accompany *cāga* itself. It is customary in Buddhist countries to encourage the recollection of generous and meritorious actions at the approach of death. Monks visit and chant for the dying person, who is asked to remember the happiness of past generosity as a way of cheering the mind, dispelling fear and allowing it to arise again as death approaches.

Buddhaghosa says that this recollection brings happiness, freedom from fear and a fortunate rebirth.[49] He recommends that the one who wishes to practise it should constantly devote himself to acts of generosity, according to his means (Vism VII 107). Upatissa says that the one who cultivates this meditation acquires confidence and is always undisturbed (see PF 154).[50] No single text advocates the recollection on its own, though the canon contains many texts on the importance of the appropriateness and timing of generous acts.[51] A generous, rich man is compared to a beautiful lake which lies near a village where others can drink and bathe (see S I 90–1). The greatest act of giving is said to be the gift of the teaching, the *dhamma*.[52] The householder Citta, skilled in all eight *jhānas* and a non-returner, vindicates this with his dying words, in which he encourages his family to be generous (see S IV 304).[53]

The Giving and Sharing sutta

This was said by the Exalted One, spoken by the arahat, I have heard.

'If beings knew in this way, monks, as I know, the result of giving and sharing (*dānasaṃvibhāgassa*), they would not eat without having given, nor would they allow the stain of meanness to take hold of their mind and become stuck there. Even if it were their last morsel, their last mouthful, they would not eat without having shared it, if there were someone to share it with. But, monks, as beings do not know, as I know, the result of giving and sharing, they eat without having given and the stain of meanness takes hold their mind and becomes stuck there.' The Exalted One explained the meaning and this was said too:

'If beings just knew – so the great sage spoke –
The result of sharing, that is of such great fruit,
They would remove the stain of meanness, with a brightened mind.
They would give to noble ones,
Where what is given is of great fruit.
Having given a large quantity of food, an offering to those most worthy of offerings,
When they depart from the human state here, those that give go to heaven.
Those who have gone to heaven, rejoice, delighting in the pleasures there.

The fruit of sharing with others: those who are not mean experience this.'
This is the meaning of what was said by Exalted One: so it is said.

(It 18–19)

26. Recollection of devas (*devatānussati*)

Visitors to Buddhist temples are often impressed by pictures on the walls of sometimes sensuously beautiful figures, surrounded with a kind of 'halo' around the head, that seem to fill every available space above the level of the eye. These are *devas*, shining beings or gods that inhabit heavens where rebirth is possible from the human realm. In these depictions, as in the texts, they represent a thoroughly humanized ideal of physical beauty and happiness.[54] In some temples, both ancient and modern, more earthy and sometimes goblin-like beings are shown, depicted or carved, protecting and ornamenting doors, door brackets and the entrance ways: these are *yakkhas*, or *devas* of a lower level than the others, the realm of the Four Kings, who are considered as protectors against misfortune or evil spirits, guarding those inside from spiritual and physical harm. In order to understand these beings, and their recollection, a few words need to be said about the background to Indian life at the time of the Buddha, and indeed in many Buddhist countries to the present day.

According to Buddhist cosmology the human realm stands near the base of thirty-one realms where existence of different kinds is possible, and where one may be reborn on death. Four of these are lower than the human, and experience various degrees of unhappiness. These 'bad destinies' as they are called, include the realm of animals, the hungry ghosts (*petas*), the jealous gods (*asuras*) and the hells, whose misfortunes and bodily torments correspond most closely to Western conceptions of infernal realms. Rebirth in these realms is indefinite, but not permanent, and is produced by the force of bad *kamma*. In much temple art they are depicted underneath the others in an area that is literally lower, giving an almost gravitational sense of the darkness underlying but not dominating rebirth in the human realm. At Aluvihara, near Kandy, a visitor walks up past paintings of hells to reach the shrine at the top of the hill. Beings in these lower realms embody a life governed purely by desire, hatred or ignorance.

Above the human realm however the six sense-sphere heavens enact a form of existence where the joyful aspects of human experience are translated into a paradise where much of the suffering of humans has been excluded. Beings reborn there are not immortal, but their lifespan, of thousands of years, is vast. *Devas* are from the earliest times depicted in Buddhist art, sculpture and narrative friezes with graceful bodies whose ease of movement enacts release from physical constriction, pain or sexual torment. It is difficult to find exact counterparts in modern Western culture, though classical Greece and Rome, also polytheistic societies, seem to have had a comparable sense of the gods as beings who might and do sometimes mix with humans.[55] Rather in the manner of Greek gods, though without their addiction to vengeance, *devas* have a very good time, and with their radiant beauty, extended lifespan and spontaneous birth have many of the pleasures of human life without its disadvantages. They like to witness acts of generosity and provide blessings and encouragement to humans whose behaviour is like theirs.

The practice is given in the texts later by remembering the ascending hierarchy of sense-sphere *deva* realms, noting their happiness and pleasure. Meditators remind themselves of their proximity to these beings and their own merit that will lead to rebirth as a *deva*: faith, virtue, learning, generosity and understanding (Vism VII 116). In this recollection, the heavens also extend to a seventh, the Brahma realm, a more refined world than the sense sphere, where beings are born through practising *samatha* meditation. The heavens are those of: the Four Great Kings (*catummahārājika*); the Thirty-Three Gods (*tāvatiṃsa*); Yāma; the Contented (*tusita*); those who Delight in Creation (*nimmāṇaratin*); those who Delight in the Creations of Others (*paranimmitavasavattin*) and Brahma.[56]

We do not know the extent to which the practice was developed in the early days of Buddhism: few *suttas* cite it specifically. *Devas*, however, have always been painted and sculpted in shrine halls throughout the East. The chanting of auspicious texts such as the *Maṅgala-Sutta* and the *Ratana-Sutta* assume their presence as witnesses, rejoicing and giving blessings to skilful actions. The *Mahāsamaya-Sutta*, which involves visualization of the *devas*, can be seen as an extended exercise in this practice.[57] Their recollection is recommended by the Buddha as a practice which a layman can give to another on his deathbed, along with that of the Triple Gem (see S V 409–11). As an embodiment of a happy life to which ordinary people can aspire through the practice of giving and keeping the precepts, remembering the chance of rebirth in these realms seems always to have offered consolation in grief and encouragement in daily life. It forms an almost inevitable part of the background of lay visits to temples and shrines.

> Devas
>
> 'When a noble disciple is endowed with four things, monks, the *devas* are delighted to speak to him as one of the same company.[58] What four?
>
> 'Here, monks, the noble disciple is endowed with unwavering confidence in the Buddha . . . the *dhamma*, . . . the *saṅgha*. Now those *devas* who, being likewise endowed with unwavering faith, have deceased here in this world and risen up there, in a heaven, think in this way: "That noble disciple is endowed with just the same kind of unwavering faith in the Buddha . . . the *dhamma* . . . and the *saṅgha* on the basis of which we, deceased there in that world arose here, in a heaven: come into the presence of the *devas*."
>
> 'Then one is endowed with the virtues dear to noble ones, virtues unbroken, whole, unspotted, untarnished, purified, praised by the wise, untainted and leading to concentration of mind. Now those *devas* who, being likewise endowed with such unbroken virtues, dear to noble ones, have deceased here in this world, and risen up there, in a heaven, think in

this way: "That noble disciple possesses just the same unbroken virtues, dear to noble ones, on the basis of which we deceased there, in this world and arose here, in a heaven: come into the presence of the *devas*."

When a noble disciple is endowed with four things, monks, the *devas*, delighted, speak to him as one of the same company.'

(S V 394)

Groups of practices: a laywoman

This extract, taken from a *sutta* addressed to Visākhā, the chief female lay follower of the Buddha, pre-eminent in almsgiving and a stream-enterer (see A I 26).[59] Visākhā enjoyed a life that is regarded as exemplary for the laity in its abundance, happiness and fertility. Youthful in appearance throughout her life, she produced 10 sons, 10 daughters and, according to the commentaries, by the time of her death at a 110 had countless descendants, all living. She fed 500 monks daily at her house and in the afternoon visited the Buddha to hear *dhamma* (see Ja IV 144). The thoroughly domestic nature of most of the following images is particularly apt: the shampooing of a dirty head, the cleansing of a dirty body, the laundering of a dirty garment, cleaning a mirror; lastly, that of *devas*, like purifying gold. The highly detailed descriptions of the materials used to clean each of the first four items give us a sense of the quotidian preoccupations of a laywoman – even a wealthy one who would have had plenty of servants – and suggest something of the frequency and repetitive care with which these practices, like other meditations, should be practised. All the cleaning processes described are, in an Eastern context, energetic, dextrous and tend to be conducted with great thoroughness and *elan*. They involve a more generalized background awareness than the intent pursuit of calm or insight: perhaps a way of bringing contentment to a busy life. Oddly enough the recollection on generosity is omitted, or perhaps felt unnecessary, for this hospitable woman.

This extract occurs after the description of the *uposathas* of the herdsmen and the naked ascetics, whose recollections, the Buddha says, are without much profit. The text concludes with recommendations to bring to mind the qualities of the arahats and a description of *deva* realms. Visākhā is assured by the Buddha that those who observe *uposatha* days in this way are likely to be reborn in such realms.

The noble uposatha

'And what, Visākhā, is the noble *uposatha*?

It is, Visākhā, the cleansing of the defiled mind with a suitable approach.

And how is this done?

Here, Visākhā, the noble disciple brings to mind the Tathāgata: "By this reason the Exalted One is an arahat, fully awakened..." As he brings to mind the Tathāgata, his mind becomes clear, gladness arises, the defilements of the mind are abandoned. It is just like the shampooing of the head when it is dirty.

And how is the shampooing of the head undertaken when it is dirty? By means of a paste, special clay, water and the appropriate application of effort by the person. This is how the shampooing of the head is undertaken when it is dirty and how the cleansing of the defiled mind is undertaken, with a suitable approach.

And how is the cleansing of the defiled mind undertaken with a suitable approach? Here the noble disciple brings to mind the Tathāgata: "By this reason the Exalted One is an arahat..." As he brings to mind the Tathāgata, his mind becomes clear, gladness arises, the defilements of the mind are abandoned. This noble disciple is said to keep the Brahma *uposatha*. Living with Brahma and associating with Brahma, his mind becomes clear, gladness arises, the defilements of the mind are abandoned. This is how the cleansing of the defiled mind is undertaken, with a suitable approach.

It is, Visākhā, the cleansing of the defiled mind with a suitable approach. And how is this done?

2. Here, Visākhā, the noble disciple brings to mind the *dhamma*: "The *dhamma* is well taught by the Exalted One, visible here and now..." As he brings to mind the *dhamma* his mind becomes clear, gladness arises, the defilements of the mind are abandoned. It is just like the cleansing of the dirty body with a suitable approach.

And how is the cleansing of the dirty body undertaken with a suitable approach? It is by means of a stone, soap powder, water and the appropriate effort of the person. This is the cleansing of the dirty body with a suitable approach. It is also how cleansing of the defiled mind is undertaken, with a suitable approach.

And how is the cleansing of the defiled mind undertaken with a suitable approach?

Here the noble disciple brings to mind the *dhamma*: "The *dhamma* is well taught by the Exalted One..." As he brings to mind the *dhamma* his mind becomes clear, gladness arises, the defilements of the mind are abandoned. This noble disciple, Visākhā, is said to keep the *dhamma uposatha*. Living with the *dhamma* and associating the *dhamma*, his mind becomes clear, gladness arises, the defilements of the mind are abandoned. This is how the cleansing of the defiled mind is undertaken, with a suitable approach.

3. It is, Visākhā, the cleansing of the defiled mind with a suitable approach. And how is this done?

Here the noble disciple brings to mind the *saṅgha*: "The *saṅgha* of the Exalted One's disciples is practising the good way, practising the straight way..." As he brings to mind the *saṅgha* his mind becomes clear, gladness arises, the defilements of mind are abandoned. It is just like the cleaning of a dirty cloth with a suitable approach.

And how is the cleaning of a dirty cloth undertaken with a suitable approach?

It is by means of a saline substance, soda, cow dung, water and the appropriate effort of the person. This is the cleaning of a dirty cloth with a suitable approach. It is also how cleansing of the defiled mind is undertaken, with a suitable approach.

And how is the cleansing of the defiled mind undertaken with a suitable approach?

Here the noble disciple brings to mind the *saṅgha*: 'The *saṅgha* of the Exalted One's disciples is practising the good way…". This noble disciple is said to keep the *saṅgha uposatha*. Living with the *saṅgha* and associating with the *saṅgha* his mind becomes clear, gladness arises, and the defilements of the mind are abandoned. This is how the cleansing of the defiled mind is undertaken, with a suitable approach.

4. It is, Visākhā, the cleansing of the defiled mind with a suitable approach. And how is this done?

Here the noble disciple brings to mind his own virtues: 'The virtues are unbroken, whole, unspotted, untarnished, purified, praised by the wise, untainted and leading to concentration of mind'. As he recollects virtues his mind becomes clear, gladness arises, the defilements of mind are abandoned. It is just like the cleaning of a dirty mirror with a suitable approach.

And how is the cleaning of a dirty mirror undertaken with a suitable approach? It is by means of oil, ashes, a brush and the appropriate effort of the person. This is the cleaning of a dirty mirror with a suitable approach. It is also how cleansing of the defiled mind is undertaken, with a suitable approach.

And how is the cleansing of the defiled mind undertaken with a suitable approach? Here the noble disciple brings to mind his own virtues: "The virtues are unbroken…". This noble disciple is said to keep the virtue *uposatha*. Living with virtue and associating with virtue his mind becomes clear, gladness arises, and the defilements of the mind are abandoned. This is how the cleansing of the defiled mind is undertaken, with a suitable approach.

5. It is, Visākhā, the cleansing of the defiled mind with a suitable approach. And how is the cleansing of the defiled mind undertaken with a suitable approach?

Here the noble disciple brings to mind the shining ones (*devas*): "There are Four Great Kings, there are Gods of the Heaven of the Thirty-Three, there are Gods of Yāma's realm, there are Contented Gods, there are Gods Who Delight in Creation, there are Gods Who Delight in the Creations of Others, there are Gods of the Brahma realms and there are gods beyond that. There exists in me such faith as the faith, endowed with which, those shining ones died in this world and were reborn in that world. There is found such virtue in me, I have listened to as much teaching. There is found such generosity in me and such wisdom." As he brings to mind his own faith, virtue, the fact that he has listened to the teaching, his own generosity and wisdom, his mind becomes clear, gladness arises, the defilements of mind are abandoned.

It is like the purification of impure gold with a suitable approach. And how is the purification of impure gold undertaken with a suitable approach?

By means of a furnace, salt, red chalk, a cooling pipe, tongs and the appropriate effort of the person. This is the purification of impure gold with a suitable approach. It is also how cleansing of the defiled mind is undertaken, with a suitable approach.

And how is the cleansing of the defiled mind undertaken with a suitable approach?

Here the noble disciple brings to mind the *devas*:" There are Four Great Kings, there are Gods of the Heaven of the Thirty Three..." This noble disciple is said to keep the *devatā uposatha*. Living with the *devas* and associating with the *devas* his mind becomes clear, gladness arises, the defilements of the mind are abandoned. This, Visākhā, is how the cleansing of the defiled mind is undertaken, with a suitable approach.'

(A I 206–11)

Groups of practices: in a house with children

The last twenty-five years have seen an unprecedented increase in lay practitioners of meditation.[60] This text is of particular interest because it describes practices for a domestic context, with children around. According to Buddhaghosa, Mahānāma was a stream-enterer, a stage for which these six recollections are considered particularly suited (see Vism VII 111).

The *sutta* is one amongst several including these recollections. Another, given to the businessman Nandiya, should be mentioned for its slight modification of the usual formulae for two of the recollections, indicative of the way the Buddha 'tailors' practices for different people.[61] Nandiya is encouraged to practise, not recollect, virtue. He is told not to recollect the *saṅgha* but '...good friends, compassionate, who wish for my well being, who encourage and exhort me. In this way, Nandiya, you should keep mindfulness of good friends steady inside' (A V 336). This advice, presumably phrased in this way for his lay-practice, provides us with another illustration of how canonical meditation guidance sometimes eludes too rigid classification, for it is given in the usual place of the *saṅgha* recollection, after that of the Buddha. There is no separate category for this recollection in the usual classifications found. The recollection of *devas* is also expressed differently: speaking of *devas* who arise who live on 'material food' (*kabaliṅkāra*) and who rise up again in a certain mind-made body he should remember they 'observe nothing more to do for the self and no need to repeat what is done'.[62] The variety within this series of *suttas*, all addressed to different householders, indicates the fluidity in the form and mix of practices in the canon: the Buddha clearly adapts meditation objects with flexibility, though, as in the latter case, the circumstances might not be obvious now.

Mahānāma

At one time the Exalted One was staying amongst the Sākyans at the Deer park at Kapilavatthu. At that time the Venerable Mahānāma had risen from a sick bed and had just recovered from illness. At that time a large group of monks were sewing robes for the Exalted One, for, they said, 'When the rains are over the Exalted One will go on the almsround'.

Now Mahānāma heard what was going on and went to see the Exalted One, greeted him and sat to one side. Seated, he spoke to the Exalted One.

'I have heard, sir, the report that a large group of monks are sewing robes for the Exalted One and that when the rains are over the Exalted One will go on the almsround. So, sir, how should those of us who are in varied walks of life spend our time?'

'Very good, very good, Mahānāma! It is very suitable that a man of good family comes to ask the Exalted One the question, "How should those of us who are in varied walks of life spend our time?" The successful man has faith and does not lack faith.[63] He has effort stirred up and he is not lazy. His mindfulness is steady,[64] and he is not confused. He is composed and not discomposed. He is strong in wisdom and not weak in wisdom.

When you are grounded[65] in these five qualities, Mahānāma, you should cultivate six more.

'Here, Mahānāma, you should recollect the Tathāgata in this way, "By this reason the Exalted One is an arahat..." At the time when a noble disciple brings to mind the qualities of the Tathāgata in this way, at that time his mind is not possessed by desire, his mind is not possessed by hatred, his mind is not possessed by delusion: at that time his mind becomes straight, taking as its object the Tathāgata. The one who has a straight mind takes joy in his practice, takes joy in the *dhamma*, and finds gladness in association with *dhamma*. In the one who is glad, joy arises, in the one with a joyful mind the body becomes tranquil, the one who has a tranquil body feels happiness. The one who is happy concentrates the mind. So you, Mahānāma, should cultivate this recollection of the Buddha when walking, standing, sitting, lying down and as you go about your business. You should develop it while you live as a householder, in a place with children all around.[66]

'Here, Mahānāma, you should recollect the *dhamma* in this way, "The *dhamma* is well taught by the Exalted One..."…. So you should cultivate this recollection of the *dhamma* when walking, standing, sitting, lying down and as you go about your business. You should develop it while you live as a householder, in a place with children all around.

'Here, Mahānāma, you should recollect the *saṅgha* in this way, "The *saṅgha* of the Exalted One's disciples is practising the good way..." ... So you should cultivate this recollection of the *saṅgha* when walking, standing, sitting, lying down and as you go about your business. You should develop it while you live as a householder, in a place with children all around.

'Here, Mahānāma, you should recollect your own virtues in this way: "The virtues are unbroken, and whole..." ...So you should cultivate this recollection of virtues when walking, standing, sitting, lying down and as you go about your business. You should develop it while you live as a householder, in a place with children all around.[67]

'Here, Mahānāma, you should recollect generosity in this way: "It is a gain for me, a very good gain for me, that amongst those possessed with the stain of meanness, I live as a householder with the stain of meanness removed from my mind, freely generous, pure handed, delighting in letting go, giving what is asked, rejoicing in giving and sharing"...So you should cultivate this recollection of generosity when walking, standing, sitting, lying down and as you go about your business. You should develop it while you live as a householder, in a place with children all around.

'Here, Mahānāma, you should recollect the *devas* in this way: "There are Four Great Kings, there are the Gods of the Heaven of the Thirty Three...."...So you should cultivate this recollection of the devas when walking, standing, sitting, lying down and as you go about your business. You should develop it while you live as a householder, in a place with children all around.'

(A V 332–4)

9

THE RECOLLECTIONS

The four mindfulnesses

27. Mindfulness of death (*maraṇasati*)

All cultures and religions address the problem of death and mortality. It is a measure of the practicality of the Buddhist tradition that death is employed as one of the meditation objects, to be used as a reminder of the death of all beings and as an object to arouse urgency (*saṃvega*). This is then, through the application of skilful attention, stilled to arouse joy and peace.

In Buddhism, the subject is knitted in to the definition of the central doctrine. It is included with birth, old age and sickness as one of the principle manifestations of *dukkha*, the first noble truth, the 'dis-ease' that characterizes existence of any kind, whose manifestation through these events afflicts all beings.[1] Even the gods experience death, though without the physical suffering of humans and animals.[2] Death is also part of the chain of dependent arising, and, with birth, forms one of the twelve linked causes that are brought into being by ignorance and that lead to the renewal of the cycle of craving and becoming. 'The passing away of beings from the various ranks of beings, their passing away, breaking up, disappearance, dying, coming to their time, the breaking up of the aggregates, the putting aside of the body – this is called death' (M I 49). The moment of death, at which this cycle may be broken, is therefore of great import within the Buddhist tradition: if there is peace at that moment a fortunate rebirth will ensue.[3] Within the Buddha's life story, the knowledge of death given by the sight of a dead body is one of the signs that prompts him to question his own existence. This idea of the dead body as a 'messenger' for humans is found in the *suttas*. Lord Yama, the god of death, is described questioning the wrong doer about the *deva* messengers (*devadūtā*) sent to remind those that are badly conducted in body, speech and mind to remedy their ways.[4] The dead body is the fifth in the list that cites birth, old age, illness, and the visible and horrific kammic results of unskilful actions as messengers to humans. As in many other traditions, the word pertaining to 'death' is used in an adjectival sense to describe the principles which militate against wholesome and skilful behaviour as well: Māra, that great opponent of meditation practice, whose lordship extends over any realm of the sense sphere, is described as death and his name is derived from it.[5] Defilements of mind (*kilesā*) are described as the armies of death, an image which supplies a further dimension to the description of the absence of death as one of the defining features of *nibbāna*, the deathless (*amata*) (see S IV 91 and Sn 425–49).

Perhaps as a reflection of its potential to arouse insight or calm, the meditation is described with two terms in the canon. The most complete list of meditation objects in the *nikāyas*, the *Jhānavagga*, lists death as a meditation practice three times: twice as a perception and once as a recollection (see A I 41). It is not clear in what way the two are distinguished. Meditations occur twice where they feature as components of two separate lists: the formless meditations, for instance, are included as deliverances and on their own. Here the two occurrences of the perception of death appear to arise from a conflation of two lists that appear elsewhere.[6] The nature of the distinction between a perception and a recollection could be a matter of emphasis, with the perception (*saññā*) suggesting a stress on awareness of death as a challenge to views, where the recollection may have been addressed to the area of feeling (*vedanā*) and upon the calming of the energy that arises at the prospect or news of a death. The perception occurs in lists that seem aimed at the purification of view through the labelling or identifying part of the mind, and so slanted more towards the cultivation of *vipassanā*.[7] It is a delicate subject, but can be seen in hearing news of a death of someone not very close, that one saw every day. This can unsettle a 'view' of the world as much as a feeling. As a recollection it is regarded as a *samatha* practice and is taken that way by both Buddhaghosa and Upatissa. They say it weakens avarice, makes the practitioner fearless, undeluded and less attached to the body. It is said by the two commentators to lead only to access concentration. Buddhaghosa claims that this is because the object is 'states with individual essences' and because it arouses too much urgency.[8] Upatissa says such an object cannot bring sufficient peace. Both insight (*vipassanā*) and calm (*samatha*) are suggested by the passages used here. It is one of the most frequently recommended meditations in Sri Lanka, though it is given with other practices, such as *mettā* (31), *asubha* (11–20) and the recollection of the Buddha (21) (see BMTP 312).

The *Visuddhimagga* says that it is suitable for those of temperaments inclined towards intelligence (see Vism III 121). Upatissa concurs, but adds that it is also suitable for the one who is deluded, who has acquired some wisdom (see PF 69). Buddhaghosa makes an important proviso for the practice, warning against the unwise recollection of death in the case of someone whose death arouses great grief, as for one's own child, or gladness, as for someone hated. He also advises against considering one's own death as too fearful an object for direct consideration. He says that death is of two kinds, timely and untimely. Eight ways in which to reflect upon death are recommended: (1) as having the appearance of a murderer; (2) as the ruin of success; (3) by comparison with someone great who has suffered death; (4) the body being shared with many, in the form of parasites and worms; (5) the frailty of life; (6) as signless, in that it cannot be predicted; (7) as to the limitedness of extent, in that our lifespans are short and (8) the shortness of the moment. For this last, Buddhaghosa employs one of his most powerful images by way of comparison, communicating the extraordinarily vast and cyclic nature of the Buddhist conception of *saṃsāra*: the human lifespan is like the moment of contact that a large chariot wheel makes as it touches the ground. After that brief contact, life is over and the wheel moves on.

It is the only practice for which Buddhaghosa recommends considering other beings, and the inevitability of their death, before oneself: for practices such as loving-kindness (31) he recommends starting with oneself (see Vism IX 8–10). The refrain he suggests for recitation is impersonal, however: either 'death, death' or 'death will take place' (Vism VIII 4–6).[9] Upatissa's description applies death as a possibility both for others and for oneself.[10] The Buddha's description of the practice varies. Like many other meditation subjects in the canon it is simply expressed and described. Some judiciousness seems to accompany the giving of the practice: the assembly at Nādika, in the texts that follow, appear to have needed a bit of a shock, and the meditation is presumably given to arouse urgency. Many texts that cannot be included in this anthology are of this kind. In one the aspect of death as a dramatic and irreversible process is described with awesome majesty by being compared to mountains crashing in from all sides (see S I 102). In another context, however, the layman Mahānāma, who is frightened of death, is reassured that his continued practice will bring about a good rebirth, and that he need not live in terror of it (see S V 370–1).

Mindfulness of death (1)

The Buddha addresses an assembly at Nādika on mindfulness of death, which leads, he says, to the destruction of the corruptions (*āsavas*), a statement which emphasizes the element of insight for this practice. The text impresses the sense of the moment that sometimes accompanies the way meditation practices are given. The first four options, of living aware of the Buddha's teaching by day and night, throughout the day, for so long as one eats a meal and so long as one eats a few morsels, are all rejected as careless. The last two, being aware of the Buddha's teaching for the space of one mouthful or in the momentariness of observation of one breath, are not: as if to prevent large, vague ambitions, the present is stressed as the time for conducting this practice. Upatissa cites it for this sense of momentariness, for, he says, 'Nothing exists for two moments. All beings sink in the conscious moment' (PF 169). This text is cited by Buddhaghosa as a means of arousing mindfulness of death in its seventh aspect, the brevity of the human lifespan (see Vism VIII 36–7).[11]

(1)

At one time, the Exalted One was staying at Nādika in the Brick Hall. And there the Exalted One addressed the monks. 'Monks.' 'Sir,' the monks replied.

'Mindfulness of death, monks, when cultivated and made much of, is of great fruit and great reward: it associates with the deathless and has as its conclusion the deathless. Monks, cultivate mindfulness of death.

When he had spoken a certain monk said this to the Exalted One. 'Sir, I do cultivate mindfulness of death.' 'And how, monk, do you cultivate mindfulness of death?' 'Here, sir, I reflect, "If I were to live, day and night, paying attention to the teaching of the Exalted One, a great deal would be done by me". This is how I cultivate mindfulness of death, sir.'

And another said, 'I do cultivate mindfulness of death, sir'. And the Exalted One replied, 'And how, monk, do you cultivate mindfulness of death,

'Here, sir, I reflect, "If I were to live, throughout the day, paying attention to the teaching of the Exalted One, a great deal would be done by me". This is how I cultivate mindfulness of death, sir.'

And another: 'Here, sir, I reflect, "If I were to live, for such time as it takes to eat one almsmeal, paying attention to the teaching of the Exalted One, a great deal would be done by me". This is how I cultivate mindfulness of death, sir.'

And another: "If I were to live, for such time as I chew and swallow five mouthfuls, paying attention to the teaching of the Exalted One, a great deal would be done by me". This is how I cultivate mindfulness of death, sir.'

And another: "If I were to live, for such time as I chew and swallow one mouthful, paying attention to the teaching of the Exalted One, a great deal would be done by me". This is how I cultivate mindfulness of death, sir.'

And another: "If I were to live for just such time as, having breathed in, I breathe out, and having breathed out, I breathe in, paying attention to the teaching of the Exalted One, a great deal would be done by me". This is how I cultivate mindfulness of death, sir.'

When they had spoken the Exalted One said this:

'The one who cultivates mindfulness of death, monks, reflecting, "If I were to live, day and night, paying attention to the teaching of the Exalted One...", or the one who cultivates mindfulness of death, monks, reflecting, "If I were to live, throughout the day, paying attention to the teaching of the Exalted One..." or the one who cultivates mindfulness of death, monks, by reflecting, "If I were to live, for such time as it takes to eat one almsmeal, paying attention to the teaching of the Exalted One..." or the one who cultivates mindfulness of death, monks, reflecting, "If I were to live, for such time as I chew and swallow five mouthfuls, paying attention to the teaching of the Exalted One..."

These monks, who speak like that, live carelessly, monks, and are lazy in their practice of mindfulness of death, in order to destroy the corruptions.

'The one who cultivates mindfulness of death, monks, reflecting, "If I were to live, in the time that I chew and swallow one mouthful, paying attention to the teaching of the Exalted One, a great deal would be done by me". And the one who cultivates mindfulness of death, monks, reflecting, "If I were to live for just such time as, having breathed in,

I breathe out, and having breathed out, I breathe in, paying attention to the teaching of the Exalted One, a great deal would be done by me".

These monks, who speak like that, live carefully, monks, and are alert[12] as they practise mindfulness of death, in order to destroy the corruptions.

Therefore monks, it should be practised in this way:

"We live carefully and are alert as we practise mindfulness of death, in order to destroy the corruptions." This is how you should practise, monks.'

(A III 303)

Mindfulness of death (2)

The Buddha addresses monks at Nādika again on mindfulness of death, which should be practised, he says, by thinking of ways that death may come. Here he uses physically explicit reminders: death by scorpions, snakes falls, choking and dysentery. The *sutta* differs from the treatment of death in the *Visuddhimagga* in that the one who will experience death is at first taken as oneself rather than other beings (see Vism IX 8–10). The word for oneself (*me*) is used.[13] The language is stark and uncompromising in its description of the means of possible death. The image of the 'head on fire' is used, presumably to arouse *saṃvega*, the sense of urgency associated with this practice. This text suggests considering the manifold possibilities of early death as a means of arousing energy, mindfulness and clear comprehension. If the monk reviewing (*paccavekkhamāna*) knows that he has done what he should, however, the practice brings joy and gladness and leads to the deathless (*amata*): the wording suggests a weight towards the cultivation of *samatha*.

(2)

At one time, the Exalted One was staying at Nādika at the Brick Hall. There the Exalted One addressed the monks:

'Mindfulness of death, monks, when cultivated and made much of, is of great fruit and great reward: it associates with the deathless and has as its conclusion the deathless. And how is mindfulness of death cultivated, how is it made much of? How is it of great fruit and great reward, associating with the deathless and having as its conclusion the deathless?

'Here, monks, when the day is ending and night falling, a monk reflects in this way: "There are many causes of death for me. A snake, a scorpion or a centipede might bite me and bring death and be an obstruction for me. I may trip and fall; eating something I may become sick from food; bile may upset me; phlegm may choke me; cutting winds may rack me, so that I may die of this and it would be an obstruction for me." Monks, a monk should reflect in this way: "Have I given up harmful and unskilful states, which, were I to die tonight, would be an obstruction for me?" And if, monks, a monk, reviewing in this way, knows that he has not, he should arouse great willingness, effort, endeavour, resolve, heroic exertion, indefatigableness, mindfulness and clear comprehension.

'But if a monk, reviewing in this way, knows that he has given up harmful and unskilful states, which, were he to die that night, would be an obstruction for him, then, monks, may such a monk live in joy and gladness, training himself, day and night, in skilful states.

'Here monks, when the night is ending and day is dawning, a monk reflects in this way: "There are many causes of death for me. A snake, a scorpion or a centipede might bite me and bring death and be an obstruction for me. I may trip and fall, eating something I may become ill from food, bile may upset me, phlegm may choke me, cutting winds may rack me, so that I may die of this and it would be an obstruction for me." Monks, a monk should reflect in this way: "Have I given up harmful and unskilful states, which, were I to die in the day, would be an obstruction for me?" And if, monks, a monk, reviewing in this way, knows that he has not, he should arouse great willingness, effort, endeavour, resolve, heroic exertion, tirelessness, mindfulness and clear comprehension.

'Suppose his clothes or his head were on fire: he would arouse great willingness, effort, endeavour, resolve, heroic exertion, tirelessness, mindfulness and clear comprehension to put the fire out. So, monks, just in this way a monk should arouse great willingness, effort, endeavour, resolve, heroic exertion, tirelessness, mindfulness and clear comprehension to abandon harmful and unskilful states.

'And if a monk, reviewing in this way, knows that he has given up given up harmful and unskilful states, which, were he to die that day, would be an obstruction for him: then, monks, may such a monk live in joy and gladness, training himself, day and night, in skilful states.

In this way, monks, mindfulness of death, when cultivated and made much of, is of great fruit and great reward: it associates with the deathless and has as its conclusion the deathless.'

(A III 306)

28. Mindfulness of body (*kāyagatāsati*)

One of the distinguishing features of the Buddha's system of meditation is the emphasis placed upon the physical body both as a foundation for practice and the means of experiencing and exploring reality. The body, the texts stress, needs to be well maintained and looked after; it then provides the basis by which the mind may be calmed; through sense impressions it provides the data for the cultivation of wisdom and it then continues, in daily life, to give a support whose care and well-being is of the utmost importance for the practice of meditation and development of insight. To this day most practices involve remembering to look after the bodily base as part of their preliminary instructions. They also recommend a careful return to everyday life and normal bodily activities after the meditation has finished.[14] A substantial section of the *Mahāsatipaṭṭhāna-Sutta* reminds us that human existence is, for a large part, made up of basic activities like eating, walking, washing and performing various bodily functions. Good meditation practice involves being aware of these, allowing mindfulness to become established as a flow in all the activities of the day and keeping a balance between sitting practice and awareness in other postures. This direction of attention to awareness of the body, both in being mindful of its needs and in attentiveness to the data it provides the mind, is constantly described and reiterated.[15]

This can be seen in a variety of different ways in texts we can see in this anthology and in the canon generally. For instance, the practice of *sīla* enjoined in the *Sāmaññaphala-Sutta* involves a level of respect for one's own body and that of others that is also the underlying principle of all the precepts. In addition to this, throughout the canon, emphasis on bodily experience assumes that, as a preliminary to meditation, practices are being conducted to be aware of the body and the perception of objects at the sense doors.[16] Guarding the sense doors and the preparations for meditation involve continued awareness of what is going on around and the ways that sense objects are being experienced. Many of the texts in the six sense-base section of the *Saṃyuttanikāya* describe the closeness of attention required to maintain mindfulness at the five senses and at the mind door, for the mind in this section is also taken as a sense. These are worth reading as a series for the memorability of the images used to illustrate the six senses: the lute, the fishhooks and the charioteer. The texts also, however, apply these images, with great precision of observation, to experience of the impingement of each sense in turn.[17] When we read such texts we should remember that the slightly negative slant on physical experience they can suggest to a new reader depends upon the underlying assumption of early Buddhist thought that a human rebirth is particularly fortunate, a happy destiny (*sugati*) and difficult to obtain. Most of human experience, according to *Abhidhamma* theory, is the result (*vipāka*) of the skilful or wholesome (*kusala*) mind necessary for a human rebirth. So simply being aware of the various activities at all of the senses will have a tendency to produce the pleasant or neutral feeling that accompanies the skilful mind. Because there is also a mixture of painful and happy experience, the human bodily form is considered the most suitable for spiritual development.[18] Gethin has shown that the canon regards the practice of mindfulness of body both as needing some initial calm (*samatha*) and producing it too (see Gethin 1992a: 55–7). As one of the texts here says, it anchors the mind so that it is possible to be fully alert to whatever happens at each of the sense doors and to allow attention to be free to experience what is going on without excitement, irritation or confusion.

Observation at the sense-doors is also thought integral to the development of wisdom: indeed the word that often accompanies the term *sati* in the *suttas*, that is usually translated as clearly comprehension, *sampajañña*, is taken by the *Abhidhamma* under the category of the mental factor (*cetasika*) of wisdom (see DhS 53). Much of the description of the sense door process involves practical investigation (*dhammavicaya*) of the way in which the mind responds to bodily feeling that is both pleasant and unpleasant, and bodily feeling as a base for noticing the nature of rise (*samudaya-dhamma*), the nature of fall (*vaya-dhamma*) and the nature of arising and fall (*samudaya-vaya-dhamma*): the experience of bodily sensations in a flow from one moment to the next. This observation of physical process develops the aspect of wisdom (*paññā*) and is described in the canon as involving close discrimination of the stages of the sense-door thought process: the way in which objects are received and examined by the mind. Without this, it is not possible to identify the source of attachment in the sixth sense, the mind, and to observe and understand things as they actually are (*yathābhūtaṃ*). It is only through touch, taste, sounds, smells and sights that we perceive and process information about the way attachment forms and where we can investigate, over time, how this process occurs and at what point we interfere or become pulled in different directions by what is perceived. This aspect of investigative insight is stressed throughout the canon.[19] It should be noted that the *suttas* of the Pāli canon do not dismiss bodily and sensory experience as an illusion, or a delusion, or sensory experience as in itself negative or debilitating. The Buddha actively discouraged quietism or the withdrawal from the world of the senses on a day to day level.[20] This comprehensiveness of the practice, and its applicability to so many diverse areas of life is, I think, also peculiarly Buddhist. Buddhaghosa says that as a meditation subject it is only taught in the dispensation of a Buddha (Vism VIII 42).

As a *kammaṭṭhāna* Buddhaghosa, however, takes the practice to refer specifically to the parts of the body in its thirty-two aspects: in this sense he considers it as a *samatha* practice that can lead to any of the first four *jhānas*.[21] He takes the recommendations for daily life in the four postures and the four kinds of clear comprehension as well as the practice of the four elements as it is described in the *Mahāsatipaṭṭhāna-Sutta*, included in that *sutta* under body mindfulness, as insight practices. The charnel ground meditations he considers under foulness (11–20) (see Vism VIII 43). Certainly the importance attached to this specialized understanding of the practice by the tradition may be seen in the wording of the ordination ceremony: the new monk is formally and publicly given the first five of hairs of the head, body hair, nails, teeth and skin (*kesa*, *loma*, *nakkha*, *danta* and *taca*) as his first meditation practice.[22] I have not been able to find out why it is these first five. Perhaps, as the hard, external parts of the body, they are those that are most obvious, and most visibly subject to decay. Interestingly, part of the ritual preparation for becoming a monk that occurs immediately preceding ordination is the complete shaving of the head: the first object has just been relinquished when the instruction is given. Buddhaghosa examines the practice with a careful precision by taking each part of the body in turn and describing it in detail. He compares the process to a man considering a garland of flowers knotted on a single string: each one appears separate but the whole may be considered simultaneously (Vism VIII 139). He adds the brain to the list of thirty-one parts described in the canon, so bringing the list up to thirty-two. Each one, however, may then be used as an object, which, if developed, leads to the first four *jhānas*. There is a further breakdown of these thirty-two parts into the four elements: this is discussed under the fortieth meditation subject in this book.

Mostly in the canon, however, 'body mindfulness' refers to all the instructions for daily life in the general awareness of postures and, with clear comprehension, in activities throughout the day. In one text Kassapa is told to train himself with the thought, 'I will never relinquish mindfulness directed to the body associated with joy' (S II 220). Practising this, with other instructions that he should practise shame (*hiri*) and dread (*ottappa*) with regard to other monks, whatever their status, and listen attentively to the *dhamma*, he becomes an arahat seven days later. For the cultivation of happiness and joy in daily life, awareness of the body is recommended: one text recommends guarding the sense doors, along with moderation in eating and wakefulness (see S IV 175–7). In the *Kāyagatāsati sutta* ten benefits are described for the one with body mindfulness established: (i) he overcomes dislike and liking; (ii) he overcomes fear and dread; (iii) he bears cold, heat, hunger, thirst, gadfly, mosquito, wind and sun, creeping things and harsh speech; (iv) he bears sharp and painful feeling; (v–viii) he acquires the first four *jhānas*; (ix) he experiences the various forms of psychic power (*iddhis*); (x) he destroys the corruptions (*āsavas*): clearly it is a practice with elements of both *samatha* and *vipassanā*.

For reasons of space the *Kāyagatāsati-sutta*, the *locus classicus* for this practice, has been reluctantly omitted from this anthology, but it is well worth considering for its roundedness and amplification of the methods pertaining to the body found in the *Mahāsatipaṭṭhāna-Sutta* (M III 88–99). As Bodhi notes, the inclusion of the full description of the *jhānas* as well as the presence of the *iddhis* in the list quoted in the previous paragraph, neither of which is found in the *Satipaṭṭhāna-sutta*, weight the *sutta* on body mindfulness much more towards the practice of *samatha* than that one does.[23] There is a much less austere tone to the text entirely devoted to body mindfulness. The underlying common sense of practising mindfulness of body in all postures is suggested through a series of mundane, domestic images, such as the overturning of a pot or failure to light a fire, to describe ways in which Māra, who represents obstructions to practice, can defeat the one without mindfulness of body and fail to overturn one established in it.[24]

The subject is very large but it is hoped that this account at least indicates the comprehensiveness of the early Buddhist attitude towards the body. Mindfulness of body is considered to this day the foundation stone of the Buddha's teaching on meditation. It is the first of the thirty-seven constituents of enlightenment and, according to the way it is treated in the canon, is capable of taking the meditator to arahatship.[25] It is the first practice listed in the *Saṃyuttanikāya* series of factors said to lead to the unconditioned.[26] The body gives the starting point for meditation, the tool for practising it, a source of many of the meditation objects for calming the mind and a means of providing data for the cultivation of wisdom. It is also the place in which the effects of meditation may be felt and discerned both within meditation and in daily life. As we have seen, the bulk of each the standard passages or pericopes pertaining to the first four *jhānas* is devoted to description of the bodily effects of each meditation. The body also reflects the benefits of any moment of mindfulness. According to the *Abhidhamma*, for instance, the skilful mind, which may arise at any time in daily life as well as in *jhāna*, is said to be accompanied by tranquillity, softness, lightness, manageability, proficiency and straightness of body.[27]

Six animals
It is just as if, monks, a man with his limbs wounded and festering, should enter a jungle of reeds. The grasses and thorns might pierce his feet and the reeds scratch his limbs. In this way, monks, that man might experience all the more pain and unhappiness because of that. In this way, monks, a monk might go to a jungle or village and meet one who speaks up at him: 'This venerable monk, acting in such a way and behaving in such a way, is a thorn to the village'. Having understood him in this way as a 'thorn', so restraint and lack of restraint are to understood.[28]

And how, monks, is there lack of restraint? Here, a monk, having seen a form with the eye, inclines towards forms that are dear and turns away from those that are not dear. He practises without having established mindfulness of body, with a limited mind. He does not know as it really is that deliverance of mind, that deliverance by insight whereby harmful, unskilful states that have arisen cease, without remainder. Having heard a sound with the ear...having smelt an odour with the nose...having tasted a flavour with the tongue...having touched a sensory object with the body...having become aware of an object of the mind with the mind, he inclines towards forms that are liked and turns away from those that are not liked.

It is just as if, monks, a man were to catch six animals, each from a distinctive terrain and different feeding ground, and bind them with a strong rope.[29] He catches a snake and binds it with a strong rope and then a crocodile, a bird, a dog, a jackal and a monkey: he binds each with a strong rope. Having done this, monks, he would tie the ropes together, with a knot in the middle, and let them go.

Now, monks, those six animals, with their distinctive terrain and different feeding grounds, would each pull to get to their own terrain and different feeding grounds. The snake would pull one way, 'I'll enter an anthill'. The crocodile would pull another, 'I'll enter water. The bird would pull another, 'I'll fly in the air'. The dog would pull another, 'I'll enter the village'. The jackal would pull another, 'I'll enter a charnel ground'. The monkey would pull to try and get to a forest.

Now, monks, when those six animals become worn out and tired, they would all follow the one who was the stronger, go to him for leadership and become subject to him. In just this way, monks, when a monk does not cultivate mindfulness of body and does not make much of it, the eye pulls him to pleasing forms and unpleasing forms repel him. The ear pulls him...The nose pulls him...The tongue pulls him...The body pulls him...The mind pulls him to pleasant objects and unpleasant objects repel him. This, monks, is lack of restraint.

And how, monks, is there restraint? Here, monks, a monk, having seen a form with the eye, does not incline towards forms that are dear nor turn away from those that are not dear. He practises having established mindfulness of body, with a measureless mind. He does know as it really is that deliverance of mind, that deliverance by insight whereby harmful, unskilful states that have arisen cease, without remainder. Having heard a sound with the ear... having smelt an odour with the nose... having tasted a flavour with the tongue... having touched a sensory object with the body... having become aware of an object of the mind with the mind, he does not incline towards forms that are liked and turn away from those that are not liked.

It is just as if, monks, a man were to catch six animals, each from a distinctive terrain and different feeding ground, and bind them with a strong rope. He catches a snake and binds it with a strong rope and then a crocodile, a bird, a dog, a jackal and a monkey: he binds each with a strong rope. And having done this he binds them fast to a strong stake or pillar. Now, monks, those six animals, with their distinctive terrain and different feeding grounds, would each pull to get to their own terrain and different feeding grounds. The snake would pull one way, 'I'll enter an anthill'. The crocodile would pull another... the bird... the dog... the jackal... the monkey would pull another to try and get to a forest.

Now, monks, when those six animals become worn out and tired, they would all stand, sit or lie down by that strong stake or pillar. In just this way, monks, when a monk does cultivate mindfulness of body and make much of it, the eye does not pull him to pleasing forms and unpleasing forms do not repel him. The ear does not pull him... the nose does not pull him... the tongue does not pull him... the body does not pull him... the mind does not pull him to pleasant objects and unpleasant objects do not repel him. This, monks, is restraint.

'The stake or pillar': this, monks, is a way of describing mindfulness of body. Therefore, monks, you should train in this way: 'We will cultivate and make much of mindfulness of body, we will make it our vehicle, make it a basis, ensure it is stable, increased and really set going'. Thus you should train yourselves.

(S IV 198–200)

Anuruddha

At one time Venerable Anuruddha and Venerable Sāriputta were dwelling at Vesālī in Ambapālī's Grove.[30] Then, Sāriputta emerged from seclusion in the evening and went to visit Anuruddha and, approaching him, greeted him and sat down to one side. Seated, he said to Anuruddha, 'How serene your features are![31] Your complexion is clear and bright. In what way of living does the Venerable Anuruddha usually spend his time?'

'Now, sir, I usually spend my time with my mind well grounded in the four foundations of mindfulness. What four? Here, sir, I practise contemplating body in the body... feeling in feelings... mind in mind... *dhamma* in *dhammas*, ardent, clearly comprehending, mindful, having removed longing and discontent with regard to the world. In these four foundations of mindfulness, sir, I now usually spend my time.

The monk, friend, who is an arahat, who has eliminated the corruptions, who has lived the holy life, done what has to be done, laid down the burden, reached his own aim, and has eliminated the fetters of existence, completely released by proper knowledge: such a man usually spends his time well grounded in these four foundations of mindfulness.'

It is a gain for us, sir, a great gain, sir! That in the presence of Venerable Anuruddha we have heard him roar like a bull![32]

(S V 301–2)

29. Breathing mindfulness (*ānāpānasati*)

The practice of breathing mindfulness is the most popular meditation to accompany the spread of Buddhism in recent years, a pre-eminence encouraged within the canon. In the *Ānāpānasaṃyutta* the Buddha says, 'If anyone, monks, speaking rightly could say of anything: "It is a noble abiding, a divine abiding, the Tathāgata's abiding", of concentration by mindfulness of breathing one could rightly say this' (S V 311–41). It is said to establish all four foundations of mindfulness:

> If a cart or a chariot comes from the east, west, north or south, it would flatten that mound of soil. So too, Ānanda, when a monk dwells contemplating the body in the body, feelings in feelings, mind in mind, *dhamma* in *dhammas*, he flattens harmful, unskilful states.
>
> (S V 324–5)

It is also said to provide a basis for all eight *jhānas* and for *nirodha samāpatti*.[33] The practice is particularly associated with the suppression of discursive thoughts: the canon and the commentaries of Buddhaghosa and Upatissa describe it as useful for this.[34] Upatissa compares this to the soothing of a heavenly musician's mind with sweet sounds, or like a 'person walking along the bank of a river. His mind is collected, is directed towards one object and does not wander' (PF 166). As we saw in the section on foulness (11–20), it is to this as a *samatha* practice that the Buddha immediately resorts when there is an emergency: it is, he says, 'peaceful and choice: it is a sublime and happy abiding too, that disperses and settles harmful, unskilful states whenever they arise' (S V 321–2).

The meditation is conducted by being aware or mindful of the in-breath (*ana*) and being aware or mindful of the out-breath (*pana*). In the *Satipaṭṭhāna-Sutta*, we saw the first tetrad in the sequence known as the sixteen stages of breathing mindfulness. These are associated with the establishment of the first foundation of mindfulness, that of the body. The next twelve stages cover the other three foundations: the second tetrad mindfulness of feeling, the third tetrad mindfulness of mind and the fourth mindfulness of *dhammas*. A different emphasis directs the practice in various ways: as a *samatha* practice, the meditator pays attention to the peaceful and enlivening aspect of the breath. An image (*nimitta*) is produced in the mind's eye that is a reflection of the unificatory calm that is present in the mind (Vism VIII 214–16). This develops and settles over time so that the meditator enters *jhāna*. The second and third tetrad of the sixteen stages are particularly associated with this process. When it is taken as an insight practice, attention is directed to the moving and unsatisfactory aspect of the breath. Any images that arise are ignored or regarded as objects of impermanence. This then allows the mind to be trained through the stages of insight, so that the nature of the mind and the attention that comes to bear on the breath is itself observed, and the aspect of not-self understood. This process is suggested, as we shall see, by the last tetrad of the sixteen stages of the practice delineated in the *suttas*. The benefits of the practice, conducted with either emphasis, are stressed, though a modern teacher, Saddhatissa, emphasizes, 'in the early stages of meditation, when the mind is still uncontrolled and restless, the only course open to the meditator will be to practise *samatha*' (Saddhatissa 1971: 81).

Buddhaghosa recommends that the meditator spend some time with the teacher learning each part of this practice: the meditator should learn the subject, ask questions about it, establish it in himself, become absorbed it and see its characteristics. These instructions continue to apply in the way the practice is usually taught now: each stage is said to take some time and attention (Vism VIII 187–8).[35]

Four stages

Four techniques are associated with the practice, which, although non-canonical, are said to be ancient by Upatissa; he delineates them in sequence (PF 159–60). The first, the counting (*gaṇanā*), 'suppresses uncertainty. It causes the abandoning of uncertainty'. The second, the pursuing or following (*anubandhanā*), involves following the flow of the breath as it moves in and out of the body continuously; this 'removes gross discursive thinking and causes unbroken mindfulness of respiration'. The third, the contacting or the touching (*phusanā*) involves allowing attention to rest at the nose-tip or the point of the mouth where the air passes in and out of the body; it 'removes distraction and makes for steady perception. One attains to distinction through bliss'. The fourth is the establishing or settling (*ṭhāpaṇa*), which prepares the mind for the attainment of *jhāna*. These stages are maintained in forms of the practice found today. Buddhaghosa adds another four: observing, turning away, purification and looking back (Vism VIII 189).

Buddhaghosa explores each stage with a detailed consideration that bears the stamp of considerable experience, whether his own or derived from others' accounts. At each stage, it provides practical help and similes. Counting, for instance, involves counting each breath as it occurs: under five and the thoughts become too cramped, like, Buddhaghosa says, a confined herd of cattle, while beyond ten the mind wanders. Buddhaghosa says that counting may be rapid or slow. If the meditator counts slowly, he is like a measurer of grain, carefully emptying the measure and then counting. If he counts quickly, he is like a cowherd letting his herd out of a pen: he needs to count them rapidly, as they leave so quickly. There are some slight differences in approach between the two. For the start of practice, for instance, Upatissa says that one begins with an outgoing breath and ends with an ingoing breath (PF 160); Buddhaghosa says that one chooses whichever appears most plainly first (Vism VIII 191).[36] The canonical formula mentions the ingoing breath first. Buddhaghosa's explanation also includes the famous image of a gong. The object of this practice is, he says, like listening to the ebbing reverberation of the sound of a gong when it has been struck: just as you need to be increasingly attentive to listen to the subtle sounds when the gross ones have gone, so the meditator needs to be aware of the breath becoming more subtle and fine as the practice develops (Vism VIII 207–10). The nature of the attention is compared to someone using an ever-finer needle for embroidery work (Vism VIII 212).

In order to demonstrate the care with which even one stage of the sixteen is treated in modern and traditional practice, some instructions are given here from one of the leading teachers of breathing mindfulness in the twentieth century, Buddhadāsa. His book, *Mindfulness of Breathing*, explores each stage of the practice as described in the *sutta* from an experiential point of view, in what one might call a meditator's exegesis of the text. This extract communicates something of the leisured exploration that, he says, is needed to practise the first stage with the kind of attention that it requires:

> The first lesson is the contemplation of the long breath. Having learned how to make the breath long and keep it long we are able to breathe long whenever we need to. In this first lesson, we will study exclusively the nature of the long breath. When a breath is long, how pleasant is it? Is it natural and ordinary? What kinds of calmness and happiness arise? In what ways is it different from a short breath? We begin by studying just the long breath to find out its properties, qualities, influence, and flavor. We should sit and investigate only the long breath. This is lesson one: understanding all matters connected with long breathing.
>
> Finally, we observe how the body works in relation to the long breath. How does the body move when there is a long inhalation? In what places does the body expand? Where does it contract? When there is the deepest possible long breath, does the chest expand or contract? Does the abdomen expand or contract? These are things to examine. In studying the breath carefully . . . we find that in taking a very long inhalation, the abdomen will contract and the chest will expand. We find the reverse of what common sense teaches. Then, we investigate the very long breath, the longest possible breath, to see what changes occur. We do not take anything for granted but instead learn these basic facts for ourselves.
>
> In order to know the nature of the long breath, we study all the secrets and attributes of the long breath. We are able to contemplate its long duration, learning to protect and maintain it . . . we learn the happiness

> and comfort the long breath brings. We learn in a deeper way, through personal experience rather than through thinking, that the breath is intimately associated with the body.
>
> (Buddhadāsa 1997: 54–5)[37]

It is worth noting that Buddhadāsa constantly emphasizes care in pursuing a single meditation sitting from beginning to end. All the practices that explore the subsequent fifteen stages of breathing mindfulness require that each sitting begins with this long breath and he recommends returning to it repeatedly to bring about confidence and a sense of achievement (ibid.: 79).

The techniques of breathing mindfulness in practice are precise, requiring a fine tuning and innate balance that cannot be considered here: a teacher is usually needed for anyone who would like to try it. Another renowned modern teacher, Ajahn Lee, writes of breathing mindfulness:

> Experience has shown me that the most productive, shortest, most pleasant and easiest path – the path least likely to lead you astray – is to keep the breath in mind, the path the Buddha himself used with such good results.
>
> (Dhammadharo 1956–60: 1)

Upatissa concludes,

> What are its benefits? If a man practises mindfulness of respiration he attains to the peaceful, the exquisite, the lovely and the blissful life. He causes blissful evil and demeritorious states to disappear and to perish as soon as they arise. He is not negligent as regards his body or his organ of sight. His body and mind do not waver and tremble.
>
> (PF 155–66)

The discourse on breathing mindfulness

It is often illuminating to consider the ways a particular teaching is introduced, and the extent to which a particular narrative context or genre of text is considered to be the best way of addressing a single theme or meditative practice. Whoever constructed the *Satipaṭṭhāna-Sutta*, for instance, eschewed any setting or backcloth, as if deliberately presenting us only with the essentials required to arouse and sustain the quality described. The introduction to the *Ānāpānasati-sutta*, however, describes the breadth and attentiveness of its audience in memorable detail. It opens on a particularly atmospheric night in the Buddhist calendar, the full moon of the Pavāraṇā ceremony, towards the end of the rains retreat. This is the period when the community of monks does not travel but stays in one place, often developing individual practice. All around monks are teaching groups of younger monks thus, of course, ensuring the health and longevity of the tradition; the Buddha, noting with pleasure the progress and standard of those present, announces that he will stay until the next full moon, of Kamudī; at that time he gives his account of the practice of breathing mindfulness.[38]

The Buddha opens his talk with one of the most extensive eulogies of the merits of his order, as it is represented in a given assembly, to be found in the canon. The opening sections are, in effect, an exercise in the recollection of the *bhikkhusaṅgha* (23), working at its best and most unified, after the retreat of the rains. The Buddha notes that the community is worthy of homage, in the formula usually associated with the recollection; that any gift given to such a community becomes much greater, that it is hard to find an equal and that it is worth travelling to find. Attainments within that group are then described: some have become arahats, some have destroyed the five lower fetters (non-returners), some the first three (once-returners), and some are stream-enterers.[39] Others dwell in each of the thirty-seven constituents of enlightenment: the four foundations of mindfulness, the four right efforts, the four bases of spiritual power, the five faculties, the five powers, the seven enlightenment factors and the noble eightfold path. Some practise each of the divine abidings (31–4), some meditation on the foul (11–20), some impermanence – and some breathing mindfulness.

The warmth and appreciative tone of his greeting to his followers is striking. The practice of breathing mindfulness itself seems to be being introduced as the 'heartwood' of the teaching, just as the receptive and alert audience are so described by the Buddha.[40] The Buddha describes the full sixteen stages of breathing mindfulness. The *Satipaṭṭhāna-Sutta* had, by introducing the first four stages alone, emphasized the aspect of mindfulness of body. The four tetrads that comprise the sixteen stages are in this *sutta* allocated to the four foundations of mindfulness: (1–4) mindfulness of body, (5–8) mindfulness of feeling, (9–12) mindfulness of mind, (13–16) mindfulness of *dhammas*.

The first tetrad

The first tetrad is described in the same terms employed in the *Satipaṭṭhāna-Sutta*, though the image of the wood turner is not used. It is also associated in this *sutta* with mindfulness of body. The meditator knows firstly when he breathes in and out with a long breath and then secondly when he breathes in and out with a short breath. The third stage is the breathing in and out that experiences the whole of the breath body and the fourth the breathing in and out that tranquillizes the bodily formation. In modern practice the techniques are highly varied with each stage, according to the method that is taught, and the acquisition of slightly different skills concerning the breath vary.

The second tetrad

The fifth stage associates the in- and out-breath with joy, the third *jhāna* factor, that is present in the first and second *jhāna*. The sixth associates the in- and out-breath with happiness (*sukha*), the fourth *jhāna* factor that is present in the first three *jhānas*. Buddhadāsa writes of this that '*Pīti* has varying levels, but all are characterized as stimulating, as causing the *citta* to tremble and shake. *Sukha* is the opposite; it calms and soothes the mind' (ibid.: 69–70, 71). For the fifth stage he says, 'there is a very pleasant feeling of well-being when this step is practiced. This work is fun to do; it is a most enjoyable lesson'. The next stage is needed to calm this: 'Taste the tranquil flavor of *sukha* with every inhalation and exhalation'. The seventh stage associates the in- and out-breath with the experience of the mental formations (*cittasaṅkhārā*), which Buddhadāsa links to the joy and happiness which have just occurred, and which need to be viewed themselves.[41] The eighth stage involves the tranquillization of these. This tetrad is important, Buddhadāsa says, because it teaches mastery of feeling and the ability to recognize how and when it occurs in any situation (see ibid.: 77).

The third tetrad

The third tetrad is related by the *sutta* to mindfulness of mind: the awareness of the nature of the mind that is perceiving and responding to the object. In these stages the meditator successively experiences, gladdens, concentrates and liberates the mind with each in an out breath. This tetrad is described in modern and ancient meditation manuals as involving awareness of the nature and quality of consciousness at each stage. The skill in attention in this tetrad, it is said, is gradually to allow the experience of the mind to deepen into gladness, to concentrate the mind that perceives that and then to transform the attitude towards the object itself.[42] Upatissa, for instance, writes of the twelfth stage, liberating the mind:

> If his mind is slow and slack he frees it from rigidity; if it is too active, he frees it from restlessness. Thus he trains himself. If the mind is elated, he frees it from lust. Thus he trains himself. If it is depressed he frees it from hatred. Thus he trains himself. If the mind is sullied he frees it from lesser defilements. Thus he trains himself. And again, if his mind is not inclined towards the object and is not pleased with it, he causes his mind to be inclined towards it.
>
> (PF 162)

The fourth tetrad

The fourth tetrad involves the contemplation of impermanence, dispassion, cessation and letting go, or relinquishment, in association with each in- and out-breath. Buddhaghosa notes that the last has two aspects: it means both the giving up of defilements, and the entering into of *nibbāna*, the state where there are no defilements. He says that the last tetrad is primarily concerned with insight, while the first three link both *samatha* and *vipassanā* (Vism VIII 236–7). Buddhadāsa suggests that each of the sixteen may be pursued with different emphasis. With an urgency that reflects the Buddha's own enjoinders to his followers, he writes on the last stage, of relinquishment,

> Let us understand clearly and perfectly that whenever we are foolish, we pick up weights and pile them up as burdens of life. Once we know what they are doing to us, we throw them off. Now we no longer have any burdens.... Whoever wants to be free, to be at ease, to be above the world, ought to try their best to practice according to this truth as much as possible – starting right now.
>
> (Buddhadāsa 1988: 98)

A sense of interplay between calm and insight continues as the text considers the factors of enlightenment. The 'great fruit' of breathing mindfulness is that it arouses these, which of themselves correct any imbalances or distortions in perception in the mind. The list is an application of the seven to the list of four, to make twenty-eight. The links from mindfulness to investigation of *dhamma*, from that to strength and from that to joy, are made by investigating each state thoroughly, with wisdom (*paññāya*). The links from joy to tranquillity, from that to concentration and from that to equanimity are described as a process that occurs naturally through the consequent joyfulness of mind and body, happiness and concentration. So the first three links are described through the arising of wisdom, the last three through calm (*samatha*). This is significant for our understanding of the practice: through this expansion of the four foundations by each of the enlightenment factors, the text provides us with such a fusion and interchange of approaches it would be impossible to say whether it was primarily *samatha* or *vipassanā* in its orientation.

The practice of breathing mindfulness can seem immensely complex and to involve a number of different possible variations at each stage, depending on the emphasis towards insight or calm. When considering the many different accounts in the way it is described and taught now it is useful to come back to the image of the wood turner, employed by the Buddha in the *Satipaṭṭhāna-Sutta* to describe the awareness of the long and the short breath. If one were to write a detailed account of the whole process of wood turning and the states associated with the job – the smoothing of an object, the shaping of it, the enjoyment and tranquillity that is aroused by the work and the final relinquishment of the object at the end when it is recognized as complete – one would probably come up with a list not unlike the sixteen stages of breathing mindfulness. At each stage it is possible to look more closely at technique: to examine the relationship with the object and the extent to which the wood governs and shapes the mind and body of the wood turner, who in turn influences and controls the object so that it is made good. The techniques described here, and, more fully, in the *Paṭisambhidāmagga* examination of imbalances within each breath, reinforce this sense of finely tuned and responsive craftsmanship (see Patis I 163–7). At some point, however, whatever the technique, the whole needs to be relinquished, and seen as not-self. The Buddha seems to teach this practice as a craft and while the details of method might vary, we can gain a sense of this by reading a text such as this.

Ānāpānasati sutta

Thus have I heard. At one time the Exalted One was living in Sāvatthī in the Eastern Park, in the palace belonging to Migara's mother, along with many distinguished elder disciples: the Venerables Sāriputta, Moggallāna, Mahākassapa, Mahākaccāna, Mahākoṭṭhita, Mahākappina, Mahācunda, Anuruddha, Revata, Ānanda and other distinguished elder disciples.

Now on that occasion elder monks were teaching and giving instruction to younger monks. Some elder monks were teaching and training ten monks, some were teaching and training twenty monks, some were teaching and training thirty monks, some were teaching and training forty monks. And the new monks who had been taught and trained by the elder monks became aware of the distinctive excellence of each stage in its sequence.

At that time, the *uposatha* day of the fifteenth, on the full moon night of the Pavāraṇa festival, the Exalted One was sitting in the open air, surrounded by the community of monks. Then, after surveying the silent community of monks, he addressed them in this way: 'I am pleased with this progress, monks. My heart is pleased with this progress. So arouse even more energy to attain the unattained, to realize the unrealized. I shall wait here at Sāvatthī for the full moon at the time of the blossoming of the white lotus (Komudī) in the fourth month.'

The monks from the countryside heard the report that the Exalted One would wait there at Sāvatthī for the full moon of the white lotus, in the fourth month. And so they streamed into Sāvatthī to see the Exalted One. And those who were the elder monks taught and trained the new monks still more. Some elder monks taught and trained ten monks, some taught and trained twenty monks, some taught and trained thirty monks, and some taught and trained forty monks. And the new monks who had been taught and trained by the elder monks also became aware of the distinctive excellence of each stage in its sequence.

Now, at that time the Exalted One was sitting in the open air surrounded by the community of monks on the night of the full moon of the white lotus, the *uposatha* of the fourth and final month of the rains. Then, after surveying the silent community of monks, he addressed them in this way:

'Monks, this assembly is not chaff. This assembly is free from any chatter. This assembly is settled, the most excellent heartwood. Such is this community of monks, monks, such is this assembly, an assembly that is worthy of gifts, worthy of hospitality, worthy of reverence, an incomparable field of merit for the world: such is this community of monks, monks, such is this assembly. It is such an assembly that even a small gift becomes great and a great gift greater: such is this community of monks, monks, such is this assembly. It is such an assembly that is difficult to see in this world: such is this community of monks, such is this assembly. For just a glimpse of such an assembly, monks, it would be worth travelling many leagues with a bag of provisions on one's shoulder: such is this community of monks, such is this assembly.

'There are in this community of monks those who are arahats, with the corruptions destroyed, who have lived the holy life, who have done what has to be done, laid down the burden, attained their own goal, destroyed the fetters of existence, and who are freed by right knowledge: there are such monks in this community of monks. There are in this community of monks those who, with the five fetters connected with this side of existence destroyed, will be born spontaneously in the Pure Abodes and from there attain *nibbāna*, without returning from that world; those who have destroyed three fetters, who, with the reduction of greed, hatred and delusion are one-returners, who will return once to this world to make an end of suffering; those who have destroyed three fetters, stream-enterers, not bound for an unhappy rebirth and destined for enlightenment; those who live dedicated to the cultivation of the four foundations of mindfulness, the four right efforts, the four bases of success, the five faculties, the five powers, the seven factors of enlightenment, the Noble Eightfold Path, loving-kindness, compassion, sympathetic joy, equanimity, meditation on foulness, the perception of impermanence: there are such monks in this community of monks.

'There are, monks, in this community of monks those who live dedicated to the cultivation of mindfulness of breathing. When mindfulness of breathing is cultivated and made much of, it is of great fruit and great reward. When mindfulness of breathing is cultivated and made much of it fulfils the four foundations of mindfulness; when the four foundations of mindfulness are cultivated and made much of they fulfil the seven factors of enlightenment.

'When the seven factors of enlightenment are cultivated and made much of they fulfil knowledge and deliverance.

'And how, monks, is breathing mindfulness, cultivated? How is it made much of? How is it of great fruit and great reward? Here, monks, a monk goes to a forest, or the roots of a tree or an empty place and sits, folding his legs in a cross-legged position, making his body straight and sets up mindfulness in front of him.

'Mindful, he breathes in; mindful, he breathes out. As he breathes in a long breath, he knows, "I am breathing in a long breath", or, as he breathes out a long breath, he knows, "I am breathing out a long breath". As he breathes in a short breath, he knows, "I am breathing in a short breath", or, as he breathes out a short breath, he knows, "I am breathing out a short breath". He trains thus: "Experiencing the whole body I shall breathe in", he trains thus, "Experiencing the whole body I shall breathe out". He trains thus: "Tranquillizing the bodily formation I shall breathe in", he trains thus, "Tranquillizing the bodily formation I shall breathe out".

'He trains thus: "Experiencing joy I shall breathe in"; he trains thus: "Experiencing joy I shall breathe out". He trains thus: "Experiencing happiness I shall breathe in"; he trains thus: "Experiencing happiness I shall breathe out". He trains thus: "Experiencing the mind formation I shall breathe in"; He trains thus: "Experiencing the mind formation I shall breathe out". He trains thus: "Tranquillizing the mind formation I shall breathe in"; he trains thus: "Tranquillizing the mind formation I shall breathe out".

'He trains thus: "Experiencing the mind I shall breathe in"; he trains thus: "Experiencing the mind I shall breathe out". He trains thus: "Gladdening the mind I shall breathe in"; he trains thus: "Gladdening the mind I shall breathe out". He trains thus: "Concentrating the mind I shall breathe in"; he trains thus: "Concentrating the mind I shall breathe out". He trains thus: "Liberating the mind I shall breathe in"; he trains thus: "Liberating the mind I shall breathe out".

'He trains thus, "Contemplating impermananence I shall breathe in"; he trains thus: "Contemplating impermanence I shall breathe out". He trains thus: "Contemplating dispassion I shall breathe in"; he trains thus: "Contemplating dispassion I shall breathe out". He trains thus: "Contemplating cessation I shall breathe in"; he trains thus: "Contemplating cessation I shall breathe out". He trains thus: "Contemplating letting go I shall breathe in"; He trains thus: "Contemplating letting go I shall breathe out". This is how, monks, mindfulness of breathing is cultivated and made much of, so that it is of great fruit and great reward.

'And how is breathing mindfulness cultivated? How is it made much of, so that it fulfils the four foundations of mindfulness? At whatever time, monks, a monk breathes in a long breath... he trains thus, "Tranquillizing the bodily formation I shall breathe out". At that time, monks, a monk practises contemplating the body in the body, ardent, clearly comprehending and mindful, putting away longing and discontent in the world. I say that this is a particular body amongst bodies: that is the in- and the out-breath.[43] Therefore, monks, at the time when a monk practises contemplating the body in the body, ardent, clearly comprehending and mindful, he puts away longing and discontent in the world.

'At whatever time, monks, a monk trains thus: "Experiencing joy I shall breathe in." ... he trains thus: "Tranquillizing the mind formation I shall breathe out". At this time, monks, a monk practises contemplating feeling amidst feelings, ardent, clearly comprehending and mindful, putting away longing and discontent in the world. I say that this is a particular feeling amongst feelings: that is proper attention to the in- and the out-breath.[44] Therefore, monks, at the time when a monk practises contemplating feeling amongst feelings, ardent, clearly comprehending and mindful, he puts away longing and discontent in the world.

'At whatever time, monks, a monk trains thus: "Experiencing the mind I shall breathe in"... "Liberating the mind I shall breathe out". At that time, monks, a monk practises contemplating the mind in the mind, ardent, clearly comprehending and mindful, putting away longing and discontent in the world. I do not say, monks, that the cultivation of mind that is mindfulness of the in- and out-breath is for one of confused mindfulness or the one who lacks clear comprehension. Therefore, monks, at the time when a monk practises contemplating the mind in the mind, ardent, clearly comprehending and mindful, he puts away longing and discontent with regard to the world.

'At whatever time, monks, a monk trains thus: "Contemplating impermanence I shall breathe in".... At that time, monks, a monk practises contemplating *dhamma* amongst *dhammas*, ardent, clearly comprehending and mindful, putting away longing and discontent in the world. He, having seen, with wisdom, the abandonment of longing and discontent, is one who looks on with perfect equanimity. Therefore, monks, at the time when a monk practises contemplating *dhamma* amongst *dhammas*, ardent, clearly comprehending and mindful, he puts away longing and discontent with regard to the world. Cultivated and made much of in this way, monks, breathing mindfulness brings to fulfilment the four foundations of mindfulness.

'And how, monks, do the four foundations of mindfulness, which have been cultivated and made much of, bring to fulfilment the seven factors of enlightenment?

'At whatever time, monks, that a monk practises contemplating the body in the body, ardent, clearly comprehending and mindful, putting away longing and discontent in the world, then the mindfulness established in him at that time is not confused. At whatever time, monks, that the mindfulness established in a monk is not confused, at that time the enlightenment factor that is mindfulness is stirred in him, at that time he cultivates the enlightenment factor that is mindfulness, the enlightenment factor that is mindfulness comes to fulfilment.

'This monk, mindful in such a way, looks into, takes up and comes to examine that state with wisdom. At whatever time, monks, that a monk who is mindful in this way looks into, takes up and comes to examine that state with wisdom, at that time the enlightenment factor that is investigation of *dhamma* is stirred in him, at that time he cultivates the enlightenment factor that is investigation of *dhamma*, the enlightenment factor that is investigation of *dhamma* comes to fulfilment.

'When he looks into, takes up and comes to examine that state with wisdom, at that time unflinching strength is stirred in him. At whatever time, monks, that unflinching strength is stirred in a monk who looks into, takes up and comes to examine that state with wisdom, at that time the enlightenment factor that is strength is stirred in him, at that time he cultivates the enlightenment factor that is strength, the enlightenment factor that is strength comes to fulfilment.

'When strength is stirred, the joy that is free from sense desire arises. At whatever time, monks, that the joy that is free from sense desire is stirred in a monk who looks into, takes up and comes to examine that state with wisdom, at that time the enlightenment factor that is joy is stirred in him, at that time he cultivates the enlightenment factor that is joy, the enlightenment factor that is joy comes to fulfilment.

'In the one who has a joyful mind both the body becomes tranquil and the mind becomes tranquil. At whatever time, monks, that both the body and the mind becomes tranquil in the one who has a joyful mind, at that time the enlightenment factor that is tranquillity is stirred in him, at that time he cultivates the enlightenment factor that is tranquillity, the enlightenment factor that is tranquillity comes to fulfilment.

'The mind of the one whose body is tranquil and happy comes to concentration. At whatever time that the mind of one whose body is tranquil and happy comes to concentration, at that time the enlightenment factor that is concentration is stirred in him, at that time he cultivates the enlightenment factor that is concentration, at that time the enlightenment factor that is concentration comes to fulfilment.

'The one who has concentrated his mind in this way looks on that concentrated mind with equanimity. At whatever time, monks, that the one with concentrated mind looks upon that concentrated mind with equanimity, the enlightenment factor that is equanimity is stirred in him, at that time he cultivates the enlightenment factor that is equanimity, at that time the enlightenment factor that is equanimity in him comes to fulfilment.

'[The same for:] At whatever time that a monk practises contemplating feeling amongst feelings... mind in mind... *dhamma* amongst *dhammas* ardent, clearly comprehending and mindful, putting away longing and discontent in the world, then the mindfulness established in him at that time is not confused... at that time the enlightenment factor that is equanimity in him comes to fulfilment. When the four foundations of mindfulness are cultivated in this way and made much of, monks, in this way the seven factors of enlightenment are fulfilled.

'And how, monks, when the seven factors of enlightenment are cultivated and how, when they are made much of, do they fulfil knowledge and deliverance? Here, monks, a monk cultivates the mindfulness dependent on seclusion, dependent on dispassion, dependent on cessation, that leads to letting go.[45] Here, monks, a monk cultivates the investigation of *dhamma*... the strength... the joy... the tranquillity... the concentration... the equanimity dependent on seclusion, dependent on dispassion, dependent on cessation, that leads to letting go. When the seven factors of enlightenment are cultivated in this way, monks, when they are made much of, they fulfil knowledge and deliverance.'

Thus spoke the Exalted One. Delighted, these monks rejoiced in what the Exalted One had said.

(M III 78–88)

Mahākappina

The arahat Mahākappina is pointed out by the Buddha for his ability to teach, his supernormal powers and his radiance (see S II 284).[46] He is particularly associated with the practice of breathing mindfulness and for the steadiness of his bearing. The Buddha once asked the monks whether they ever see any shaking or trembling in Mahākappina: they aver that they do not, and that his posture is always steady, both in the presence of the *saṅgha* and on his own (see S V 315–6). The Buddha attributes this to the concentration of mind achieved by mindfulness of breathing.

In one of ten verses attributed to this elder Mahākappina explains his serenity:

> The one who has perfected, fulfilled, and practised in due order mindfulness of breathing, as taught by the Buddha, illuminates this world, just as the moon is released from a cloud.
>
> (Th 548; quoted in Patis III 171; also Dhp 382)

30. Recollection of peace (*upasamānussati*)

A sense of the value of peace informs the canon: it is often associated with *nibbāna*, enlightenment, the life of a monk and as a state that may be present whenever there is a sense of the path, even if it has not been attained. It is this quality which impresses Ajātasattu so deeply when he approaches the assembly of the *saṅgha*, 'calm like a lake', in the *Sāmaññaphala-Sutta*, and which he wishes that his son might find, although as a parricide he is denied it himself (D I 50). In the *Ariyapariyesanā-Sutta* the Buddha says that one of the reasons he left his first teachers was because their respective teachings on nothingness and the sphere of neither perception nor non-perception did not lead to peace (see M I 164). The eightfold path is said to lead to peace (M II 82–3). The *Paṭisambhidāmagga* says that the enlightenment factor of tranquillity (*passadhi*) is the same as peace (Patis 1 26). Simply keeping the five precepts of the laity are, according to this text, to follow the way that leads to peace (see Patis I 265). It is a word sometimes used to describe meditation: so the divine abidings (31–4) are said to lead to the internal peace (M I 284 and this anthology 168–9). The second *jhāna*, where the various kinds of thinking – which also give rise to speech – are abandoned, is also traditionally described as possessing internal peace (*vūpasamaṃ ajjhattaṃ*).

We do not find in the canon, however, its description as a practice in the manner of the first six recollections: a sense of peace is everywhere, but advice for its cultivation elusive. Although the canon gives us no instructions, as Vajirañāṇa points out *upasamānussati* is frequently implied as a practice (see BMTP 259–62). It is included in the list of subjects, which if practised by a monk 'even for a finger snap' render him worthy of his way of life (A I 41). In a text included earlier in this section of the anthology, it is said to be one of the 'single things' that lead to enlightenment (see A I 28 and this anthology 110). Indeed *nibbāna*, often described as and even synonymous with the word for peace, is as important a presence, if such a word is possible for the unconditioned, in the Buddhist texts as the more often discussed truth of dis-ease or suffering. The noble truth of suffering and its end is only really penetrated and understood at stream-entry. Most of us feel an immediate recognition of the truth of *dukkha*, bodily and physical, and this noble truth is one of the most discussed and debated elements in modern discussion about Buddhist philosophy. It carries implications that range from the most obvious forms of suffering, as seen in the troubles of birth, old age, sickness and death, to the mild dis-ease or tension that is the characteristic of all experience, whether pleasant or unpleasant. We can sometimes overlook, however, the omnipresent sense of *nibbāna* as a truth that underlies any perception of the world as *dukkha*. This separation was clearly not intended: it is always worth stressing that the four noble truths tend to be taught together.[47] We are constantly invited within the canon to consider the possibility of the end of suffering, *nibbāna*, in association with the other three truths: any awareness of suffering implies some intimation of its absence, just as a path of freedom is dependent upon a sense of being lost or enslaved.[48] As Walpola Rahula notes,

> Buddhism is quite opposed to the melancholic, sorrowful, penitent and gloomy attitude of mind which is considered a hindrance to the realization of Truth. On the other hand, it is interesting to remember here that joy (*pīti*) is one of the seven *bojjhaṅgas* or "Factors of Enlightenment", the essential qualities to be cultivated for the realization of *Nirvāṇā*.
>
> (Rahula 1967: 28)

Nibbāna, at the end of *dukkha*, is the greatest form of peace: the formless realm is more peaceful than the form realm, one text says, but the end of suffering is the most peaceful of all (It 61–2 and this anthology 181–2). Buddhaghosa recommends that this practice should be conducted by bringing to mind its qualities according to one's ability (see Vism VIII 250).

Upatissa says little about the practice, applying it immediately to bodily experience: peace is the stilling of the activities of body and mind found by the recollection of seclusion of body and mind (PF 177–9). The one who practises its recollection sleeps and wakes happily, is calm, has tranquil faculties and can fulfil his aspirations: 'He is pleasant of mien, modest of demeanour and is esteemed by others. He fares well and approaches the ambrosial' (PF 178). It leads, according to this text, to access concentration – a state not recognized in the *suttas* – and is practised by bringing the peace of one's own meditative attainments to mind, starting with the first *jhāna*, then moving through all the meditations on to *nibbāna* (PF 179). Buddhaghosa also states that it does not lead to *jhāna*, and advises that this practice can only really come to success in a stream-enterer: for the one who has not known true peace cannot fully recollect it. He says, however, that it nevertheless can be brought to mind by an ordinary person who values peace, as the mind gains confidence from peace even by hearing of it (see Vism VIII 249). For those that have not attained such states, the recollection of any peaceful state of mind is helpful.

Taking an overview of the range of practices and stages of the path with which it is associated, it becomes clear that while its recollection as a meditation subject is not described in detail in the canon, peace is considered both as a product of Buddhist practice, and susceptible of cultivation at any stage, as both the hallmark of the path and its goal.

The unconditioned

This sutta is taken from the *Udāna*, a collection where an 'inspired utterance' is given to accompany the teaching. It is chosen for its simple and concise description of the attributes, or rather the lack of attributes, which characterize *nibbāna*. It has that quality peculiar to Indian philosophical texts of evocation through juxtaposed negatives, where pairings usually considered mutually exclusive or antithetical, such as this world and the next world and the sun and the moon, are both denied.[49] The components that are discussed are also those which would make the basic building blocks of existence as understood by the ancient Indian world: the elements, the spheres of rebirth, the sun and the moon, coming and going.[50] Literary criticism founders in the presence of short *suttas* such as these. It employs the most succinct kind of poetic writing that manages to challenge and disturb a level of logical understanding in the mind while at the same time communicating a sense of the very peace and freedom it describes.

> Nibbāna
> Thus have I heard. At one time, the Exalted One was staying in the Jeta Grove at Anāthapiṇḍika's monastery near Sāvatthī. At that time the Exalted One was teaching, stirring, inspiring, and electrifying the monks with a *dhamma* talk connected with *nibbāna*, and those monks, receptive, attentive and settling their minds wholeheartedly on the subject, listened to the *dhamma*.
>
> Then, understanding its meaning, the Exalted One uttered at that time this inspired utterance:
>
> 'There is, monks, that sphere where there is no earth, no water, no fire, no air; no sphere consisting of the infinity of space, no sphere consisting of the infinity of consciousness, no sphere consisting of nothingness, no sphere consisting of neither perception nor non-perception; neither this world nor another world nor both; neither sun nor moon.

Here, monks, I say that there is no coming, no going, no remaining, no deceasing, no arising. Not fixed, not moving, without an object: just this, indeed, is the end of suffering.'

(Ud 80)

Proof of the unconditioned

This talk was, according to the commentary, given to brahmins of the Lokāyata school who held that *nibbāna* was mere talk.[51] That which is called *nibbāna* could not, according to them, exist 'in the highest sense, on account of its own nature failing to be discovered' (Masefield 1994b: 2 1018). The commentary gives what it terms logical reasons for the existence of *nibbāna*: it argues, for instance, that given the inability of the *jhāna* to eradicate defilements completely, because of the conditioned nature of the *dhammas* involved, or because of having conventional truth as its object, there has to be an object that is unconditioned (see ibid.: 1021).

Nibbāna

Thus have I heard. At one time the Exalted One was staying in the Jeta Grove at Anāthapiṇḍika's monastery near Sāvatthī. At that time the Exalted One was teaching, stirring, inspiring, and electrifying the monks with a *dhamma* talk connected with *nibbāna*, and those monks, receptive, attentive and settling the mind wholeheartedly, listened to the *dhamma*.

Then, understanding the meaning, the Exalted One uttered at that time this inspired utterance:

'There exists, monks, a not born, a not coming into being, a not made, an unconditioned. If monks, there were no 'not born', no 'not coming into being', no 'not made' and no 'unconditioned', no escape would be discerned from what is born, coming into being, made or conditioned. But since there is a 'not born', a 'not coming into being', a 'not made', an 'unconditioned', therefore an escape is known from what is born, what is coming into being, what is made and what is conditioned.'

(Ud 80–1)

Peace

This extract from a poem in the *Sutta Nipāta* describes the tranquil condition (*santipadaṃ*), or *nibbāna*, and the life of the monk who has attained it. In this case the peace suggested is not associated with any particular meditational state, but with a whole way of life and in an attitude towards oneself and others. It is the enlightened monk who is described as one who does not despise others, does not become involved in proliferations, and who does not think himself better, inferior or equal, but clearly it could as well be applied in daily life for anyone.

This text is not mentioned by the commentaries but its simple evocation of ease of mind render it useful for anyone at any stage of meditative practice. Buddhaghosa's commentary implies that it does not have to be practised by someone who has attained a particularly advanced stage of meditation: any moment of peace that has been experienced can be brought to mind.

Tuvaṭakasutta
915. I ask that kinsman of the sun, the great seer,
about solitude and the tranquil state.
In what way does a monk, when he has seen, become cooled,
not grasping at anything in the world?
916. 'He stops the entire root of proliferation', said the Exalted One,
'that is, the thought, "I am".
Constantly mindful, he should train himself,
free from whatever cravings there are inside.
917. Whatever teaching he might understand,
within himself and in the outside world,
He should not be obstinate about:
this is not called "cooling" by the good.
918. He should not for that reason think that he is better, or worse, or even equal.
When he has contact with various forms,
he should not keep on conjuring images in his mind about himself.[52]
919. A monk should look for peace only in himself and not in another.
For one who is at peace within himself nothing is taken up:
How then can anything be laid down?
920. Just as in the middle of the ocean no wave arises:
the waters remain still,
so he remains still and unperturbed.
A monk should not make a swell anywhere.'

(Sn 915–20)

10

31–34. THE FOUR DIVINE ABIDINGS (*BRAHMAVIHĀRĀ*)

The divine abidings (*brahmavihārās*) are amongst the most popular of *samatha* practises. They are the meditations on loving-kindness (*mettā*), compassion (*karuṇā*), sympathetic joy (*muditā*) and equanimity (*upekkhā*). In the worldly sense (*lokiya*), each can be present in any activity.[1] The first, *mettā*, is considered throughout Buddhist countries as providing a basis for all dealings with other beings. Bodily, verbal and mental acts of loving-kindness are to be cultivated towards other practitioners, so that they live 'in harmony, with mutual appreciation, without arguing, blending like milk and water, viewing each other with kindly eyes' (M I 207). Upatissa says that 'the four immeasurables are of one nature though their signs are different. Thus owing to the suppression of tribulation, owing to the object which comprises beings, owing to the wish to benefit, they fulfil one characteristic' (PF 194). Although some progression is implied, they enact four aspects or modes of the purification of the emotions: different ways that one being may respond and react to another, according to what is appropriate. In daily life compassion is the appropriate response to the presence of suffering, sympathetic joy to another's happiness. Equanimity may arise at any time, not as indifference or boredom, but as feeling undifferentiated by pleasantness or unpleasantness. As a meditation, however, they all involve a sitting practice in seclusion, usually taking as an object living beings in all directions. The object of all beings becomes simple, because it is infinite. So one moves from a limited object, such as one person, to many and then yet more: it is then that the object becomes immeasurable (*appamāṇa*), pertaining to the form-sphere. This makes it a basis for *jhāna* where each of the four can become a deliverance of the mind (*cetovimutti*).

Loving-kindness (mettā)

The first, *mettā*, is usually translated as loving-kindness.[2] If a monk indulges a thought of *mettā* even for a finger snap, his meditation is not 'empty of result' (A I 10). One canonical text, the *Haliddavasana-Sutta*, also recommends that it be practised alongside and as a support for each of the seven enlightenment factors (S V 119–21). *Mettābhāvanā* is endowed with immense respect throughout

Buddhist countries, and, inasmuch as it is possible to know details of private practice, is said to be one of the most commonly pursued meditations in Sri Lanka.[3] The *Mettā-Sutta*, one of the most frequently chanted of all Buddhist texts in Theravāda countries, is regarded as possessing a particular potency as a means of bringing good fortune, dispelling bad dreams and protecting against ghosts and evil spirits. Like one other immeasurable, equanimity (*upekkhā*), it is included as one of the *pāramīs* in later traditions, the ten perfections pursued by the Bodhisatta over a period of lifetimes. In this worldly sense, it is described as having an almost magical efficacy in counteracting the hostility present in other beings. Many *Jātaka* stories describe the Buddha in earlier rebirths as an animal whose *mettā* is so unwavering that it affects the murderous intent of others: in the *Nandiya Jātaka* (no. 385), his unflinching practice of loving-kindness as a deer renders a hunter king incapable of releasing the fatal arrow (see J III 273). Stories are told throughout the East of famous abbots or monks who similarly defend themselves from tigers and wild beasts in the forest through the power of their *mettābhāvanā*.[4] There is even a canonical chant, often recommended by lay people in Sri Lanka as the best protection against bites and stings, which wishes well to snakes, spiders and other small predators in the area and asks them to depart (A II 72)!

Within the canon, it warrants special treatment. The *Mettā-Sutta*, translated later, advocates what is to be done by the one who has attained, or wishes to attain, 'that tranquil condition', *nibbāna*. The practitioner, it is suggested, may practise this at all times, in all postures, to all beings, just as a mother extends loving-kindness to her only child. It is the way to experience a higher heaven, the *brahma* world, in this lifetime, a statement which is the nearest canonical reference to draw a direct parallel between the heavenly realms and experience possible amongst humans. Vajirañāṇa writes, '[*mettā*] is not an evanescent exhibition of emotion, but a sustained and habitual mental attitude of service, good will and friendship, which finds expression in word, deed and thought' (BMTP 280). Descriptions as to how to conduct the practice are less common, aside from the simple instructions in the standard canonical formula. These are included here with sections from the *Paṭisambhidāmagga*, which describes some permutations on this. Broadly speaking, in the canon it is given on a directional basis: each of the four directions is pervaded with loving-kindness, and then above, below and all around. On a personal basis, it is practised by wishing for the well-being of someone dear, then someone neutral, then someone inimical. Upatissa says that the meditator should first reflect on the disadvantages of fostering hatred and resentment: he 'will be laughed at by enemies and cause his friends to be ashamed of him' (PF 182). Buddhaghosa suggests first bringing to mind the disadvantages of ill-will and consider ways of overcoming it (Vism IX 14–39). According to Buddhaghosa, *mettā*, like the other immeasurables, should not be cultivated through attention to a member of the opposite sex, as it will reinforce attachment (Vism IX 6). Its near enemy is desire, as both see virtues; its far enemy is ill-will, which can await in ambush for him or her (IX 98). Like the other immeasurables, it cannot be practised on a dead person (Vism IX 7). In order to break down barriers, to prepare the mind for the attainment of *jhāna*, it should be practised towards four beings: first oneself, then a dear person, then a neutral and then an enemy (Vism IX 11–13; 40–3).

Compassion

Compassion is compared to the feeling a mother experiences when her child is suffering (PF 190–1; Vism IX 108). Buddhaghosa says that it is manifest as non-cruelty and succeeds when cruelty subsides. Using his favourite punning word plays (*nirutti*) he says that *kāruṇā* makes (*karoti*) the hearts of good people moved (*kampana*) and attacks (*kiṇāti*) others' suffering. It is scattered (*kiriyati*) upon them, like a pervasion (see Vism IX 92/PP 343–4). Again, if resentment arises for an enemy he should consider the disadvantages it brings to oneself (Vism IX 14–39). Indeed, he suggests starting the practice towards an evildoer, who will surely experience unfortunate *kamma*, and so is suffering despite apparent happiness (IX 79–80). The meditator then goes through the series of dear, neutral and hostile person as object. Both commentators say compassion fails if there is sadness and that it is not the same as being afflicted by others' sorrows (IX 94; PF 191). The near enemy of compassion is grief, as both see suffering: its far enemy is cruelty (Vism IX 99). Upatissa argues, interestingly, that all beings may be the object of compassion as all suffer at some stage or in some way (PF 192). The Great Compassion of the Buddha is described in the *Paṭisambhidāmagga* (Patis I 126–31).

Sympathetic joy

Sympathetic joy is compared by Upatissa and Buddhaghosa to the gladness a mother experiences at her child's happiness (PF 191; Vism IX 108). Upatissa says that it destroys dislike and is cultivated by taking delight in another's good behaviour and the fact that another's qualities are esteemed (PF 192). Buddhaghosa says that if a dear person is unhappy, one can still practise this by remembering his or her past gladness and anticipating his or her future happiness (Vism IX 86). The near enemy of sympathetic joy is joy in the home life as both see success: aversion and boredom are the far enemy (Vism IX 100).

Equanimity

Indian lists of four are too dynamic and interrelated to be regarded as purely hierarchical. In the four noble truths, for instance, the internal pattern of relationships between each truth is more like that to be found in the kind of four-petalled flower, or the swastika design. This is also the case for these four, which are seen as different ways of viewing or considering other beings. The last, however, equanimity, does encompass and transcend the others: the development of the equanimity is linked to the fourth *jhāna* and is considered essential for the cultivation of the higher knowledges. Buddhaghosa says the first three immeasurables lead directly only to the first three *jhānas*. The fourth *jhāna* is cultivated on the basis of equanimity, with the others like a framework upon which the rafters of a roof are based (see Vism IX 104). Upatissa says that equanimity is like the attitude to parents to any one of a group of their children: 'neither too attentive nor inattentive' but with an 'even mind' towards them all (PF 193). Buddhaghosa, as for each, indicates the qualities which may be mistaken for or vitiate the arising of equanimity: its near enemy is unknowing, as this shares its disregard of the good and bad features in another being. Its far enemies are desire and resentment (see Vism IX 101 and PP 346 n. 16).

Buddhaghosa's approach in seeing the enemies of each has canonical precedent: the *Mahārāhulovāda-Sutta* gives loving-kindness as an antidote to ill-will, compassion as an antidote to cruelty, sympathetic joy as an antidote to discontent or boredom and equanimity as an antidote to aversion (M I 424 and this anthology 000). Buddhaghosa advocates, however, the practice of equanimity to one given to desire (Vism IX 108). Buddhaghosa also says that each divine abiding has a natural relationship with certain other meditations. Citing the *Haliddavasana-Sutta*, he says that loving-kindness has affinities with the beautiful deliverance of the colour *kasiṇa*; compassion, through its awareness of suffering even in the form sphere, has affinities with the sphere of infinite space (35); sympathetic joy, which develops familiarity with others' consciousness, with the sphere of infinite consciousness (36); equanimity, which makes the mind skilled in not adverting to existent things, leads naturally to the sphere of nothingness (37) (S V 119–21; Vism IX 121–2). This rare example of an association between the divine abidings and the form sphere perhaps indicates that, in practice, there was some variation in the more usual use of a *kasiṇa* as the basis for formless meditation.

The imagery with which the practice of the divine abidings is associated reveals a robust lack of sentimentality. They may be cultivated just as a strong conch blower sends his sound to all directions (D I 251; S IV 322). *Mettā* is compared variously to the pull of a cow udder (S II 189), a tough catskin bag (M I 129) and in one text later, to a tough spear. As with all meditation practices, they can be developed by someone from any caste (M II 151). The divine abidings themselves can be the object of insight, and seen as conditionally and volitionally produced, and hence impermanent (see M I 351). They are never jettisoned, however, and are considered an essential support and instigator for the first factor of the path, right view. As Aronson points out, the Buddha liked to practise them after his enlightenment (see A I 181–3).[5]

Mettā-Sutta

These verses, the *locus classicus* for the practice of loving-kindness, comprise the most famous Buddhist *sutta* in the Pāli canon. It is chanted on all occasions and is supposed to ward off bad luck, evil spirits and misfortune.

143. He who is skilled in welfare, who wishes to attain that calm state (*nibbāna*), should act in this way: he should be able, upright, perfectly upright, of noble speech, gentle and humble.

144. Contented, easily supported, with few duties, of simple livelihood, with senses calmed, discreet, not impudent, he should not be greedily attached to families.

145. He should not pursue the slightest thing for which other wise men might blame him. May all beings be happy and secure, may their hearts be wholesome!

146–7. Whatever living beings there be: feeble or strong, tall, stout or medium, short, small or large, without exception; seen or unseen, those dwelling far or near, those who are born or those who are yet to be born, may all beings be happy!

148. Let one not deceive another, nor despise any person, whatsoever, in any place. Let him not wish any harm to another out of anger or ill-will.

149. Just as a mother would protect her only child at the risk of her own life, even so, let him cultivate a boundless heart towards all beings.

150. Let his thoughts of boundless love pervade the whole world: above, below and across without any obstruction, without any hatred, without any enmity.

151. Whether he stands, walks, sits or lies down, as long as he is awake, he should develop this mindfulness. This they say is the noblest living here in this world.[6]

152. Not falling into wrong views, being virtuous and endowed with insight, by discarding attachment to sense desires, he never again knows rebirth.

(Sn 143–52)

Five ways of getting rid of resentment[7]

There are five ways of getting rid of resentment, by which a monk may get rid of all resentment that arises. What five?

If resentment arises towards any person, then one should cultivate loving-kindness . . . or compassion . . . or equanimity . . .[8] In this way he may get rid of resentment that has arisen towards any person.

Or one should cultivate lack of awareness (*asati*) of him and not give attention (*amanasikāra*) to that person. In this way, he may get rid of resentment that has arisen towards any person.

Or one should fix in one's mind the fact of his ownership of *kamma*: 'This venerable sir is the owner of his deeds, the heir to his deeds: his deeds are his progenitor, his kinsmen and his refuge. Whatever he does, good or bad, he will be the heir of that.' In this way, he may get rid of resentment that has arisen towards any person.

By these five ways of getting rid of resentment, a monk can get rid of all resentment that arises within him.

(A III 185)

Extract from Cūḷa-Assapura Sutta

'He sees himself purified of those harmful, unskilful states, he sees himself delivered from them. When he sees this, gladness is born in him. When he is glad, joy is born in him; in the one whose mind is joyful the body becomes tranquil, the one whose body is tranquil feels happy; in one who is happy the mind goes to concentration.

'He abides with a mind filled with loving-kindness, suffusing one quarter, likewise the second, likewise the third, likewise the fourth. So above, below, all around and everywhere, to all as to himself, he abides suffusing the whole world, in every direction, with a mind filled with loving-kindness, abundant, made great, immeasurable, free from hostility, free from ill-will.

'He abides with a mind filled with compassion, suffusing one quarter, likewise the second, likewise the third, likewise the fourth. So above, below, all around and everywhere, to all as to himself, he abides suffusing the whole world, in every direction, with a mind filled with compassion, abundant, made great, immeasurable, free from hostility, free from ill-will.

'He abides with a mind filled with sympathetic joy, suffusing one quarter, likewise the second, likewise the third, likewise the fourth. So above, below, all around and everywhere, to all as to himself, he abides suffusing the whole world, in every direction, with a mind filled with sympathetic joy, abundant, made great, immeasurable, free from hostility, free from ill-will.

'He abides with a mind filled with equanimity, suffusing one quarter, likewise the second, likewise the third, likewise the fourth. So above, below, all around and everywhere, to all as to himself, he abides suffusing the whole world, in every direction, with a mind filled with equanimity, abundant, made great, immeasurable, free from hostility, free from ill-will.

'It is just like, monks, a pond with clear, pleasant cool water, translucent, with smooth banks, delightful. If a man, overpowered and exhausted by the heat, weary, parched and thirsty, should come to that pond, he would remove his thirst for water and allay his fever. Whether he came from the east, the west, the north or the south or whichever direction, overpowered and exhausted by the heat, weary, parched and thirsty, having come to the pond he would quench his thirst for water and allay his fever. In just this way, monks, a man of family, going forth from the home into homelessness, comes to the discipline and teaching taught by the Tathāgata and, cultivating in this way loving-kindness, compassion, sympathetic joy and equanimity, finds internal peace. That internal peace, I say, is the way proper to the ascetic.'

(M I 283–4)

Extract from 'The Treatise on Loving-kindness'

This is an extract from a lengthy section of a canonical work on the *Abhidhamma* that examines the way that loving-kindness is developed and its relationship to other aspects of meditative practice. Glossing this passage, Buddhaghosa says the methods it describes are suitable for someone already experienced in *jhāna* (Vism IX 49–58). Traditional practice has, however, applied the principles described in various ways. Modern monks and meditation practitioners usually 'localize' an exercise in *mettā*, and name some of the towns, areas or kinds of beings in each direction (see James 1986: 94).

Mettā

There is the deliverance of mind by loving-kindness which suffuses undifferentiated objects.[9] There is the deliverance of mind by loving-kindness which suffuses differentiated objects. There is the deliverance of mind by loving-kindness which suffuses the directions.

In what ways does the deliverance of mind by loving-kindness suffuse undifferentiated objects? In what ways does it suffuse differentiated objects? In what ways the directions? The deliverance of mind by loving-kindness suffuses undifferentiated objects in five ways, differentiated objects in seven ways and the directions in ten ways.

In what five ways does the deliverance of mind by loving-kindness suffuse undifferentiated objects?

'May all beings be free from hostility, may all beings be free from ill-will, may they be free from trouble; may they live happily. May all breathing beings . . . all who have come into existence . . . all individuals . . . all who have a sense of self . . . be free from hostility, may they be free from ill-will, may they be free from trouble; may they live happily.'

In these five ways the deliverance of mind by loving-kindness suffuses undifferentiated objects.

In what seven ways does the deliverance of mind by loving-kindness suffuse differentiated objects?

'May all women be free from hostility, may they be free from ill-will, may they be free from trouble; may they live happily. May all men . . . noble ones . . . those who are not noble ones . . . all gods . . . all human beings . . . all those in unhappy rebirths be free from hostility, may they be free from ill-will, may they be free from rage; may they live happily.'

In these seven ways the deliverance of will by loving-kindness suffuses differentiated objects.

In what ten ways does the deliverance of mind by loving-kindness suffuse the directions?

'May all beings in the eastern direction be free from hostility, may all beings be free from ill-will, may they be free from trouble; may they live happily.

May all beings in the western direction . . . in the northern direction . . . in the southern direction . . . in the intermediate eastern direction . . . in the intermediate western direction . . . in the intermediate northern direction . . . in the intermediate southern direction . . . in the direction below . . . in the direction above be free from hostility, may all beings be free from ill-will, may they be free from trouble; may they live happily.

(Apply for each of five and the seven in lists above)

In these ten ways the deliverance of mind by loving-kindness suffuses the directions.

It is loving-kindness since it is friendly in these eight ways:

1. For all beings, it avoids harming for the sake of non-harm.
2. For all beings, it avoids injury, for the sake of kindness.
3. For all beings, it avoids torment for the sake of non-torment.
4. For all beings it avoids exhausting for the sake of non-exhausting.
5. For all beings, it rejects cruelty for the sake of mercy.[10]
6. 'May all beings be free from hostility and may they not be hostile.'
7. 'May all beings be happy and may they not suffer.'
8. 'May all beings live in a state of happiness and may they not live in a state of unhappiness.'

It is mind (*ceto*), because it uses the mind (*cetayati*) for that state.[11] It is deliverance since it is delivered from all obsession with ill-will. Loving-kindness, mind and deliverance: these are the deliverance of mind by loving-kindness.

(Patis II 131–3)

The spear

Staying at Sāvatthī. 'Suppose, monks, there was a sharp-bladed spear, and a man came along, thinking, "I will bend back this sharp-bladed spear with my hand or fist, knock it out of shape and twist it around." What do you think, monks, would it be possible for that man to do so?'

'No, sir.'

'For what reason? Because it is not easy to bend back a sharp-bladed spear with the hand or fist, knock it out of shape and twist it around. That man would only become tired and annoyed. So too, monks, when a monk has cultivated and made much of the deliverance of the mind by loving-kindness, made it a vehicle, made it a basis, ensured it is stable, increased and really set it going, if a non-human thinks he can overthrow his mind, he will only become tired and annoyed.

Therefore, monks, you should train yourself in this way: "We will cultivate and make much of the deliverance of mind by loving-kindness, make it our vehicle, make it our basis, ensure it is stable, increased and really set going:" thus you should train yourselves.'

(S II 265)

Advantages

If, monks, the deliverance of mind by loving-kindness is practised, cultivated and made much of, made a vehicle, made a basis, ensured as stable, increased and really set going, eleven advantages are to expected. What eleven?

He sleeps happily, he wakes happily, he sees no bad dream, he is dear to humans, he is dear to non-humans, the gods protect him, fire, poison or sword do not harm him, his mind goes easily to concentration, the expression on his face is serene, he dies unbewildered and, if he does not penetrate the supreme state, he will be reborn in a Brahma realm.

These eleven advantages, monks, are to be expected if the deliverance of mind by loving-kindness is practised, cultivated and made much of, made a vehicle, made a basis, ensured as stable, increased and really set going.

(A V 3)

The cultivation of loving-kindness

This was said by the Exalted One, spoken by the arahat, I have heard. The Exalted One explained the meaning and this was said too:

'Whatever bases there are for making merit for a future rebirth, monks, all are but a sixteenth part of the deliverance of mind by loving-kindness. For the deliverance of mind by loving-kindness surpasses them all, shining forth, bright and radiant.

Just as, monks, the light of all the stars does not equal a sixteenth part of the radiance of the moon, but the light of the moon surpasses them all, shining forth, bright and radiant: even so, whatever bases there are for making merit for a future rebirth, all of these do not equal a sixteenth part of the deliverance of mind by loving-kindness.

Just as, monks, in the autumn, in the last month of the rains, when the sky is clear and the clouds have gone, the sun, on rising, dispels the darkness that has been in the sky and then alone shines forth, bright and radiant: even so, whatever bases there are for making merit for a future rebirth, all of these do not equal a sixteenth part of the deliverance of mind by loving-kindness.

Just as, monks, in the night, at the time towards dawn, the healing star shines forth bright and radiant: even so, whatever bases there are for making merit for a future rebirth, all of these do not equal a sixteenth part of the deliverance of mind by loving-kindness.

The deliverance of mind by loving-kindness surpasses them all and shines forth, bright and radiant.

Whoever, mindful, cultivates immeasurable loving-kindness,
Seeing the destruction of attachment,
The fetters are diminished in him.

The one who extends loving-kindness to just one being,
With a mind that is uncorrupted: through that he is skilful.
The one who extends a compassionate mind to all beings:
Through that, he produces an abundance of merit.

Whatever royal seers, who conquered the thicket of the earth, filled with beings,
Then went around making sacrifices:
Sacrifices of the horse, the man, the water, soma,
And the unobstructed:

They do not experience a sixteenth part of a heart
Where loving-kindness has been brought into being,
Just as the radiance of the moon surpasses the whole host of stars.

Whoever does not kill, nor causes to kill,
Whoever does not conquer, nor causes to conquer:
Extending loving-kindness to all beings, there is no enemy for him.'

This is the meaning of what was said by Exalted One: so I have heard.
(It 19–22)

11

35–38. MEDITATION ON THE FORMLESS (*ARŪPASAMĀPATTI*)

All the meditations discussed so far have clearly defined and recognizable objects as a starting point. Some have involved an object with a complexity of attributes, as in those recollection practices recommended for daily business, as a preliminary to meditation or for arousing a particular quality such as faith or a sense of urgency. Others are so simple that the mind can rest entirely on the object, to the exclusion of others, and need to be undertaken in seclusion. The formless meditations refine attention further: they do not at first sight start from an easily identifiable physical object at all. Unlike the *rūpa* realms, they are described as spheres (*āyatanāni*):

5 The sphere of infinite space (*ākāsānañcāyatana*)
6 The sphere of infinite consciousness (*viññāṇañcāyatana*)
7 The sphere of nothingness (*ākiñcaññāyatana*)
8 The sphere of neither perception nor non-perception (*nevasaññānāsaññāyatana*).

The fifth *jhāna* takes as an object the sense of space left behind when the *kasiṇa*, the object of the form realms, has been withdrawn for the attainment of the 'sphere of infinite space'. The sixth takes as an object the nature of the attention that is required for the experience of boundless space: the sphere of 'infinite consciousness'. The third, the sphere of nothingness, examines the sphere that is present when the relationship between the object and its perceiver is withdrawn. This is the *jhāna* that the Buddha practised with one of his first teachers before his enlightenment, but rejected as a sole means of finding release from suffering. The last, the eighth, appears to be an examination of the arising of perception in the mind: the sphere of neither perception nor non-perception, also practised by the Buddha before his enlightenment but also rejected as the sole means of ending suffering.

We tend to think of the realms of Buddhist cosmology in vertically ascending order. If the rebirths after death in various heaven realms are taken as a counterpart for the different levels of meditation they are certainly the most refined.[1] But it is difficult to see that which is without form only in terms of 'up': they describe experience unbounded by any kind of spatial differentiation, and appear to move the meditation into another dimension altogether. They are of the world (*lokiya*) and not thought essential to the path but they are described as the most peaceful form of meditative experience, all characterized by imperturbability (*ānenjam*) (Vibh 135).[2]

We find almost nothing about these highly developed and subtle forms of meditation in modern manuals of practice. There is an obvious reason for this: in the Buddhist tradition, they are practised only on the basis of the attainment of the fourth *jhāna*. Only from this point of stability of mind is the meditator ready to examine the object and the nature of the attention on that object in an entirely different way. The canon is also economical in description of these states, and gives only hints at method. In explanation of this Khantipālo says that they are ineffable – and that meditators can think they have attained path on reaching them. He comments: 'Teachers in Northeast Thailand usually do not identify any of these attainments when asked by a pupil about some meditative experience' (Khantipālo 1981: 61). A ninth element is often added to the list in the canon: cessation, *nirodha samāpatti*, said to be accessible only to arahats.[3] Buddhaghosa and Upatissa describe how these practices have traditionally been conducted: in this instance the commentators are really essential, as we shall see later in this section, as their discussion gives some idea of what these highly specialized meditations involve.[4]

The *suttas* provide little in the way of elucidation. Few images refer solely to the formless realms, with the exception of one which says they are outside the influence and sight of Māra, that great mythical opponent to meditative practice, whom they are said to blindfold (see A IV 434; M I 174). They are, however, frequently mentioned within the canon. We know from his own account that two of the meditations predate the Buddha: he was taught the seventh *jhāna* by Āḷāra Kālāma and the eighth by Uddaka Rāmaputta before embarking on his own method, which involved a starting point in the simple happiness of the first *jhāna*. On the night of the enlightenment he practises all eight *jhānas* – though starts, significantly, with the first. Although he had rejected his two earlier teachers, he considered them the only people capable of grasping the teaching after his enlightenment, an indication of the high esteem with which he held the practice of these meditations: both teachers had in fact just died, Āḷāra Kālāma seven days before, and Uddaka Rāmaputta the night before (see M I 169–70). The realms feature again just before his death. The Buddha ascends through all eight *jhānas*, then back down again just before his *parinibbāna*. He enters into the fourth *jhāna*, however, the traditional starting point for the formless realms and for so much of the Buddhist path, for the moment of death.[5] From the evidence of the texts the Buddha constantly practised and taught the formless realms, though the fact that they are so often described after the first four confirms their dependency on a form-sphere basis. They are usually described in the list of eight: Moggallāna, for instance, works his way through each one in turn, overcoming difficulties at each stage before attaining the next (S IV 262–9). The following text compares the meditator who attempts any of the *jhānas* after the first without a sound footing in the one before to a 'foolish cow' who slips while climbing a mountain: perhaps also a reason for the paucity of description of these states within the canon (A IV 418–9). Other evidence in the canon emphasizes the relationship between this practice and a starting point in the form-sphere *jhānas*. The list of the eight deliverances, frequently mentioned in the canon alongside one or both the lists of the spheres of transcendence and the *kasiṇas*, implies that formless meditation is a development from skills associated with *kasiṇa* practice (1–10).[6]

So what do the *suttas* say about these subtle levels? The method of obtaining the first is described routinely with a formula that is sparse. The usual description is that 'completely surmounting the perception of material forms, by leaving behind perceptions of sensory impact and by not paying attention to perceptions of diversity, reflecting, "space is infinite" he enters upon and abides in the sphere of infinite space'.[7] The vocabulary used for this first and subsequent formless *jhānas* reflects the shift in emphasis from earlier states. Termed spheres (*āyatanāni*), they are also denoted by a new verb. Two verbs are routinely applied to all *jhānas*. *Viharati*, which means to dwell or abide, is commonly used for residing or staying in a particular location like a house: it is the word from which *vihāra*, a monastery, is derived. The other is *upasampajjati*, to attain or enter into. Each of the formless spheres, however, is also obtained by the meditator who 'passes beyond' or 'surmounts' (*samatikkama*) the state before.[8] A different kind of movement seems to be operating, not necessarily upward. It is difficult to draw conclusions about these changes, other than noting that they occur, and that they are always applied: it appears that the transcendence of the object of the one before which had operated in the first four *jhānas* is of a different kind. Another noteworthy feature is that these realms do not appear to be concerned with the refinement of feeling, purified in the first four *jhānas*, but rather with exploration of the *khandhas* of consciousness and perception. Each of the first four *jhānas* are standardly described with the factors of joy, happiness and equanimity: this last is assumed as a basis for the formless *jhānas*. Indeed, according to the *Abhidhamma* the mental factors present in these realms are the same as for the fourth *jhāna* (see DhS 265–8). The effects on the mind and body that perceive and experience the object, so memorably evoked for the first four *jhānas*, are not described for these states at all. Rather, a new dimension of exploration is implied, involving the ability to discard the object which had previously occupied the mind through a more subtle and refined attention as much to the means by which the object is perceived as to the object itself. Many objects are said to lead to the richly varied unification of the first *jhāna* (1–10, 11–20, 27, 29, 31–40). These *jhānas*, however, are each defined not by associated mental factors, but by the single feature which is both their object and their sphere.

These few points tell us that the nature of the experience involved is of a different order than the first four *jhānas*, though it needs them and their object as a basis. The usual building blocks by which we measure and define our world and which give us some understanding of the *rūpa* realm are successively examined and then transcended, so that the mind enters into an experience which concerns the very nature of perception and consciousness itself. Buddhaghosa's commentary is particularly helpful here, as his instructions in this case are practical, do take a common solid object as their starting point, and at each stage give figurative analogies to make the next step in the process clear. The procedure is much the same as with other meditations, in that an easily recognizable object and a straightforward premise introduces the practice, which is then carried through from stage to stage until a more subtle object is discerned.

Nirodha samāpatti

Before considering his comments, mention should be made of the state often described alongside the eight *jhānas* as a culmination of their work, *nirodha samāpatti*. This seems to be an experience of *nibbāna* within the world that does not, however, constitute the attainment or the fruit of any of the paths. In the lists we considered briefly earlier, it is taken as the consummation of meditational attainment, in which it appears difficult to distinguish the state from *nibbāna* itself. One *sutta* concerns two brahmins: Pūraṇa Kassapa is said to subscribe to the view that 'with infinite knowledge I abide knowing, seeing a finite world', while the Jain, Nāṭaputta, declares, 'with infinite knowledge I abide knowing, seeing an infinite world' (A IV 428). The Buddha compares the situation to four men standing at each corner of the world, who think they can run to the other end, but never will in their own lifetime: both views placed at the beginning are, the *sutta* implies, still limited by the parameters with which they circumscribe their understanding. Mentioning each *jhāna* in turn, the Buddha states that even the one who transcends the allure and pleasure of shapes, sounds, smells, tastes and touch to attain each *jhāna* has still not crossed over the world: the one who practises *nirodha samāpatti* can be said, 'to have come to the end of the world and abide at the end of the world, having crossed over clinging in the world' (A IV 432).

Buddhaghosa and Upatissa: the sphere of infinite space

Both Buddhaghosa and Upatissa cite the problems of the sense-sphere realm as like the pains and threats that encompass gross physical existence. Buddhaghosa says that although these have been overcome in the form sphere, they have not been entirely surmounted (see Vism X 3–4). It is, he says, like a man who lives in a village where he is ill-treated, and escapes to another, where he meets another man of similar appearance and becomes fearful and anxious. So the monk escapes from the threats of the sense sphere by the fourth *jhāna*. However, the earth *kasiṇa* – always a paradigm for the basis of form-sphere meditation – still reminds him of the sense sphere, and he wishes to escape from that too. This meditation on boundless space, he says, is practised not by removing the earlier object 'like a mat or by removing a cake from a tin' but by becoming aware of the space it occupies (Vism X 7). The meditator strikes at this, with initial and sustained thought, repeating the word 'space'. The rest of the process is the same as for the *kasiṇa* practice, except that, it is said, he becomes like a man who has stuffed a coloured rag into a hole. When the rag is removed, he finds himself looking at space. He notes that sense objects disappear here, and through this observation the practice becomes imperturbable.[9]

Buddhaghosa says that the practice is conducted on the basis of nine *kasiṇas*, omitting limited space.[10] Upatissa, who describes the practice more simply than Buddhaghosa, says, 'But depending on space, one liberates oneself peacefully' (PF 113). The meditator then abandons the earth *kasiṇa*, its sign and dwells upon space as an infinite object, with a mind untouched by the four elements, of fire, water, earth and air, like an empty hole (PF 115 n. 2).

The sphere of infinite consciousness

Whereas the first formless *jhāna* looks to an infinite object without, that of space, the second takes the attention within to that which perceives that space. According to the instructions we are given the meditator first considers the flaws and tribulations of the sphere of infinite space: there is still an element of form, it is still gross and the meditator is not completely free from a sense of diversity and contact: so 'he surpasses the spatial object' (PF 117). The next sphere is found, according to Buddhaghosa, by mastering the sphere before in five ways, then by becoming aware of the consciousness that had perceived and pervaded that space, repeating the word 'consciousness'.[11] The object, which is, according to the terminology of these realms, itself infinite, is one of the *khandhas* that constitute the basic components of a being: the means by which one experiences the world is being investigated. As for other formless attainments the mind (*citta*) is, according to the *Abhidhamma*, still characterized in the same way as that of the fourth *jhāna* (see DhS 266).

The sphere of nothingness

Again the meditator perceives the problems of the state before: it is not completely free from a sense of space and consciousness, so, seeing the freedom of nothingness, he attains it and surmounts the sphere of infinite consciousness and attains to, or 'enters into' the sphere of nothingness that is 'without the nature of consciousness and is empty' (PF 118). It is a state of 'holding to nothing'. He then 'dwells peacefully in the enjoyment of the reward of concentration'. Adverting to the consciousness that has been present, he should say 'there is not, there is not' and 'emptiness, emptiness' or 'secluded, secluded'. Two words Buddhaghosa recommends repeating during the practice, *n'atthi* and *suññatā*, are highly suggestive in ancient Indian thought.[12] The object then becomes the empty, secluded, non-existent state of the past consciousness that pervaded space. Buddhaghosa compares it, evocatively, to going back to a hall where there has been an assembly of monks, which is now empty. Sue Hamilton suggests that 'the meditator is learning to suspend, so to speak, the operating of his cognitive apparatus in the usual making manifold (thing-like) way' (Hamilton 2000: 155). Cousins suggests the term 'poverty' for this realm in the sense it is sometimes taken in a Christian context – a state of owning nothing at all (Cousins: 2001). This is supported by a kind of joke in the *Parosahassa Jātaka* (no. 99). The Bodhisatta assures his disgusted fellow practitioners that he has attained 'nothing' on his deathbed, a comment they misconstrue as indicative of lack of meditative skill. His meditation ensures, however, that he is reborn in the radiant heavens (J I 405–7).[13]

The sphere of neither perception nor non-perception

The tranquillity of the last formless realm is such that perception is at the bare minimum: the meditator is compared by Buddhaghosa to a king, riding through a city, who admires the beautiful work of dusty craftsmen working on ivory around him, but does not wish to abandon the majesty of his status to become one (see Vism X 46). So, he says, the meditator gives attention to the peace of his attainment, but does not make any resolves to attain to it, to emerge from it or to review it. Buddhaghosa continues his analysis through a variety of simple similes. A novice smeared a bowl with oil, so when requested to bring it by his teacher, he says he cannot, because there is oil in it; but when told to bring some oil he says there is no oil. Or it is like a monk who, seeing a puddle, warns his teacher of water ahead, so that he should take off his sandals; when the teacher proposes a bathe, the monk says that there is no water. Or it is like tepid water, where the heat element is not strong enough to burn. This is like perception in this state, Buddhaghosa says, which is sufficient to be aware, but does not wish to make that perception decisive: so there is neither perception nor non-perception.

The sparse accounts communicate a simplicity that can be sensed even in a short summary: the formless realms explore the very nature of our consciousness and the way the mind constructs. The first examines the measurelessness of the space that is apparent when a physical object is withdrawn from the visual field and a sense of the space it occupies is extended. The second takes as an object the nature of the attention that is applied to that object, the third the sphere that is present when the relationship between that object and its perceiver is withdrawn and the last, it seems, the arising of awareness at the threshold of consciousness itself. Each stage of formless meditation is dependent on earlier attainments; careful preparation is involved in making the shift from one to the next, and each is described by Buddhaghosa through simple and even homely analogies. The meditation on these objects seems to use as its basis activities of the mind which are most mundane and familiar, but which we never see or understand precisely because they underlie all our sensory activities: we live in space, we are conscious, we would like to own or identify things around and within us, and we perceive. It is oddly reminiscent of the way children ask what is there when that is not, and go on and on trying to find a solution, but in this case the reassurance that underlies the questions is eventually found in the most refined, the *nirodha samāć patti*, the experience of freedom in this world. Another dimension of meditation is being described: not essential for the attainment of enlightenment, but which the Buddha frequently practised and made use of himself. Vajirañāṇa writes, 'According to Buddhist teaching the disciple should bear in mind that the object of attaining these stages is to achieve the mastery of *Samādhi*; for without this mastery of *Samādhi* his training would be incomplete' (BMTP 335).

The eight *jhānas* and the cessation of perception and feeling

Buddhaghosa quotes from the first part of this *sutta* while discussing the masteries of meditation applied to the first *jhāna*, suggesting that the meditator should not try to review that state too much when it has first been attained. He emphasizes the need to mature and stabilize one state before trying to enter another (see Vism IV 130).

> *The foolish and the wise cow*
> Suppose, monks, a foolish, inexperienced mountain cow, with no knowledge of the terrain and no skill in wandering in craggy mountains, were to think, 'What if I were to visit a place where I have never been before, eat grasses I have never eaten before and drink waters I have never drunk before?' And, without placing her front leg carefully, she would lift her back leg. Then she would not visit the area she had never visited before, nor eat grasses she had never eaten before, nor drink water she had never drunk before: and nor would she return to the place where she had formerly thought, 'What if I…?', and where she had been safe.
>
> And what is the reason for this? It is because, monks, that foolish and inexperienced mountain cow has no knowledge of the terrain and no skill in wandering in craggy mountains. And in just this way, monks, if some foolish and inexperienced monk, with no knowledge of the terrain and no skill, secluded from the senses and secluded from unskilful states, were to enter and abide in the first *jhāna*, accompanied by initial and sustained thought, with the joy and happiness born of seclusion; but were not to practise, develop and make much of that mental image nor settle it properly.[14] And then he thinks, 'What if I, with the subsiding of thoughts, were to enter and abide in the second *jhāna*…?' but he cannot, with the subsiding of thoughts, enter the second *jhāna*. Then he thinks, 'What if I, secluded from the senses and secluded from unskilful states, were to enter and abide in the first *jhāna*…?' but he cannot, secluded from the senses and secluded from unskilful states, enter and abide in the first meditation, accompanied by initial and sustained

thought, with the joy and happiness born of seclusion. So it is said, the monk has fallen down at both, failed at both.[15]

But suppose, monks, a wise, experienced mountain cow, with knowledge of the terrain and skill in wandering in craggy mountains, were to think, 'What if I were to visit a place where I have never been before, eat grasses I have never eaten before and drink waters I have never drunk before?' And, placing her front leg carefully, she would lift up her back leg. Then she would visit the area she had never visited before, eat grasses she had never eaten before, drink water she had never drunk before: and she would also return to the place where she had formerly thought, 'What if I . . . ?', where she had been safe. And what is the reason for this? It is because, monks, she is a wise and experienced mountain cow, with knowledge of the terrain and skill in wandering in craggy mountains. And in just this way, monks, some wise and experienced monk, with knowledge of the terrain, skilful, secluded from the senses and secluded from unskilful states, enters and abides in the first *jhāna*, accompanied by initial and sustained thought, with the joy and happiness born of seclusion; but he does practise, develop and make much of that mental image and he settles it properly.

He thinks, 'What if I, letting initial and sustained thought subside, were to enter and abide in the second *jhāna* . . . ?' And without harming the second meditation, letting initial and sustained thought subside, he enters and abides in the second *jhāna* . . . .and he does practise, develop and make much of that mental image and settles it properly'.[16] He thinks 'What if I abandon...? and enters the third jhāna . . . . And without harming the third *jhāna*, abandoning joy, he enters and abides in the third *jhāna* and he does practise, develop and make much of that mental image and settles it properly'. He thinks, 'What if I, abandoning happiness, enter and abide in the fourth *jhāna* . . . . And without harming the fourth *jhāna*, abandoning happiness, he enters and abides in the fourth *jhāna* . . . and he does practise, develop and make much of that mental image and settles it properly'. Then he thinks, 'What if I, completely surmounting the perception of material forms, by leaving behind perceptions of sensory impact and by not paying attention to perceptions of diversity, enter upon and abide in the sphere of infinite space, reflecting, 'space is infinite' . . . . What if I, completely surmounting the sphere of infinite space, reflecting, 'consciousness is infinite', enter upon and abide in the sphere of infinite consciousness . . . What if I, completely surmounting the sphere of infinite consciousness, reflecting that 'there is nothing', enter upon and abide in the sphere of nothingness . . . What if I, completely surmounting the sphere of nothingness enter upon and abide in the sphere of neither perception nor non-perception . . . 'What if I, completely surmounting the sphere of neither perception nor non-perception enter upon and abide in the cessation of perception and feeling?' . . . Without harming the cessation of perception and feeling, completely surmounting the sphere of neither perception nor non-perception he enters upon and abides in the cessation of perception and feeling.

Indeed, monks, when a monk both enters into and emerges from an attainment, his mind is soft and manageable, and with a soft and manageable mind his concentration is well cultivated and limitless.[17] And with well cultivated, limitless concentration he inclines his mind with higher knowledge to whatever state that can be realized by higher knowledge: and in each case he acquires the possibilities of an eyewitness, in whatever that sphere may be.[18]

If he should wish, 'May I experience the various manifestations of the psychic powers, being one, may I become many, becoming many may I become one . . . the divine ear . . . the knowledge that encompasses the minds of others . . . the knowledge of the recollection of past lives . . . the divine eye . . . the elimination of the corruptions . . . ' with well cultivated, limitless concentration he inclines his mind with higher knowledge to whatever state that can be realized by higher knowledge: and in each case he acquires the possibilities of an eyewitness, in whatever that sphere may be.

(A IV 418–9)

Two happinesses

Monks, there are these two happinesses. What two? The happiness of having a visible object and the happiness of having a formless object. These are the two. Of these two the latter has pre-eminence.

(A I 80)

Peace

This was said by the Exalted One, spoken by the arahat, I have heard.

'The formless realms, monks, are more peaceful than the form realm and cessation is more peaceful than the formless.' The Exalted One explained the meaning and this was said too:

'Both those beings who reach the form realm
And those established in the formless:
If they do not know well cessation
They come once more to further becoming.

Those who fully understand forms
And do not linger in the formless:
They are released into cessation;
They leave death behind.

Having touched with his own body
The element that is deathless, free from clinging,
Having realized for himself the relinquishment of clinging,
Free from corruptions, the Fully Awakened One teaches
A state without sorrow, free from stain.'

This is the meaning of what was said by the Exalted One: so I have heard.

(It 61–2)

12

THE ONE PERCEPTION AND THE ONE DEFINING

39. The perception of loathsomeness in food (*āhāre paṭikkūlasaññā*)

This meditation is mentioned rarely in the canon, and involves consideration of the bodily function of eating as a means of enabling the mind to become free from entanglement in the senses.[1] It occurs twice in the *Aṅguttaranikāya* list of meditation subjects, where two lists are conflated.[2] Elsewhere in the *Aṅguttaranikāya* it is described as one of several other meditations, also termed 'perceptions' (*saññā*), such as perception of the foul, impermanence and death (see A III 82). It is also described as one of ten ideas (*dhammā*) leading to the deathless (see A V 105).

As this meditation is described in the commentaries – our only early textual sources for its practice – it is not pursued while eating but is a *samatha* practice to be undertaken as a sitting meditation. According to Buddhaghosa, it leads to access concentration, not *jhāna*. Edible food, he recommends, should be considered in a tenfold aspect.[3] This involves going to a secluded place and bringing to mind all the difficulties and undesirable properties of the search for food and its consumption: there are risks of death and struggle involved in its pursuit; food soon goes stale or becomes putrefied and maggot-ridden if it remains uneaten; when it is eaten and chewed it loses its beauty and becomes disgusting; while it is being digested it is mashed up in the body; it then sustains not only each part of the body but any parasites that happen to be living in the body; finally it is turned into excretion before being expelled. As Upatissa says, 'impure urine and excrement are due to drink and food' (PF 206).

We do not know if this is exactly how the practice was conducted at the time of the Buddha. I understand from monks with whom I have discussed this subject that some variation on this exercise is often undertaken while monks are eating, to prevent the enjoyment of food from engulfing the senses. It is rarely recommended to lay people. In the canon, it is never given without other meditations. It is striking in that like the meditation on the foulness of dead bodies, it violates all sorts of little social taboos, and in loosening attachments to the sense-sphere explores a subject we usually consider a little unwholesome to examine in too much detail: children are much more willing to consider the whole process of digestion than adults are, and indeed like to joke about it. For the meditator this is not a bad thing to bear in mind: the whole process can exercise considerable power over mental state during an extended period of meditation. The *vipassanā* teacher, Sayadaw U Pandita, comments:

> Food can be one of the most difficult areas of meditators, especially on retreat. Leaving aside the whole problems of greed, yogis often feel strong disgust toward food...alternatively, when yogis experience strong rapture, this rapture becomes a nourishment for their minds, such that they entirely lose their appetite. Both of these types of yogis should try to overcome their initial reactions and make a concerted effort to eat sufficient food to maintain their energy. When the body is deprived of physical nutriment it loses strength and stamina, and eventually this undermines the meditation practice.
>
> (Sayadaw U Pandita 1992: 115)

It is perhaps hardly surprising that more commonly attention to moderation in eating is recommended in the texts, as in the *Sāmaññaphala sutta* (D I 71 and 69).[4] Often the monk is enjoined to eat not for amusement or adornment, but enough to sustain the body and aid his practice, thinking, 'In this way I shall destroy any old feeling without producing new feeling. I shall be healthy, without blame and live in comfort' (M I 273).[5] In the *Vatthūpama-Sutta* the monk trained in virtue (*sīla*), *dhamma* and wisdom (*paññā*) is said to be able to eat even the finest almsfood without it being a stumbling block (see M 1 38). Moderation in eating is said to be one of the ways to live in happiness (It 23–4). The *Vinaya* rules for monks advise ways of eating that require some relinquishment of greed: while the *Vinaya* is concerned with behaviour rather than inner state, the seventy-five *sekhiya* injunctions to eat with good manners, without gobbling or chomping, with appreciation and so on, require, as do many *Vinaya* rules, considerable alertness and a lack of overwhelming desire if they are to be put into practice.[6] Many monks I have spoken to regard these, like the fulfilment of other *Vinaya* rulings regarding simple bodily activities such as washing the bowl and even wearing their robes, as like meditation practices in themselves, needing mindfulness, energy and confidence to get right.[7] It is not commonly observed that rules about the consumption of food, along with the almsround and the daily ritual of receiving *dāna*, also ensure that monks take care of their body properly, do not lose contact with other people, and eat without rushing. For the *saṅgha* the way food is often eaten in company, under conditions of great good humour and generosity, would be an important element in the background for any meditation practice undertaken.[8]

In some ways, early Buddhism had its origins in a revolutionary attitude towards food, in that the Buddha, unlike many other seekers of wisdom at the time, denied that depriving the body of nourishment could aid enlightenment.

He did not recommend fasting and stressed the importance of the middle way in the consumption of food. While the practice suggested here may suit a monastic context, for the laity moderation is recommended. I was at a meal given to a monk who paused after the food had been offered, looked at all the variety of dishes and said before starting his meal: 'Let's see if we can eat together, enjoy the taste in each mouthful of the meal and not allow the arising of greed'.[9]

> *Seven perceptions*
> These seven perceptions, monks, to be cultivated and made much of are of great fruit, great reward, leading to the deathless and having their conclusion in the deathless.
>
> What seven?
>
> The perception of the foul, the perception of death, the perception of loathsomeness in food, the perception of disaffection for the world,[10] the perception of suffering in impermanence, the perception of not-self in suffering.
>
> When a monk, monks, often spends his time with the perception of the foul collected[11] around the mind, the mind draws back, bends back, turns back from sexual intercourse and does not stretch out towards it; and either equanimity or reluctance[12] are established. Just as a cock's feather or piece of gristle, thrown on the fire, draws back, bends back, turns back and does not stretch out towards the fire; even so, when a monk often spends his time with the perception of the foul collected around the mind, the mind draws back, bends back, turns back from sexual intercourse and does not stretch out towards it; and either equanimity or reluctance are established.
>
> If a monk, monks, often spends his time with the perception of the foul collected around the mind, and his mind flows towards sexual intercourse, and very little reluctance is established, the monk should understand, 'I have not cultivated the perception of foulness; I have not attained the successive stages of distinction; I have not won the fruit of my meditation.' So he has clear comprehension about the situation. And if a monk often spends his time with the perception of the foul collected around the mind, and the mind does draw back, bend back, turn back from sexual intercourse, and does not stretch out towards it, and either equanimity or reluctance are established, then the monk should understand, 'I have cultivated the perception of foul; I have attained the successive stages of distinction; I have won the fruit of my meditation'. It is for this reason it is said, 'The perception of the foul, cultivated and made much of, is of great fruit, great reward, leading to the deathless and having its conclusion in the deathless'.
>
> When a monk, monks, often spends his time with the perception of death…the perception of loathsomeness in food…the perception of

disaffection for the world... the perception of suffering in impermanence... the perception of not-self in suffering... the mind draws back, bends back, turns back [so for each].... It is for this reason it is said, 'The perception of death... the perception of loathsomeness in food... the perception of disaffection for the world... the perception of suffering in impermanence... the perception of not-self in suffering, cultivated and made much of, is of great fruit, great reward, leading to the deathless and having its conclusion in the deathless'.

These seven perceptions, monks, cultivated and made much of, are of great fruit, great reward, lead to the deathless and have their conclusion in the deathless.

(A IV 46)

40. The defining of the four elements (*Catudhātuvavatthānam/ekaṃ vavatthānaṃ*)

It is a pleasing aspect of the Buddhaghosa list of meditation subjects that his list of meditation subjects concludes with a practice which revisits the first four *kammaṭṭhānas*, from an entirely different perspective: their presence together in a human body (see Vism XI 27–117).[13] The *kasiṇa* practice had introduced each of the four elements through an external object as a starting point. Here, the meditator examines the four elements as they are manifest in his own physical experience: it is the only *kammaṭṭhāna* that includes a group of specifically differentiated objects in one practice. Vajirañāṇa notes 'whatever is solid or hard is the earth element, whatever is cohesive or fluid is the water element, whatever causes maturity or is warm is the fire element, whatever is buoyant or moving is the air–element' (BMTP 319). Earth is known through the experience of the 'hard' parts of the body: hairs of the head, hairs of the body, nails, teeth, skin, flesh, sinews, bones, bone marrow, kidneys, heart, liver, diaphragm, spleen, lungs, large intestines, small intestines, stomach, excrement or, 'or whatever else belonging to oneself, that one appropriates to oneself, that is earth, earthy'.[14] Water is known by the 'wet' parts of the body: bile, phlegm, pus, blood, sweat, fat, tears, grease, saliva, mucus, oil in the joints, and urine. Heat or fire is known through warmth: it is said to be perceived when the body is excited by a fever, or when a man feels burning that makes him crave cooling ointments and the breeze of a fan. The maturing of various processes such as digestion and even ageing is regarded as a property of fire or heat. Air is explored as movement in the body, conceptualized as 'breaths'. These winds, thought to circulate throughout the physical body, include the breath, but also more subtle breaths, which according to ancient thought were seen as operating alongside and in association with the breath itself.[15] A fifth element is sometimes considered with the element of space. In terms of the body itself this element is discerned in the cavities and gaps in the physical structure, like the opening within the jaw, for instance, or the cavities in the throat and bowels.[16]

The four elements

These are, however, manifestations of the elements: what are the four elements themselves? The *Mūlapariyāya-Sutta*, which, as the opening text for the *Majjhimanikāya* may be regarded as particularly significant, opens with the assertion that the Buddha is distinguished by his knowledge of the earth element as earth, the water element as water, the fire element as fire and the air element as air, and the fact that he regards none of them as 'mine' (M I 1). There is something very simple about seeing the body in this way: from the point of view of the meditation, things which are hard and resist the sense of touch are considered earth; that which coheres and binds things together is regarded as the element of water; that which is warm is the element of heat or fire, and that which is perceived as moving, like wind or the breath, is the element of air. As a way of describing experience, however, it may seem strange to the modern mind, so it is helpful here to give some explanation of the important position the four elements occupy in ancient Indian thought, and what that would have meant in practice. For the ancient Indian of any tradition the four elements, the great primaries (*mahābhutāni*) as they are called, are the basic constituents of all matter. Our bodies come from the four elements and are what they return to at death: to this day when ashes are scattered in the river Ganges the body is said to be returning to the four elements. According to a late *Upaniṣadic* view, the four elements, along with space, make up *ātman* as well.[17] Poṭṭhapāda, in the *sutta* of the same name, proposes one view, not a Buddhist one, which was presumably current at the time: 'I go back, sir, to the idea of a self, having form, composed of the four elements, nourished by solid food' (D I 186).

From the Buddhist point of view, the four elements are not considered self, and, according to both Buddhaghosa and Upatissa, the effect of practice upon them frees the mind from a sense of an individual being (see Vism XI 30 and PF 204). A standard description of form is that it is 'the four great elements and whatever is secondary to, or derived from, those four elements' (S III 53). As Sue Hamilton points out, their presence is considered so interwoven with any kind of experience in the sense sphere that enlightenment is defined as the condition where there is no earth, water, fire nor air.[18]

How it is practised

Much of this practice, called also by Buddhaghosa 'the one defining (*ekaṃ vavatthānaṃ*)', has fallen under the category of body mindfulness and in the *Satipaṭṭhāna-Sutta* the description of the four elements is placed next to this practice of the thirty-one parts of the body. According to the canon, the practice is conducted by becoming aware of the properties of each element in turn, thus loosening attachment to the body as a whole. Indeed Buddhaghosa claims that if one has quick understanding one just needs to follow the instructions provided in the *Satipaṭṭhāna-Sutta* (M I 57–8). For those of less quick understanding, he recommends three other *suttas*.[19] It is, he says, just like someone who is not so good at chanting: he needs to go over each section in detail, with repetitions (see Vism XI 39–44). All these further *suttas*, one of which is included later, specify which part of the body is associated with each element, as has been described: earth for bones, water for phlegm etc.

As with so many meditations described in the canon, context is crucial. Each of the *suttas* recommended by Buddhaghosa employs the same formula and recommends that the meditator consider, 'this is not mine, this am I not, this not my self' for each. How the formula is exploited in each however varies considerably, weighting the texts in quite different directions. The *Dhātuvibhaṅga-Sutta*, after the standard description of four elements, describes the element of space and then a sixth, that of consciousness, in order to examine that element further. The *Mahāhatthipadopamā-Sutta*, delivered by Sāriputta, stresses the calamities that occur when one element becomes excessive or deficient – in droughts or floods, for instance. The fragility of the balance of the elements in the outside world – and hence in ourselves – is thrown into stark relief: a suitable use of the pericope in a text delivered by the master of insight, stressing the aspect of impermanence and the second noble truth of craving.[20] The *sutta* reproduced later, to Rāhula, gives an altogether different slant: the elements are shown in a benign aspect as emotional qualities to be cultivated, rather than feared. This text is also intended to remove attachment to the body.

Buddhaghosa assigns this practice for the intelligence type (see Vism III 121). Upatissa also recommends it for this type, or the deluded type with some wisdom (See PF 69). Although, like Buddhaghosa, he says that it leads only to access meditation, he calls it 'the speciality of wisdom, because of its connection with the void' (PF 68).[21] Indeed in his description of the practice he concludes with an element of insight and the famous image of the puppet that laughs, cries, moves its body and is sustained by food: this is the being that arises on the basis of the four elements. When the suffering of such beings, who are kept alive by the life faculty, is considered the meditator attains 'to the element of the most excellent' (PF 205).

So why are the four or five elements being taught together under one practice? All of the other meditation objects are single, discrete entities or principles: one element, one colour or the recollection of one quality such as virtue. Even in the case of collective objects, such as in the recollection of the *saṅgha*, or the divine abidings, which take beings in all directions as their field, one category is examined which might have manifold or even infinite aspects, such as all individual beings, but is itself defined by a single unifying principle: all beings that are sentient, or all those who have experienced path. For this practice the one unifying principle is provided by the perception of the presence in one body of the elements discerned. It has to be performed on a human body, which is live – for the element of heat to be strong enough – and that is one's own.[22] It is a suitable way for Buddhaghosa to complete his list.

The greater discourse to Rāhula

This text is recommended by Buddhaghosa for the practice on the elements. It was given to the Buddha's son, Rāhula, who was born on the night Gotama left his palace for the going forth.[23] When the Buddha visited Kapilavatthu for the first time after the enlightenment, the *Vinaya* says that Rāhula, then aged seven, was sent to ask for his inheritance from the Buddha: he was accepted by his father into the order (Vin I 82). Rāhula was known for his obedience, which, according to the *Jātakas*, was an attribute that he had exhibited in earlier lifetimes: in many of these, he had also been the son of the Bodhisatta.[24] He was also very eager to train and is described by the Buddha as being foremost in this quality (see A I 24). He was, however, infatuated with his own beautiful appearance, and it was because of this that the Buddha taught this particular *sutta*.[25] Rāhula is said to have become an arahat after hearing another discourse, the *Cūḷarāhulovāda-Sutta* (M III 277–80).

The incident that prompts the teaching shows the filial Rāhula wishing to follow his father on the almsround. After being addressed by the Buddha, he decides to sit in meditation instead and is encouraged by Sāriputta to develop breathing mindfulness. When Rāhula questions the Buddha on this practice, however, the Buddha apparently ignores the question and teaches not only four but five elements, the immeasurables (31–4), meditation on the foul (11–20) and impermanence and, only at the end of the discourse, breathing mindfulness. No comment is made in the text itself on Sāriputta's advice: the commentary suggests that Sāriputta assumed that was what Rāhula was or should be practising.[26] At any rate, the Buddha clearly felt some other supplementary practices were needed before Rāhula moves on to the practice of breathing mindfulness.

In this *sutta* the five elements are considered in two aspects: first they act as a means of arousing non-attachment, so that when each is known it is to be perceived as not self. In this way, it employs the same basic description found in the other *suttas* recommended by Buddhaghosa in this section. Another dimension is added by the second method, however, in which they are to be seen as exemplars of positive qualities that can be cultivated in dealings with contacts (*phassā*). Rāhula should 'develop meditation that is like the earth'.[27] The formula is reapplied for each of the elements, including, notably that of space. The sustaining and self-replenishing power of the elements, when emulated in the sphere of the emotions, allow operation in the sense sphere freed from partiality. Through this use of the elements as straightforward similes for corresponding attributes the external world is perceived as a mirror for our own meditative possibilities and ability to withstand difficulty. There is a *samatha* 'feel' to the reassuring strength of each as described to Rāhula, which gives a gentler interpretation to the practice than that of the *Mahāhatthipadopama-Sutta*, which seems calculated to arouse some terror in its awesome depiction of each element out of balance.[28] From here the movement into other practices appears seamless, leading finally to breathing mindfulness (29), the object of Rāhula's question: other original features of the text are its statement of the opposite quality to each *brahmavihāra* (31–4), which each suppresses, and the recommendation that breathing mindfulness can be practised at the moment of death.

These new details, peculiar to this *sutta*, and the way the pericopes are worked into them suggest the text was tailor-made for the individual concerned. Sāriputta may have felt Rāhula only needed breathing mindfulness; the Buddha, not disagreeing, sees however the need for other meditations as preparation for this. Buddhaghosa cites it as a text in which a number of meditations are given to one person, thereby making the crucial point that one temperament may need to work on a number of problems through a range of different meditation subjects, carefully selected for him (see Vism III 122). The Buddha was not partial when teaching his own son. The *Cuḷarāhulovāda-Sutta*, with its brief exposition of the relationship between the mind, the senses and corresponding sense base, employs a far more technical vocabulary and is decidedly weighted towards the development of wisdom (M I 277–80). On the basis of this, Rāhula, ready for such a finely detailed and thorough analysis, attains enlightenment: this is shortly after his full ordination, presumably at the age of twenty.

> Mahārahulovāda-Sutta
> Thus have I heard. On one occasion the Exalted One was staying at Sāvatthī at Jetavana, Anāthapiṇḍika's grove. Then, when it was morning, the Exalted One dressed, took his bowl and outer robe and went to Sāvatthī for alms. The Venerable Rāhula also dressed, took his bowl and robe and followed the Exalted One close behind.
>
> Then the Exalted One looked over his shoulder and addressed the Venerable Rāhula. 'Rāhula, whatever kind of material form, whether past, future or present, within or without, gross or subtle, inferior or superior, far or near: all material form should be seen with right wisdom just as it is: "This is not mine, I am not this, this is not my self".'
>
> 'Do you mean just material form? Just material form, Exalted One?'
>
> 'Material form, Rāhula, and, in addition, feeling, perception, formations and consciousness.'
>
> Then Rāhula reflected in this way. 'Who would go into town today to collect alms after receiving an admonishment from the Exalted One?' He turned back and sat at the roots of a tree, crossed his legs, made his body straight and established mindfulness in front of him. The Venerable Sāriputta saw him sitting there and addressed him in this way: 'Cultivate mindfulness of breathing, Rāhula. When mindfulness of breathing is cultivated and made much of, it is of great fruit and great reward'.
>
> Then, when it was evening, Rāhula rose from his meditation and went to the Exalted One. He paid homage to him, sat down to one side and asked the Exalted One: 'Sir, how is mindfulness of breathing cultivated and made much of, so that it is of great fruit and great reward?'

'Whatever, Rāhula, is internal, belonging to oneself, that one appropriates to oneself, that is earth, earthy: that is, hairs of the head, hairs on the body, nails, teeth, skin, flesh, sinews, bones, bone–marrow, kidneys, heart, liver, diaphragm, spleen, lungs, large intestines, small intestines, the contents of the stomach, excrement, or whatever else belonging to oneself, that one appropriates to oneself, that is earth, earthy: this is called the internal element of earth. Indeed both the internal and the external earth element are just that: earth. And this should be seen just as it is, with right wisdom: "This is not mine, I am not this, this is not my self". When one sees it just as it is, with right wisdom, one turns away from the element of earth and the mind is freed from the element of earth.

What, Rāhula, is the element of water? The water element may be internal or it may be external. What is the internal water element? Whatever there is that is water, or watery, belonging to oneself, that one appropriates to oneself, such as bile, phlegm, pus, blood, sweat, fat, tears, grease, saliva, mucus, oil in the joints or urine, or anything else that is water, or watery, belonging to oneself, that one appropriates to oneself: this is called, Rāhula, the internal element of water . . . and the mind is freed from the element of water.

What, Rāhula, is the element of fire? The element of fire may be internal or external. Whatever there is that is fire, or fiery, belonging to oneself, that one appropriates to oneself, such as the means by which one is warmed, the means by which one ages, the means by which one is consumed and the means by which what has been enjoyed, drunk, eaten and tasted is completely digested, or anything else that is fire, or fiery, belonging to oneself, that one appropriates to oneself: this is called, Rāhula, the internal element of fire . . . and the mind is freed from the element of fire.

What, Rāhula, is the element of air? The element of air may be internal or external. Whatever there is that is air, or airy, belonging to oneself, that one appropriates to oneself, such as winds going up, winds going down, winds in the belly, winds in the bowels, winds that flow through the limbs, or anything else that is air, or airy, belonging to oneself, that one appropriates to oneself: this is called, Rāhula, the internal element of air . . . and the mind is freed from the element of air.

What, Rāhula, is the element of space? The element of space may be internal or external. Whatever there is that is space, or spacious, belonging to oneself, that one appropriates to oneself, such as the cavities in the ears, the nostrils, the door of the mouth, the means by which what is enjoyed, drunk, eaten and tasted is swallowed, the place where what is enjoyed, drunk, eaten and tasted collects and the place from where it is excreted in the lower part of the body, or anything else that is space, or spacious, belonging to oneself, that one appropriates to oneself: this is called the internal element of space . . . and the mind is freed from the element of space.

Cultivate the meditation that is like the earth, Rāhula. Cultivating the meditation that is like the earth, Rāhula, contacts that have arisen that are pleasant and unpleasant will not take hold of the mind and remain. Just as people cast down what is clean and unclean, excrement, urine, saliva, pus and blood on the earth, and the earth is not distressed, ashamed and disgusted because of that, even so, cultivate the meditation that is like the earth, for when you cultivate the meditation that is like the earth, contacts which have arisen that are pleasant and unpleasant will not take hold of the mind and remain.

Cultivate the meditation that is like water, Rāhula. Cultivating the meditation that is like the water, contacts that have arisen that are pleasant and unpleasant will not take hold of the mind and remain. Just as, Rāhula, people wash what is clean and unclean, excrement, urine, saliva, pus and blood in water, and the water is not distressed, ashamed and disgusted because of that, even so, cultivate the meditation that is like water...

Cultivate the meditation that is like fire, Rāhula. Cultivating the meditation that is like fire, Rāhula, contacts that have arisen that are pleasant and unpleasant will not take hold of the mind and remain. Just as people burn what is clean and unclean, excrement, urine, saliva, pus and blood in fire, and the fire is not distressed, ashamed and disgusted because of that, even so, cultivate the meditation that is like fire...

Cultivate the meditation that is like air, Rāhula. Cultivating the meditation that is like air, Rāhula, contacts that have arisen that are pleasant and unpleasant will not take hold of the mind and remain. Just as air blows on what is clean and unclean, excrement, urine, saliva, pus and blood in fire, and the air is not distressed, ashamed and disgusted because of that, even so, cultivate the meditation that is like air...

Cultivate the meditation that is like space, Rāhula. Cultivating the meditation that is like space, Rāhula, contacts that have arisen that are pleasant and unpleasant will not take hold of the mind and remain. Just as space is not fixed anywhere, even so, cultivate the meditation that is like space, for when you cultivate the meditation that is like space, contacts which have arisen that are pleasant and unpleasant will not take hold of the mind and remain.

Cultivate the meditation on loving-kindness. When you cultivate the meditation on loving-kindness, any ill-will (*vyāpāda*)is abandoned.

Develop the meditation on compassion; when you cultivate the meditation on compassion, any cruelty (*vihesā*) will be abandoned.

Develop the meditation on sympathetic joy; when you cultivate the meditation on sympathetic joy, discontent (*arati*) will be abandoned.

Develop the meditation on equanimity; when you cultivate the meditation on equanimity, any aversion (*paṭigha*) will be abandoned.

Develop the meditation on foulness; when you develop the meditation on foulness, desire (*rāga*) will be abandoned.

Develop the meditation on the perception of impermanence; when you develop the meditation on the perception of impermanence, the conceit "I am" will be abandoned.

Develop the meditation on mindfulness of breathing, Rāhula. When mindfulness of breathing is cultivated and made much of, it is of great fruit and great reward. How is this breathing mindfulness, of great fruit and great reward, cultivated and made much of? Here, a monk goes to a wilderness . . . [as for breathing mindfulness (29)] . . .

In this way, mindfulness of breathing, when cultivated and made much of, is of great fruit and great reward. When, Rāhula, mindfulness of breathing is cultivated and made much of in this way, then those which are the final in-breaths and out-breaths, when they cease, are known and are not unknown.'

Thus spoke the Exalted One. Delighted, the Venerable Rāhula rejoiced in what the Exalted One had said.

(M I 420–6)

CONCLUSION

As the texts here indicate, meditation is taught by the Buddha as a kind of craft or skill. This is demonstrated both in his great love of similes derived from work in gold, ivory, wood, clay and even cooking and in the range of his teaching methods and approaches for different audiences. And just as a good cook has to relinquish his work, so the meditator's work is incomplete without the element of insight, the discernment of the marks of impermanence (*anicca*), suffering (*dukkha*) and not-self (*anattā*), found in all conditioned phenomena. Neither insight nor calm can be complete without work on virtue, both as a preparation for meditation and for a return to the world, where their effects can help others. The eightfold path is a teaching from which it is difficult to extract any one element without involving the others. The *Mahāsakuludāyi-Sutta* and the *Sāmaññaphala-Sutta* , for instance, include teachings that start with virtue and culminate in insight, the natural pattern of many canonical *suttas*. Both Buddhaghosa and Upatissa place the practice of *bhāvanā*, as it is represented by the various objects, between large sections on virtue and even larger sections on the cultivation of wisdom. The implications of this interconnectedness are profound: the notion that how we behave affects how we are and that, in turn, affects how we think, and that this process works the other way too, impresses the importance of each factor in the eightfold path.

A stress on the needs of the practitioner is found in many texts. In some, such as those concerning the six recollections (21–6), the teaching given rests primarily on an interplay between the practice of *sīla* and *samatha*, a relationship little discussed in modern times: the recollection of *sīla*, generosity and *devas* all require some prior virtue and generosity to be conducted in the first place. The commentaries say that the recollections are not developed to *jhāna*, though the Buddha stresses rather the potential of these practices (see A I 30). They appear, in modern terms, as an emotional reinforcement of the psychological effects of giving and restraint: as for other meditations, such acts 'made much of' (*bahulīkata*) and, appreciated, bring contentment.[1] This deepening of *sīla* into *samādhi* seems to have been particularly aimed at the laity: it is interesting that, in contrast to the advice given by some modern commentators, the Buddha often suggests calm, not insight, to busy people.

From the other end of the spectrum, many texts have included an element of insight, either as the culmination of other practices or as an underlying theme. The *Satipaṭṭhāna-Sutta*, taken as the principal text by many *vipassanā* schools, provides, in its stress upon mindfulness and clear comprehension at all times, an enactment of the principles it describes. It is difficult to read this text without feeling the dynamic movement of all the three signs of *anicca*, *dukkha* and *anattā* in the process of observing the rise and fall of each event, or *dhamma*, described. The five hindrances, listed under the fourth foundation, are treated not only as obstructions to *samatha* practice but to insight too. They are said to make 'the mind neither soft, nor manageable, nor shining, but brittle and not properly prepared for the elimination of the corruptions' (S V 92). The practitioner who overcomes the hindrances, 'with strong wisdom... will be able to experience for himself the excellence of the noble knowledge and vision that surpasses that of men: this has to be so' (A III 62). Arahatship is sometimes defined by the absence of the five hindrances, which are said then to be cut off, at the root, like palm stumps (S V 327).

Where other meditation instructions are given, single approaches to insight are often recommended. Rāhula and Meghiya, after receiving their various meditation objects, are instructed to be aware of impermanence, 'for the removal of the conceit "I am" '. As Meghiya is told, 'in one who perceives impermanence, the perception of not-self becomes established. And the one who perceives not-self attains the removal of the conceit "I am" and finds *nibbāna* in this very life.' (Ud 37). At the end of a discourse on overcoming sleepiness, the Buddha addresses first the symptoms Moggallāna presents and then the cause: Moggallāna should attend to the statement 'It is not fitting that things in the world should be attached to.' Then he will know each state, see its impermanence and will attain *nibbāna*. Tissa is roused from sloth and torpor by an appeal to insight, in the rigorous questioning that enables him to see impermanence and suffering in each of the *khandhas* of material form, feeling, perception, formations and consciousness (S III 106–9).

Adaptability is evident in the way some objects are taught with a varied emphasis on calm or insight. Kulla, who takes the foul as a meditation object (11–20), loses his delight in 'the five kinds of musical instruments', the senses, and, attaining knowledge and vision, becomes or already is one-pointed, when, an arahat, he 'sees things truly' (Th 393–8). Kappa, who also conducts this practice, is told that those who follow it 'will become cooled, without corruptions' (Th 567–76). The meditation on death (27) is taught as arousing both calm and insight: 'We live carefully and are alert as we practise mindfulness of death, in order to destroy the corruptions' (A III 303). In some *suttas* the balance between calm (*samatha*) and insight (*vipassanā*) is explicitly poised. Breathing mindfulness (29) leads to and develops the seven factors of enlightenment, that both characterize and awaken the enlightened mind: 'When the seven factors of enlightenment are cultivated in this way, monks, when they are made much of, they fulfil knowledge and deliverance' (M III 88). The *Satipaṭṭhāna-Sutta*, primarily intended to arouse mindfulness and clear comprehension, includes many elements usually or often treated as *samatha* objects: the breath (29), meditation on the parts of the body (28), the four elements (40) and the stages of bodily decomposition (11–20).

The extent to which *vipassanā* alone or with *samatha* is considered by the Buddha as a means to enlightenment is a vast subject and cannot be discussed here.[2] There is, to this day, a great variety of approach between different methods. In many texts, however, considerable flexibility and movement between *samatha* and *vipassanā* are evident when they are taught in practice. I can find no grounds to suggest that the Buddha intended either to be underplayed or negated: each in its own time.[3] The practice of mindfulness is constantly enjoined for both, as is that of *sīla*. The *Rathavinīta Sutta*, often taken as one of the principle texts on insight, describes seven stages of purification, which are compared to chariots in a relay race, with only one left behind as the next one is employed. The eightfold path constitutes the basis of the list: the first is the purification of virtue (*sīlavisuddhi*), the second the purification of mind (*cittavisuddhi*).[4]

A sense of careful applicability is communicated by the Buddha's teaching methods. He addressed what he was saying to his audience, a tendency reflected in the various genres and methods he employs. In teaching querents as varied as Mahānāma, Visākhā, Kulla, Kappa, Vijitasena and Meghiya he employs a variety of imagery and method directed specifically to that person's occupation, temperament and level of attainment. The fact that meditation objects are occasionally taught with an unusual slant that appears only once in the texts reinforces this impression: the *Mahārāhulovāda-Sutta* contains a number of such particularities.[5] Varied groups or clusters of meditation objects are given on different occasions. Some texts are directed to a larger audience, already experienced in meditation. The comprehensiveness of the teaching the *Ānāpānasati-Sutta* and, according to the commentaries, the *Satipaṭṭhāna-Sutta*, is a reflection of assemblies that have practised diligently beforehand. It is not, however, only experienced meditators who are the recipients of the major discourses. The teaching given in the *Sāmaññaphala-Sutta*, the most significant account of the benefits of meditation, is prompted by a question asked by a layman.

Within this discussion the *Abhidhamma* is a special case. As a teaching vehicle, it seems to have been intended to loosen rigidity of view and develop insight into not-self.[6] A sense of fluidity and manifold possibility in the application of the eightfold path, however, may also be seen in the *Dhammasaṅgaṇi*, extracts from which have been included in this anthology. Its method of describing consciousness as it develops through stages of skilfulness in daily life, to *jhāna*, to path does not distance the goal from everyday consciousness. On the contrary, the first spontaneous skilful consciousness accompanied by knowledge and joy, the basis of much human rebirth and a possibility for anyone, includes path factors such as right view and right resolve at the outset, which are deepened for the attainment of *jhāna*.

The first moment of path, stream-entry, always *lokuttara jhāna*, is described as an enrichment, perfection and coming together of factors that may arise in any moment of *kusala* consciousness accompanied by wisdom. With the first penetration of the four noble truths, all path factors, which usually appear only single or several in daily life and meditation, come to fruition, with the fulfilment of *sīla*, *samādhi* and *paññā*. One extra *cetasika*, peculiar to the first moment of path, is added: 'I shall come to know the unknown' (*anaññātaññassāmītindriyam*: DhS 277, 296). At the second path, the first two hindrances, sense desire and ill will, are diminished and another *cetasika* added: 'the knowledge that is made perfect' (*aññindriyaṃ*); at the third path, the first two hindrances are abandoned. At the fourth path, the moment of enlightenment, all passion for form and the formless, and all conceit, restlessness and ignorance are abandoned: the mind is liberated.

This is a technical way of describing the process of awakening, but highly effective. Skilful *citta*, with its innate predisposition to the path and the factors associated with it, is perceived as in itself a glimpse of the way through the jungle thicket, to pursue the analogy for the eightfold path that the Buddha gives to Tissa. It describes the human mind, working at its best, as in itself healthy and 'good' but needing training and skill to realize its full potential. Awakening occurs when all path factors, with the two extra to form a tenfold path, work together: in meditation or daily life skilful consciousness gives glimpses of path, but there may still be foliage or branches that prevent a complete view of the 'delightful stretch of ground', *nibbāna*. This only becomes clear at stream-entry, a moment of *jhāna*, where *sīla*, *samādhi* and *paññā* at last operate in unison. The texts suggest many possible combinations of *sīla*, *samādhi* and *paññā* to reach this point. My conclusion, based on texts used here, is that the practice of virtue keeps meditation and insight true, that calmness allows virtue and wisdom to rest sometimes in happiness and that wisdom ensures that *sīla* and *samādhi* recognize things 'as they really are'.

An anthology can only give samples of kinds of texts. It is noteworthy, however, that some describe people learning from and becoming enlightened from teachings given by those taught by the Buddha. The *Ānāpānasati-Sutta* opens on a scene of monks successfully teaching younger and newer monks. Some who become arahats, such as Uttamā, are taught not by the Buddha but by someone taught by him (Thī 43). The help provided by the commentaries and the manuals of Buddhaghosa and Upatissa is a further illustration of the health of the tradition in the years after his death. Their objective in sustaining a tradition colours their approach: their manuals, for instance, place set limits on the possibilities of different meditation practices; the Buddha, teaching the meditations afresh, stresses rather the worth and potential of each (see A I 10, A I 38–42, A IV 147–8 *et al.*). The manuals supply us, however, with much information about technique and method that the canon does not.

These are varied points about the way the Buddha taught meditation. Human beings, composed of the five *khandhas* as they are, exhibit many different temperaments, needs and imperfections. The compassion of the Buddha is enacted through the scrupulous care with which he teaches various aspects of the eightfold path according to the needs he finds. He seems to have wanted meditation to be taught as a living tradition, passed on from one person to the next. As some of the modern texts quoted in the anthology have shown, meditation is taught now on many of the same principles as it was over two thousand years ago. Applicability, roundedness, flexibility, friendship and a stress on the present moment as the best and only time for awareness (A III 303): these are small but significant conclusions to draw from the Buddha's teaching on meditation.

GLOSSARY

Sequence of Pāli letters: a ā ı ī u ū e o k kh g gh c ch j jh ñ ṭh t th d dh n p ph b bh m y r l v s h

Akusala	unskilful, bad, unwholesome
Adhiṭṭhānavasī	mastery of remaining (third mastery)
Anattā	not-self
Anicca	impermanence
Anussati	recollection, remembrance (21–30)
Abhijjhā	longing, sense desire (first hindrance)
Abhiññā	higher knowledge
Abhidhamma	further *dhamma*, teaching; generic term for one of three 'baskets' of the teaching
Abhibhāyatana	sphere of transcendence
Appamāṇa	immeasurable (31–4)
Arūpa	formless
Arūpajhāna	formless *jhāna* (35–8)
Asubha	foul (11–20)
Ākāsānañcāyatana	sphere of boundless space (35)
Ākiñcaññāyatana	sphere of nothingness (37)
Āghāta	hatred, ill-will
Ānāpānasati	mindfulness of breathing (29)
Āneñja	imperturbable
Āyatana	sphere, base
Āvajjanavasī	mastery in adverting (first mastery)
Āsava	corruption
Āhāre paṭikūlasaññā	perception of loathsomeness in food (39)
Iddhi	fruit of success, psychic power
Indriya	faculty: of senses, or of mind
Uggahanimitta	learning sign, acquired mental image
Udāna	inspired utterance
Uddhacca-kukkucca	restlessness and worry (fourth hindrance)
Upakkiliṭṭha	stained, defiled

Upacāra	access concentration
Upadhi	attachment
Upasamanussati	recollection of peace (30)
Upasampajjati	enter (*jhāna*)
Upekkhā	equanimity (34: fourth divine abiding; seventh factor of enlightenment)
Uposatha	day spent taking extra precepts; full moon or fourteenth/fifteenth day of the month
Ekaggatā	one-pointedness (fifth *jhāna* factor)
Ekantanibbida	complete turning away
Ekodibhāva	unification
Kammaṭṭhāna	object for meditation
Kalyāṇa	good, beautiful
Kasiṇa	meditation device (1–10)
Kāmacchanda	sense desire (first hindrance)
Kāya	body
Kāyagatāsati	mindfulness of body (28)
Kāruṇā	compassion (32)
Kusala	skilful, healthy, good
Catudhātuvavatthāna	defining of the four elements (40)
Cāga	generosity, giving up
Cāgānussati	recollection of generosity (25)
Citta	mind, consciousness, heart
Cetasika	mental state
Cetovimutti	liberation, deliverance of mind
Ñāṇa	knowledge
Tathāgata	'Thus-Gone', epithet of Buddha
Thīnamiddha	sloth and torpor (third hindrance)
Dukkha	suffering, dis-ease
Deva	shining one, sense-sphere god
Devatānussati	recollection of *devas* (26)
Du(g)gati	unhappy destiny
Dhamma	see earlier
Dhammavicaya	investigation of *dhammas* (states), or *dhamma* (teaching). Second factor of enlightenment
Nibbāna	putting out, enlightenment
Nibbindati	turns away from
Nimitta	mental image
Nirodha	cessation
Nīvaraṇa	hindrance
Nevasaññānāsaññāyatana	sphere of neither perception nor non-perception (38)
Paccavekkhaṇavasī	mastery of reviewing, remembering (fifth mastery)
Paññā	wisdom (fifth faculty)
Paññāvimutti	liberation by wisdom

Paṭinissagga	relinquishment
Paṭibhāganimitta	counterpart sign
Pariyuṭṭhita	obsessed by
Passadhi	tranquillity (fifth factor of enlightenment)
Pātimokkha	monastic code
Pāpaka	harmful, bad
Pīti	joy (third *jhāna* factor, fourth factor of enlightenment)
Bala	power, strength
Bojjhaṅga	factor of enlightenment
Bodhipakkhiyādammā	thirty-seven constituents of enlightenment
Brahmavihāra	divine abiding (31–4)
Bhāvanā	cultivation, practice
Maraṇasati	mindfulness of death (27)
Muditā	sympathetic joy (33)
Mettā	loving-kindness (31)
Yakkha	demon
Yonisa manasikāra	judicious, systematic attention
Rūpa	form
Rūpajhāna	form *jhāna*
Rāga	passion, desire
Lokiya	of the world
Lokuttara	beyond the world; pertaining to enlightenment
Vikkhitta	scattered, distracted
Vicāra	sustained thought, examination (second *jhāna* factor)
Vicikicchā	doubt (fifth hindrance)
Viññāṇa	consciousness
Viññāṇañcāyatana	sphere of infinite consciousness (36)
Vitakka	initial thought (first *jhāna* factor; equated to second path factor in *Dhammasaṅgaṇi*)
Vinaya	discipline, monastic behaviour: generic term for third 'basket' of the teaching
Vipassanā	insight
Vipāka	result, fruit
Vimutti	release, liberation
Vimokkha	deliverance
Virāga	dispassion, fading away
Virājeti	(*virajjati*) free oneself
Viriya	effort, energy (second faculty, third factor of enlightenment)
Viveka	solitude, seclusion
Visuddhi	purification
Vihārati	abide, live, practice (as in *vihāra*, dwelling); used for *jhāna*

Vuṭṭhāna	emerging
Vuṭṭhānavasī	mastery in emerging (fourth mastery)
Vedanā	feeling
Vossagga	relinquishment, letting go
Vyāpādapa-dosa	ill-will (second hindrance)
Saṃyutta	related, connected: name of one of *nikāyas*, collections of *suttas*
Saṅkhārā	formations, volitional activities
Saññā	perception, identification
Sati	mindfulness (third faculty, first factor of enlightenment, seventh path factor)
Satipaṭṭhāna	foundation of mindfulness
Santuṭṭha	content
Saddhā	faith, confidence; first of five faculties
Samatikkama	surmounting
Samatha	calm, happy serenity
Samādhi	concentration (fifth faculty, sixth enlightenment factor)
Samāpatti	attainment, entering
Samāpattivasī	mastery of entering (second mastery)
Sampajañña	clear comprehension (equated with wisdom in *Dhammasaṅgaṇi*)
Sīla	virtue, restraint, behaviour
Sukha	happiness (fourth *jhāna* factor)
Sugati	happy destiny
Sutta	text, generic term for one of three 'baskets' of the teaching
Subha	beauty, beautiful

NOTES

1 INTRODUCTION

1 The *sutta* does not specify the object. The commentary says that he practises mindfulness of breathing (see MA II 291).

2 Bronkhorst 1993: 23. Part I: 1–30 contrasts this system with current ascetic practices, particularly those of Jainism.

3 DhS 7–11, where they are listed under the spontaneous skilful *citta* accompanied by joy. The same factors that characterize this consciousness, which can feature in daily life, are also present in the first *jhāna* when the mind enters absorption (DhS 160).

4 Nai Boonman, president of the Samatha Trust, at the Samatha Centre, Greenstreete, 1995.

5 See Asl 163–4. Dhs 1006–8 says that the three fetters of an idea of self, doubt and belief in vows and precepts are put away by insight; anything remaining is put away by *bhāvanā*. So all unskilful states (*akusalā dhammā*) are put away by insight and *bhāvanā*. See also BMTP 25–7.

6 Skilful *citta* as defined by the *Dhammasaṅgaṇi* is always characterized by one of these four (see DhS 33, 150).

7 Research conducted by the University of Wisconsin-Madison appeared in *New Scientist* in an article by Prof. Flanagan in May 2003 and received widespread publicity in American and British newspapers 22–24 May 2003.

8 I understand this from discussion with members of the Burmese *saṅgha*.

9 See Bapat 1937: 1ff. for thorough discussion of Upatissa's background, his relationship with Buddhaghosa, and the little external evidence on dating found in Dhammapāla.

10 These etymologies are not necessarily philologically 'sound' but the kind of punning word play one finds in a cryptic crossword clue, in which the meanings of words are endlessly examined for chance affinities with others that are apparently unrelated. Puns are treated with far greater respect than in our culture as a means of revealing hidden patterns between apparently unrelated words and their referents. This method is often used in the *Visuddhimagga* as a means of listing and exploring attributes: the recollection of the Buddha (21) is a good example (Vism VII 2).

11 See DhS 160–268. The *anussatis* are a curious omission. Only mindfulness of body (28) and breathing mindfulness (29) were considered to lead to *jhāna* so it is possible that the parts of the body were felt to be covered by the colour meditations (5–8) or the four elements, under which each part is classified (40). Breathing mindfulness could be included under the light *kasiṇa* (9). For a summary of the different lists see BMTP 57–75.

12 CPD I 229–33 translates it as an occupation (Skt *karmasthāna*), a sense in which it is not associated with meditation, or as a subject or cause of meditation (*ṭhāna*).

13 For the ten in canon, see M II 15 and PP 182 n. 5.
14 Upatissa's list goes: ten *kasiṇa*, ten *asubha*, ten recollections, four divine abidings (*brahmavihārā*), the defining of the elements, the perception of the loathsomeness of food, the sphere of nothingness and the sphere of neither perception nor non-perception (PF 63). He appears to exclude the first two formless realms but discusses them under space and consciousness (see PF 128–30 for light and limited space).
15 *Varaṇa Jātaka* (no. 71). The incident occurs in the story from the present, regarded as later than the canonical verses.
16 See M III 241–2. I am not aware of the 'limited space' *kasiṇa* featuring in the canon.
17 The story concerns an ascetic who, to the disgust of his followers, describes on his deathbed his meditational attainment as 'sunlight and moonlight'. He is reborn in the radiant realms (*ābhassara*), gained by those that have attained the third *jhāna* (Ja I 474).
18 See Ud 34–7 and A IV 85, this anthology, 28, 57.
19 See S III 106–9, this anthology 54–6.
20 Both commentators discuss imbalance of the elements as relating to character in a manner suggesting that some system of medicine/humours comparable to that of the Western classical system was operative. See Vism III 80–1 and PF 58.
21 See the opening of both the *Brahmajala-Sutta* (D I 1) and that of the *Sāmaññaphala-Sutta* (D I 47).
22 This compound may be interpreted variously as the good or lovely friend (*karmadhāraya*); the friend of a good man or the friend in what is good or lovely (*tatpurisa*); or the one who has good friends (*bahuvrīhi*). For a full discussion of this word and its use in the canon see Collins 1987: 51–72; see also Tin 1993: 231–48 and BMTP 95–7.
23 A III 316 and this anthology 50–1.
24 See A IV 32 and this anthology 000 for seven qualities described.
25 It says: *lajjī rakkhissati, lajjī rakkhissati*. The word *lajjī* denotes those with consciousness of *hiri* and *ottappa* (PED 580), qualities suggestive of conscientiousness and humility (the Sanskrit root *lajj*, to feel shame, blush: SED 895).
26 'The rule about money' and 'the rule about money transactions' (Norman 1999: 39).
27 'The rule about a superhuman state' (Norman 1999: 10–11).
28 This was told to me by Dr Bodhiprasiddhinand Pathompong.
29 PF 51–3; Vism III 66–73.
30 See for instance Harvey 1990: 307–21.
31 For more on this and the relationship with the *saṅgha* see Gethin 1998: 85–111.
32 D III 180–93. The *sutta* is sometimes known as the householders' *Vinaya* (*gihivinaya*).
33 See S V 151, M I 57 and D I 78, this anthology 81, 72, 52–3.
34 See Gombrich 1971: 280–2.
35 He is described as the foremost *dhamma* teacher in A I 25–6. For an account of his meditative experiences see S IV 301.
36 For story of Citta see DPPN I 865–6. See also A II 164 and A III 451.
37 By my reckoning 41 monks, 13 nuns, 11 lay men and 10 lay women feature in this list (A I 23–6).
38 See Gombrich 1971: 284: 'the comparative rarity of meditation is closely connected with the widespread belief in the decline of Buddhism'.
39 See Harvey 1990: 287–9.
40 Conversation with Ven. Dhammasami. See also Tin 1993: 39–41 and Shattock 1958: 121–38.
41 See M I 382–3 for reference to the 'highest, most excellent seat'.
42 Under the section on guarding the sign (*nimitta*) he gives the seventh way of 'guarding', through posture:

> Walking suits one; standing or sitting or lying down another. So he should try them, like the abode, for three days each, and that posture is suitable in

which his unconcentrated mind becomes concentrated or his concentrated mind more so. Any other should be understood as unsuitable.

(Vism IV 41/ PP 134)

43 The phrase *pallaṅkaṃ ābhujitvā, ujuṃ kāyaṃ paṇidhāya* is part of the standard formula for the practice on breathing mindfulness (M III 82).
44 Nyanaponika discusses variations in posture for the Burmese *satipaṭṭhāna* method (1969: 89–91).
45 The Buddha encourages the practice of the six recollections (21–6) at all times and in all postures. See A V 333ff. and this anthology 133–4.
46 See, for instance, S IV 104. PED 260 gives two meanings for *caṅkam(an)a*: the act of walking and the strip of ground designated for that purpose.
47 A III 29 lists the five advantages of a walking place: it hardens one for travel, encourages effort, is healthy, aids digestion and any concentration obtained from its use is longlasting (see also Hare 1934 (GS III): 21, n. 2).
48 See A IV 84–8.
49 See Ibid.
50 See Shearer 2000: 124–5.
51 See DPPN I 262 and DA I 9ff.
52 See Harappan sealing MD013, on display in the Ashmolean Museum, and comments on n. 1 and n. 52 in (Harle and) Topsfield 1987: 3, 52.
53 For further discussion on the subject of posture and its use in other yogic systems see BMTP: 134–8.
54 Pradhan 1986: 3 1381–5.
55 I am grateful for discussions with Dr Francis Beresford, a long-standing meditator and *samatha* teacher, on medical issues arising from the question of posture. A recent knee injury or bad sciatica can prevent the adoption of the half lotus but otherwise it just takes time to build up flexibility and confidence in sitting in that way.
56 See, for instance, M I 354.
57 For a full discussion of the subject see Cousins 1973: 115–31.
58 See discussion in this anthology 'The Formless Realms', 174–7.
59 See DhS 160–75 and Asl 179–82 for both systems. See also Guneratana 1985: 101–4.
60 For those regarded as leading to *jhāna* see Vism III 106–7 and PF 63–4.
61 Cousins 1984a: 66. See also Gombrich 1996: 96–134.

2 MEDITATION: INTRODUCTORY TEXTS

1 See DPPN I 868. For story in commentaries, see ThA I 77.
2 See Thī 112–16.
3 See, for instance, BL 2: 29–30, in which a monk obtains arahatship through seeing the mark of impermanence in a mirage and a waterfall. The fact that the stories are commentarial, so could have been written on the basis of the verse rather than the other way around, need not be seen as undermining their psychological accuracy.
4 The idea that realization comes suddenly, from an outside event, is a distinguishing feature of some Zen traditions (for good short discussion of this see Harvey 1990: 270–9).
5 See Blackstone 1998: 1, 155, n. 2.
6 See also Pruitt 1998: 65–8 and DPPN I 348.
7 See Murcott 1991: 38.
8 DPPN I 719–22.
9 See Ireland 1997: 53–6.
10 See PED 401 and Ireland 1997: 248, n. 30. For the three kinds of seclusion, of body, of mind (*citta*) and from the attachments which lead to rebirth (*upadhi*) see Nidd 1 26–7 and discussion in Collins 1982: 171–6.

11 See WD, ix.
12 See BL 3: 254–9.
13 Dhp 153–4. Steve Collins shows how the idea of the house, tenanted and untenanted, provides an effective means of reconciling apparent contradictions between the popular and philosophical conception of not-self (*anattā*). The juxtaposition of the idea of home with homelessness permeates Buddhist *suttas* and commentaries (see Collins 1982: 165–76). The body is perceived as a house or abode (M I 190; and Vism XVIII 28), as is the mind (A I 261–2).
14 See this anthology 9–10.
15 See this anthology 188.
16 See this anthology 51.
17 The whole of this *sutta* occurs at A IV 353–8 without the *gāthā* at the end.
18 See CDB II 1898–9, n. 52 and S V 72. For a full discussion of the enlightenment factors as they evolve within the *suttas* and *Abhidhamma*, see Gethin 1992a: 146–89.
19 For discussion of this text as a whole see CDB I 36–40.
20 As Mahācunda releases the Buddha from his illness (S V 81).
21 See *Sammohavinodanī* 347, Ñāṇamoli 1991: 71 and 109 n. 54.
22 See ThA I 442ff. and DPPN II 510.
23 PF 49–50; the text is also quoted in Vism III 61.
24 *piyo ca hoti manāpo ca garu ca bhāvanīyo ca vattā ca vacanakkhamo ca gambhīrañca kathaṃ kattā hoti, no ca aṭṭhāne niyojeti.* Upatissa takes this last to mean, 'not applying to useless ends' (PF 49). For *bhāvanīya* see PED 503.
25 Hare compares this to Job XIII, 15. See Hare 1935 (GS IV): 19 n. 4).
26 For more on this subject see Gethin 1994: 11–35.
27 See Asl 140–1 and, for modern description, Gethin 1998: 213–18.
28 *Āgantukehi*, sometimes translated as 'adventitious corruptions' (Exp I 185). *Āgantu* can also mean a visitor or a stranger, a sense that has been retained here (CPD II 22–3).
29 In this paragraph, the verb *āsevati* is used, suggesting practice and initial development. For the next option *bhāveti* is used, with connotations of developing. The third example uses the verb *manāsi karoti*, to fix the mind intently upon, to focus, to take to heart (PED 521).
30 *Pamādo*, contrasted with *appamādo*.
31 *Kosajjaṃ*.
32 For this story see BL 3: 47–52 (DhpA III 216ff.).
33 See Gethin 1992b.
34 Dr Friedegarde Lottermeier provided information about this.
35 For a helpful account of the relationship between the six pairs see Nyanaponika 1998: 71–81. For a practical guidance on *sobhana citta* see van Gorkom 1975: 180–191 and Rowlands 1982: 21–6.
36 Bodhi comments on a *sutta* passage describing the six pairs: 'the word "body" was intended quite literally as meaning the physical body, considered as actively contributing to the qualitative tone of the experience' (CDB II 1901 n. 61).
37 For full discussion of this see Asl 128–3.
38 The *Buddhamaṅgalagāthā* place Kondañña, in the East, Rāhula in the Northeast, Moggallāna in the North, Gavampati in the Northwest, Ānanda in the West, Upāli in the Southwest, Sāriputta in the South and Kassapa in the Southeast. See also Skilling 2000.
39 See A I 23–4 for Buddha's account of excellencies of all except Devadatta.
40 See M I 145–51 and S III 105 respectively.
41 *Serivanija Jātaka* (n. 3; Ja I 110–13), set five aeons ago, describes the onset of this rivalry (see DPPN I 1106–1).
42 See DPPN I 262 and DA I 9ff.
43 For more on this subject see Rahula 1981: 156–74.

44 Masefield 1994a: 68–70 and Masefield 1994b: II 607.
45 See ibid. 608 for *thokaṃ dukkhaṃ*.
46 For memorization and the texts as oral literature see Cousins 1983 and Gethin 1992b.
47 A *ratana* is a measure of length: 7 make up a *yaṭṭhi*, a pole length.

3 THE FIVE HINDRANCES

1 See Cousins 1973: 118ff for examination of the terminology of each.
2 See Gethin 1998: 180–1. For an account of each of the hindrances, see Nyanaponika 1961.
3 See, for instance, It 115–18, where they are described as to be guarded against in all postures.
4 See S V 92, M I 38 and this anthology 45–6.
5 Cousins (1995) demonstrates how an early association of the word with wise and clever comes also to mean 'good'. For some difficulties with the use of the word 'skilful' and the useful ambivalence of the word 'good', see Keown 1992: 119–20.
6 PED 63 cites DhS 35 to substantiate this, where greed and *abhijjhā* are taken as the same *cetasika* See also DhS 1059.
7 See PED 63 for linking of *abhijjhā* and *domanassa* and, for instance, M I 340 and M III 2.
8 A *dvandva* compound; see Cousins 1973: 129, n. 19. For separation of two into qualities of mind and body, see DhS 1156. See also Bodhi's comments CDB II 1909–10, n. 99.
9 See DhS 422–30. The *cetasika* of restlessness (*uddhacca*) in a mild or intense form underlies all unskilful consciousness.
10 See Cousins 1973: 119 and n. 21.
11 See Jerome 1998 edn: 6.
12 See A I 10 and this anthology 31–2.
13 The prefix 'a' in Sanskrit and Pāli has a much more positive force than in English, denoting not just an absence: non-harm (*ahiṃsa*), has, in Jain contexts in particular, a connotation of active goodwill (SED 125).
14 On this word see MLDB 1205 n. 229.
15 In Śankhya philosophy, for instance, five is a particularly important number, associated with the senses and with the elements. See *Svetāśvatara Upaniṣad* 1.5 and *Praśna Upaniṣad* 4.8 (Roebuck 2000: 341, 397).
16 See S V 64–7 and S V 102–8, which explore the relationship between the enlightenment factors and the hindrances by means of the image of nutriment.
17 In one of Buddhaghosa's word plays (*nirutti*), he says that it is special (*pārihāriya*) because he must carry it, *pariharitabbattā* (Vism III 60).
18 See Rahula 1981:156–74.
19 See, in particular, the *Saḷāyatana-Saṃyutta*, S IV 1–204. The hindrances are treated under the fourth foundation of mindfulness in the *Satipaṭṭhāna-Sutta.*
20 *Ajjhāruhā*. See DP I 37.
21 See DPPN II 872, ThA I 424f.
22 The *bodhipakkhiyādhammā* of faith, energy, mindfulness, concentration and wisdom, which also occur as faculties.
23 S V 90–139. See CDB, II 1898–9 n. 52.
24 For discussion of *middha*, see BPE 287 n. 3.
25 For discussion of *uddhacca*, see BPE 110–11, n. 1.
26 The word *kukkucca* is 'fidgeting, bad deportment of hands and feet'. See BPE 289 n. 3.
27 'Scratching of the mind' (*manovilekha*) which features here and in the next paragraph (1161).
28 This paragraph has been omitted from BPE. Doubt is also listed as an unskilful *cetasika*, where the state, rather than its symptoms, is described (DhS 425). See BPE 106, n. 1.
29 See Gethin 1992a: 69–80.

30 See *Vibh* 373, MA I 64–5 and notes CDB II 1900, n. 54 and Horner 1954 (MLS I): 9 n. 2.
31 There is a post–canonical idea of escape (*nissaraṇa*) for each hindrance: by suppression (*vikkhambhananissaraṇa*) through *jhāna*, in a particular respect (*tadaṅga*), through insight, and by eradication (*samuccheda*) through the path (i) The first hindrance is suppressed by the first *jhāna* based on foulness and eradicated by the path of arahatship (ii) Ill-will is suppressed by the first *jhāna* based on loving-kindness and eradicated by the path of non-return (iii) Sloth and torpor are suppressed by the perception of light and eradicated by arahatship. (iv) Restlessness and worry are suppressed by serenity: worry is eradicated at non-return, restlessness at arahatship (v) Doubt is suppressed by the defining of *dhammas* (*dhammavatthana*) and eradicated at stream-entry. See CDB II 1912 n. 113.
32 I have taken this translation of *yoniso manisikāra* from (Nyanaponika and) Bodhi (Bodhi 2000: 35). The term is also sometimes translated as systematic or wise attention.
33 This (*subhanimittaṃ*) refers to a beautiful object in the sense sphere, which may arouse desire.
34 *Asubhanimittaṃ:* the mental image produced based on the foul meditations.
35 Bodhi writes:

> In AN, persons are as a rule not reduced to mere collections of aggregates, elements, and sense bases, but are treated as real centres of living experience engaged in a heartfelt quest for happiness and freedom from suffering. The *suttas* of this collection typically address these needs, many dealing with the practical training of monks and a significant number of the daily concerns of lay followers.
>
> (CDB I 34)

36 For contemporary asceticism see Bronkhorst 1993: 45–53.
37 See this chapter, n. 17. There are four kinds of nutriment: physical food, contact, volition and consciousness (see DhS 58, 70, 646ff.).
38 See conclusion to *Satipaṭṭhāna-Sutta* and this anthology 149–50.
39 Buddhaghosa cites this text as being of use in regaining the sign where absorption has been lost or as a means of familiarizing oneself with the *jhāna* again (see Vism IV 120–2).
40 *Sūdo sakassa bhattu nimittaṃ na uggaṇhāti*. The word *nimitta* is used to denote the sign of the employer's taste and also the sign experienced during meditative practice.
41 See DPPN I 1021–22 and Ja I 316–17.
42 DhA I 37–43, BL 1 166–70.
43 See her note in Woodward 1924 (KS III): 92 n. 2.
44 This is an abbreviation: the formula should be repeated for each of the five *khandhas*, with an answer from Tissa at the end. This applies to each of the questions asked by the Buddha.
45 For Moggallāna's biographical details see DPPN II 541–7 and (Nyanaponika and) Hecker 1997: 67–105.
46 *Bahulamakāsi*. The word translated here as 'sluggishness' is *middha* (PED 533), the second part of 'sloth and torpor'.
47 Pāli is: *yathāsutaṃ yathāpariyattaṃ dhammaṃ cetasā anuvitakkeyyāsi anuvicāreyyāsi manasānupekkheyyāsi*.
48 See DP I 22: *accanta*.

4 LONGER TEXTS: I. CONCENTRATION AND THE FRUITS OF RECLUSESHIP – THE *SĀMAÑÑAPHALA-SUTTA*

1 For Sanskrit and Chinese versions of text, see MacQueen 1988.
2 The most magnificent translation is still Rhys Davids' for all its Victorianisms (Rhys Davids' 1899; DB I: 65–95). For a sensitive modern translation see Walshe

1987: 91–109. Bodhi's notes and explanatory remarks on the commentary provide an impressive introduction (Bodhi 1989).

3 Manné demonstrates the way the Buddha defeats his opponents through formal debate in the longer discourses and terms this *sutta* an example of his applied method through 'case histories' (Manné 1990, 1995).

4 For full story see Bodhi 1989: 53–8.

5 The commentary is unable to accept that the Buddha's presence could be anything other than striking: was the king, dulled by parricide, unable to recognize the marks of the Buddha? The commentary concludes this could not be possible and that the question is instigated, through royal pride, as Ajātasattu pretends not to recognize him (Bodhi 1989: 65).

6 For full accounts of these, see Basham 1951.

7 *Pātimokkha*, nn. 57–72.

8 Ariyesako 1998: 108–9.

9 The word is used in the formula for the recollection of *dhamma* (22).

10 See Nyanaponika Thera 1961: 32–4. This description also occurs at M I 275–6.

11 See Basham 1967: 45–58.

12 See for instance Gethin 1992a: 344–50.

13 T.W. Rhys Davids' notes that from §68, the section immediately before the images for the hindrances, to their abandonment in §75 is 'really one long sentence or paragraph of much eloquence and force in the Pali' (DB I 84 n.1).

14 For an explanation of this term see Griffiths 1983: 55–68. He notes eighty-six different occurrences of this unit in its shorter form in the four *nikāyas*.

15 Griffiths' helpful attempts to describe in psychological terms the *jhānas*, refer, however, to this pericope as the 'stereotyped illustrative pericope', which hardly does it justice. For comment on beauty and aptness of imagery, see Bodhi 1989: 14 and Guneratana's comprehensive account of the *jhānas* (Guneratana 1985: 49–95). Cousins 1973 provides a more extensive study of each state than is possible here.

16 This extended *pericope* is also found at M I 276–8 and M III 92–4, A III 25ff. and M II 15–17. It recurs throughout the first section of the *Dīghanikāya*.

17 For the use of imagery of water in the canon, with both negative and positive connotations, see Collins 1982: 247ff.

18 Guneratana gives a full discussion of the need for more mindfulness at this stage (Guneratana 1985: 91–2).

19 See Brereton 1987: 28–31.

20 See D II 179–80.

21 This is puzzling: lotuses only flower once they grow out of the water, so there is no colour or full flower while they are submerged. David Cooke at Kew Gardens, London, was helpful in answering queries about this. He said that the *nelumbo* lotus, like all tropical and hardy water lilies, flowers above water for pollenation, but often appears to have emerged under water if a lake or pond floods after they come out. Upatissa takes the submersion as suggesting water up to the neck rather than the tip (PF 108–9).

22 PF 96, PF 104, PF 109.

23 On the various classifications of equanimity, see Aronson 1980: 78–96.

24 D II 156.

25 See Guneratana 1985: 105.

26 D I 211–14. Gethin (1992a: 97–101) demonstrates that the Buddha did not reject the *iddhis*, merely their casual use. For detailed analysis of all the higher knowledges, see Guneratana 1985: 125–37.

27 Vin II 112, Vin III 87–109 and *Pātimokkha* no. 4 'The rule about a superior human state'.

28 Vin I 24ff.

29 See CDB II 1939–40 n. 246.

30 PED 120–1: M I 152, M I 155, A I 14, D II 177.

31 In CDB II 1939–40 n. 246.
32 I am grateful for discussion with Mahes Wijavisari and other Sri Lankans about this.
33 In Thailand *Tun sūtraya*: the *Maṅgala-Sutta, Metta-Sutta* and *Ratana-Sutta* are felt to be particularly efficacious. See also Gombrich 1988: 124–7.
34 See Saddhatissa 1971: 79–80. For discussion of some of these *iddhis*, see Nyanasampanno 1976: 52–3, 245–7; Randall 1990: 127–36 and for comprehensive account of their treatment within the canon, Guneratana 1985: 125–37.
35 See Gethin 1992a: 97–103.
36 See Hamilton 1996: 156–64 for discussion of this.
37 S IV 269–77. For Moggallāna see DPPN II 541–7.
38 The first two fruits concern the status of a slave and a householder respectively, when they have joined the order, which is higher than that of a king.
39 *Virāga*: PED 634.
40 Sue Hamilton suggests that given the context of the psychic powers discussed later, *ahīnindriyaṃ* could mean that this created body, the result of inner transformation, is endowed with special or supernormal powers. The term would then refer to the skills of this subtle body, created through meditation, as a preparatory stage in the development of the next fruit (see Hamilton 1996: 156ff.).
41 *Saṅkhittaṃ* and *nikkhittaṃ*.
42 The mind that has grown great is one that has attained *jhāna*.
43 See MLDB 1193, n. 155.

5 LONGER TEXTS: II. THE FOUR FOUNDATIONS OF MINDFULNESS – THE *SATIPAṬṬHĀNA-SUTTA*

1 MLDB 1189 n. 136.
2 See on this Gethin 1992a: 36–44.
3 As well as works cited elsewhere in this chapter, see for instance Boowa 1973: 110–32; Nyanaponika 1969: 30–57, Suvaḍḍhano 1961: 4–9, Dhammasami 1999 and 2000. For vivid personal accounts, interspersed with autobiography, see Coleman 1971: 209–27 and Randall 1990.
4 *Apilāpana*: Asl 121.
5 This is the section omitted from the shorter version of the *sutta*.
6 This raises a very interesting question, because in the end the practitioner's methods are not the same as the academic, and his or her allegiance is different: it is gratifying, however, when the two agree.
7 See MLDB 1188–95 nn. 133–65 and CDB II 1915–28 nn. 122–86.
8 See, for instance, Dhammasami 1999 and Sumedho 1987.
9 See Gethin 1992a: 29–36.
10 On this see ibid. and, specifically, MLDB 1189 n. 136.
11 The *sutta* employs the material that subsequently becomes the ten *asubhā* (11–20) in slightly different form. The practice of body mindfulness (28) is described by Buddhaghosa with a different emphasis as an umbrella for the practice of breathing mindfulness and the defining of the four elements (40).
12 The sixth sense, mind (*citta*), is the object of the third foundation of mindfulness.
13 Bhikkhu Bodhi's translation.
14 But on 'Jongrom', as it is called in Thai, see Sumedho 1987: 10 and 33–4 and Dhammasami 1999: 33–5.
15 Soma 1981: 80–100 and Nyanaponika 1969: 45–56.
16 See Nyanaponika 1969: 45–56.
17 The commentary gives some context (see this anthology 14). The people of Kuru, it is said, were so attentive and virtuous that they could be called 'monk' for the purposes of receiving this text (MA I 227–8/Soma 1981: 16–18).

18 For this *sutta* I have used the word 'practise' for *viharati* (see Saddhatissa 1971: 91ff.).
19 *Sāmisaṃ*: PED 705 says that it means (1) Holding food and (2) Fleshly, carnal. It refers to the five physical senses as opposed to the sixth, the mind (see MLS I 76, n. 2 and DP I 318).
20 Sue Hamilton posits the translation 'state of mind' for *citta* in this passage (Hamilton 1996: 110–11).
21 *Saṅkhittaṃ* and *nikkhittaṃ*.
22 The mind that has 'grown great' is one that has attained *jhāna*.
23 On these pairs see MLDB 1193, n. 155 and Soma 1981: 114–18.

6 1–10. THE TEN *KASIṆA* PRACTICES

1 See BMTP 141 n. 2. Vajirañāṇa notes one canonical use of the word in an adjectival sense (see M I 328). For his discussion of these meditations, see BMTP 139–65. See also MA III 260 for entirety (*sakalaṭṭhena*).
2 See Vism 27–37 for powers ascribed to each device.
3 See D III 268, 290; M II 14; A V 46, 60; Patis I 6, 28, 95 etc.
4 See Dhs 202 and Patis I 49, 143, 149.
5 See PF 121–31 and this anthology 8.
6 See A III 321 and S II 149–51 (this anthology 99–100). Discussed in BMTP, 143. A *Jātaka* verse cites 'moonlight' and 'sunshine' as suitable meditation objects (Ja I 474), though modern teachers stress that the sun should only be viewed at dawn or sunset to prevent damage to the eyes (Boonman 2004: 31–2).
7 On *kasiṇa* practice see Vism IV and V and PF 71–131.
8 Vism IV 22 (and PP n. 4). The *Dhammasaṅgaṇi* explains the small support (*paritta ārammaṇa*) with the same words, *suppa* and *sarāva*: Asl 184.
9 PF 76–9 and Vism IV 30–1. On the mental image (*nimitta*) see also BMTP 31–4 and Vism III 114–16.
10 The description includes the five stages of joy: minor, momentary , breaking, like waves on a shore, uplifting and finally pervading, compared to a filled bladder or a cave flooded with water (Vism IV 98).
11 This differentiation between access and *jhāna* is not made in the canon.
12 In this *sutta* the earth device is taken as the basis for the formless realms, as it is in both Buddhaghosa's and Upatissa's descriptions, where earth is regarded as a paradigm for *kasiṇa* practice. See also PF 113–19.
13 Buddhaghosa takes this passage to refer to a constructed device: Vism IV 129.
14 See Vism III 126 and PP 119 n. 35 (conversation with L.S. Cousins).
15 See BMTP 139–42 and Randall 1998. The devices do not appear to be mentioned in contemporary texts, but does the *Praśna Upaniṣad* 4: 7–8 suggest the pre-existence of such meditations (see Roebuck 2000: 397)?
16 See Ud 37, Nidd 1 359–60, Vism III 121 and PF 69.
17 See DhS 365–98, which shows that the particulars, for instance, may also occur in unskilful spontaneous greed-based consciousness accompanied by joy as well as in skilful. See also Th 157.
18 See Ud 37, this anthology 28, A I 3, this anthology 49 and Patis II 39. For unwise attention to beautiful sense object see S V 64 (and CDB II 1899–1900 n. 54).
19 *Upekkhā* in skilful consciousness is not the same as boredom or coldness: DhS 165 (BPE 46 and n. 2). For a close analysis of the highly varied presentation of equanimity in the canon that emphasizes this, see Aronson 1980: 78–96.
20 See M III 219. Buddhaghosa calls the indifference of the ordinary man, who ignores faults and virtues alike, the near enemy of equanimity (Vism IX 101).
21 See Th 13, 22, 40, 50 and 113.

22 See M I 212 and the lyrical descriptions of the forest hermitage in the *Vessantara Jātaka* (Ja VI 528–40; Cone and Gombrich 1977: 47–53).
23 See Kālidāsa's *The Recognition of Śakuntala* (Johnson 2001: 10; Act 1, l.14).
24 In both these countries rural monasteries are constantly praised for natural features.
25 The usual understanding is that the active thought-process (*javana*) that arises from a skilful resultant object (*kusalavipāka*) in the sense sphere will tend to be skilful too, generating further contact with beautiful objects. It is those thought processes which arise at the mind-door when the object is considered that may arouse greed: a beautiful flower will elicit a *kusala citta* when it is experienced at the senses, but may arouse the desire to possess after unwise attention and activity involving more mind-door processes (see Asl 270).
26 See also BPE n. 1.
27 See DhS 161–247.
28 As in A I 39–41 and M II 12–15. See BPE 53 n. 1.
29 On this subject and *Abhidharma-kośa* literature see Cousins 1973: 1267.
30 A IV 428 and the *Aggivacchagotta-Sutta* (M I 483–9), for instance, describe the views that the world is finite or that it is infinite. For explicit association between *kasiṇa* practice and view see Patis I 143–4 and M II 229–3.
31 See Khantipālo 1981: 61–2 for comment on this.
32 The instructions for awareness at all times in the *Satipaṭṭhāna-Sutta* (see this anthology 81 and M I 57) are examples of the way that mindfulness in daily life is encouraged after meditation practice as well as before.
33 See Patis I 459 and this anthology 000.
34 See, for instance, the picture of some in a Sri Lankan monastery in (Bechert and) Richard Gombrich (ed.) 1984: 118.
35 PED 201 and Pradhan 1986: 3 1181.
36 see DPPN II 159–16. For *paribbājaka* see DPPN II 957.
37 See BMTP 57–67. It does not contain the *brahmavihāras* or the twenty perceptions, found in A I 34–40.
38 Ñāṇamoli and Bodhi write: 'The first liberation [deliverance] is the attainment of the four *jhānas* using a *kasiṇa* derived from a coloured object in one's own body; the second is the attainment of the *jhānas* using a *kasiṇa* derived from an external object; the third can be understood as the attainment of the *jhānas* through either a very pure and beautiful coloured *kasiṇa* or the four *brahmavihāras* [31–34]. The remaining liberations are the immaterial attainments [formless meditations 35–38] and the attainment of cessation. See MLDB 1284–5 n. 764. The internal bodily practice is a development of meditation on the parts of the body described in the *Satipaṭṭhāna-Sutta*, whereby the colour of the bodily part is used.
39 See Dhs 248–50, BPE 58 n. 2 and, on *adhimuccana*, Asl 190.
40 See DP I 209. I have used Ñāṇamoli translation, 'transcendence' (MLDB 1285 n. 765). For a close study of this list, see An 2003: 105–9.
41 See also BMTP 163–5, 481–3.
42 DhS 204–47 and Asl 187–90.
43 The text is constructed around a series of lengthy visualizations, each pertaining to different meditation objects. One sentence, from the middle of the 'Exercise on Elements' III (*dhātuprayoga*), gives some indication of the fluidity with which external and internal aspects of the colour *kasiṇa* were visualized in relation to one another: 'Above him appear mountains, which are filled with the essence of the colours blue (yellow, red and white). The image of the mountains in the mirror [visualized by the practitioner] fills his body with the essence of various colours . . .' (Lindop (and Cousins) 1998: Sect 91, 19).
44 See ibid.

45 For more on the *Abhidhamma* understanding of this, see DhS 223–53, BPE 55 n. 3; Asl 189.
46 For discussion of the commentarial application of this list, see MLDB 1285 nn. 765–7.
47 See also DhS 204–50. This text is of particular interest because it makes explicit the association of *kasiṇa* practice with *jhāna*, and describes forms as limited. See Asl 189 and BPE, 53 n. 1.
48 PF 130–1. He lists sixteen skills associated with the *abhibhāyatanas*.
49 See this anthology 8.
50 These are the first three of the *abhibhāyatanas*, described in the following section, which occur before *appanā-samādhi*, the steadying and attainment of meditation. Buddhaghosa explains that this is through not finding, or not wishing to find, the preliminary object for meditation, *parikamma*, in his own body (Asl 188).
51 The word used is *adhimutto*. The 'beautiful' is the object of the *kasiṇa* practice. See MA III 256 and Horner 1957 (MLS II): 213 n. 3.
52 MLDB 639 gives 'luminosity' (*nīlanibhāsāni*).
53 From tree *Pterospermum acerifolium*.
54 The plant *Pentapetes phoenicea*.
55 See Vism V 131–8; Upatissa takes sixteen ways that meditation can be mastered, through such exercises as being able to ascend and descend through the *jhānas*, even missing some out as he does so (PF 130–1). See also BMTP 39–42.
56 Cousins 1973: 124 for discussion of this list and related commentarial and canonical material.
57 See S III 264–78.
58 See entry in DP I 340–1 that shows association of word with the fourth stage of what subsequently became the seventeen moments of the thought-process.
59 See BL 3: 39–47.
60 See Vism XII 106–17. This post-canonical story describes the arahat's ability to quell the fiery serpent through the ease of his *jhānic* attainment .
61 DP I 88–9.
62 See Cousins 1973: 124.
63 A III 24 and D III 278–9.
64 See Hare 1934 (GS III): 19 n. 2.
65 This information was given to me by Dr Jeff Kuan, who allowed me to see his translation while preparing his Oxford University DPhil (2004).
66 See A IV 34. Texts pertaining to these are A III 311, and for an extended 'wheel' of permutations of eleven skills in meditation, see S III 263–78 (for useful notes see CDB I 1103–05, nn. 297–308).
67 See BMTP 143, 158; CDB II 1946 n. 273 and this anthology 57.
68 See CDB I 791–2, nn. 231–2.

7 11–20. THE TEN FOULNESS (*ASUBHA*)

1 In some cases it is not specified which one is intended: In It 80–1 and 92–3 the foulness appears to be that of one's own body.
2 M I 424, this anthology 192.
3 The skull was used in Western Europe throughout the mediaeval period as an emblem of mortality: its association with Saturn and the aspect of *melancholia* linked it to concerns beyond the sense-sphere. Albrecht Durer's famous engraving of St Jerome (1514) show the skull apparently being used in this way. For background see Panofsky *et al.*: 1964. The bones of dead monks from many centuries are displayed in the crypt of Santa Maria della Concessione, Rome.

4 See Basham 1967: 176–7.
5 Ibid.: 177.
6 See BMTP 166–7, S V 320–2, included in this section, and Vin III 68.
7 See *Maitri Upaniṣad*, I: 3 (Roebuck 2000: 410).
8 See this anthology 82.
9 See Dhs 263–4. See also PF 132–9.
10 M I 58 and this anthology 82.
11 MLDB 1191 n. 150.
12 See fragments of text in Lindop (and Cousins) 1998.
13 T15, 316c 1–11, quoted and discussed further by Deleanu 1993: 3–12.
14 See PP 191 n. 6.
15 See Gombrich 1996: 155ff.
16 Ven Dhammasami gave this information to me.
17 See for instance M I 237–51. I am grateful for the discussion with Sister Esmé from the Anglican Convent of the Incarnation, Oxford for her comments on this.
18 See ThA I 521ff, and DPPN I 521.
19 See Murcott 1991: 143–5.
20 See DPPN II 1649 and ThA I 444ff.
21 See CDB, II 1951, n. 301, which summarizes the story as glossed by the commentary.
22 A commentarial *Dhammapada* story also involves the unsuitability of loathsomeness of the body as a meditation subject for some temperaments (see BL 3 161–3).
23 The commentary said that some killed each other, though the noble ones did not do so. For discussion see CDB II n. 301 and n. 302.

8 THE RECOLLECTIONS: THE FIRST SIX

1 PF 64. Mindfulness of body and of the breath and are said by Upatissa to lead to the first and fourth *jhāna* respectively.
2 These are considered in each section.
3 The asterisk denotes the recollection of good friends in the place of that of the *saṅgha* (A V 338).
4 The order, as in the *Jhānavagga* (A I 42), is different from Buddhaghosa's, with the breath as the seventh and body mindfulness as the ninth. Upatissa takes the canonical order.
5 See also Rahula 1967: 80.
6 This extract, from the *Paramatthajotikā*, the commentary on the *Khuddaka-Pāṭha* 22, is quoted and translated in Carter 1982: endpiece.
7 This formula is widespread in the canon wherever there is discussion of the Triple Gem. See, for instance, M 1 37, D III 250.
8 For more on this important but overlooked subject see Palihawadana 1997: 493–515 and Gethin 1992b: 149–72. Discussion with Phra Maha Lau, chanter from the royal monasteries in Thailand, at present Abbot of the Birmingham *Buddhavihāra* Temple, England, has been helpful in communicating a sense of the training and expertise involved in this highly skilled form of daily and occasional practice.
9 In order to appreciate the sound of chanting, it is best to hear it 'live'. Recordings of chants, however, may be obtained from many monasteries. In Britain this includes the Buddhist Society, 58, Eccleston Square, London SW1V 1PH and the Birmingham *Buddhavihāra* Temple, 5, Hampton Road, Aston, B6 6AN.
10 Wan Doo Kim, Korea.
11 J I 97. I am grateful to Dr Justin Meiland for pointing out the importance of this passage to me.
12 See DhS 160–268 and this anthology 7 and 203 n. 11.

13 Images of 'washing' tend to be associated with the description of virtue. See Keown 1992: 48–54 on the range of imagery associated with canonical accounts of *sīla*.
14 A I 206–11; this anthology 129–32.
15 A III 312: *idampi kho, bhikkhave, ārammaṇaṃ karitvā evamidhekacce sattā visujjhanti.*
16 For full account of each element and how this practice is conducted see also Dhammasami 1999: 36–48 and Khantipālo 1981: 100–3.
17 PF 148. See PF xlv and 148–9, n. 3 which cites A III 285. The formula is also found in A V 329ff.
18 For life story of Buddha see Ja 1 1–94, Jayawickrama 1990, Thomas 1927, and Strong 2001.
19 For full list see M II 136–7.
20 Kālidāsa, *Raghuvaṃsa*: 3 34.
21 According to Indian folklore gods may be identified by the fact their feet do not touch the ground. A well known instance of this is in the Nala and Damayantī story, *Mahābhārata* III 53 1.
22 D II 143–5 and, for his final words, D II 156.
23 This miracle, performed only by Buddhas, involves exhibiting mastery of the elements of fire and water, which arise from his body at the same time. See Patis I 125–6, Ja IV 263–7 and BL 2: 35–56.
24 I am grateful to Dr Sally Mellick Cutler for telling me about this text. For more on this little known collection, see Mellick Cutler 1994.
25 See D III 14. For the idea of the Buddha being the seventh seer see the culminating poem of the *Upāli Sutta*, which includes one hundred epithets for the Buddha (M I 386–70), presumably representing an attempt to mirror the Jain concept of seven seers (*isisattamassa*). For account of twenty-four earlier Buddhas see *Buddhavaṃsa* and Horner 1975: xxvi–lii.
26 See, for instance, Williams 1989: 265, 268–9. For an extensive discussion of the whole subject of the recollections see Harrison 1978: 35–57.
27 See Harrison, ibid.
28 See Harvey 1990: 266–7.
29 See, for instance, pictures in (Bechert and) Gombrich 1984: 30, 49, 61, 145, 174, 179, 185, 192.
30 See DPPN II 199.
31 On visualization practice see Beyer 1978: 68–79
32 In a later Sanskrit fragment that is possibly of this poem, found at Turfan, a list of the thirty-two marks of the great man has been included: see GD 359.
33 See Harrison 1978. Wickramagamage describes some of the folklore that has developed in various Buddhist countries concerning the creation of Buddha images and their empowerment (in Wickramagamage 1984: 249–54).
34 All of these are arahats whose main path has been one of faith (*muttasaddha*). Vakkali is addressed by the Buddha in It 90–2, quoted under the recollection of *dhamma* (22).
35 See Carter 1982: 33–40.
36 There are various commentarial versions of the story: one says that he is about to throw himself off the precipices of Gijjhakūṭa when the Buddha appears to him with the words, 'come monk'; at this Vakkali is filled with joy and becomes an arahat (AA I 140 and for similar account Ap II 465). The version here, chosen because it links with the verses, is in ThA I 420. See also DPPN II 799–800.
37 See Vism VI 89–100 and PF 150–2.
38 See M III 78–9 and this anthology 153.
39 Some may prefer the word *sīla*. The traditional understanding of the benefits of keeping *sīla*, which means variously nature, behaviour and habit, carry however, many of the same associations as the old English word virtue. This was once applied to gems

and plants as well as people, and encompassed meanings ranging from sap or vitality to the value of a precious jewel (see OED II 3639–40 and the first two lines of the Prologue to Chaucer's *Canterbury Tales*, on the *vertu* of plants in April). For discussion of *sīla* and the five precepts see Gombrich 1988: 76–7, 108, 192, Harvey 1990: 196–216 and Keown 1992: 29–31.

40 See A V 335–7, where Nandiya is told to be practice virtue before other recollections, while in the text before Mahānāma is told to recollect it.

41 See Sn 782, for criticism of boasting: conceit, however, is one of the last defilements to go at arahatship.

42 With such global changes in understanding I do not know if this is true so much now – but I am grateful to older Thai friends for discussions about this!

43 See for instance S I 103–4, D III 4–5.

44 See A III 48–50. For a discussion of the place of *dāna* in the Buddhist tradition see Bodhi 1990.

45 PED 264 gives two meanings: a) abandoning, giving up, renunciation and b) liberality, generosity, munificence. Desire and greed are described as abandoned (*catta rāga*; Nidd I 54, and *catta gedha* Nidd 2 54). A verse of the elders asserts 'I shall give up my thousandfold evils': *soham cajissāmi sahassapāpaṃ* (Th 868). Both senses sometimes come together: 'The unity consisting in establishing the will-to-relinquish a gift (*dānavossaggupaṭṭhānekattaṃ*) belongs to those resolute in giving up (*cāgādhimuttānam*)' (Patis III 167/PD 169).

46 On skilful roots see BPE 19 n. 20 and Ireland 1997: 255, n. 53. Buddhaghosa also speaks of the importance of the actual act of relinquishing (in Vism VII 112).

47 See for instance the first of these stories, 'The first Divan *Vimāna*', Masefield 1989: 11–14.

48 See Zimmer 1960: II, plates 80–5.

49 He quotes A III 287 to support this. For his description of practice see Vism VII 107–14. For short account see also BMTP 206–7.

50 His treatment of the meditation is in PF 153–4.

51 As one of six recollections see A III 312–14, A V 328–32; as one of five A V 334–7. For *cāga* as one of seven treasures see A IV 5. Elsewhere it is seen as one of three, four or five (see PED 264). For the gift of *dhamma* see A IV 364. This *sutta* describes one of the best good deeds as encouraging generosity (*cāga*) in the mean. See also A II 34, A III 40–2, A III 181.

52 'The gift of *dhamma* surpasses all gifts' (Dhp 354).

53 For Citta as non-returner see S IV 301 and CDB II 1448 n. 329.

54 See Collins 1998: 304–16.

55 See 'Gods and Goddesses', Griffin 1979: 144–78.

56 See Gethin 1998: 116–17, table 2, for a list of all the realms, their lifespan and a schema of the *kamma* associated with rebirth in each one. Above the sense sphere are the sixteen Brahma or *rūpa* realms, of even greater beauty and radiance, where beings are reborn through the practice of meditation and success in attaining any of the form-sphere *jhānas*.

57 D II 253–62. The lower Buddhist heavens are sensuous and festive locations; the higher ones are more subtle, leading to the refinement of the Brahma realms. There is, perhaps, some affinity with the ascending ranks of heavens visualized in the mediaeval system of memory. Francis Yates quotes Johannes Romberch in *Congestorium artificiose memorie* (1520), on the visualization of 'imaginary places' (*ficta loca*): 'For the invisible things of Paradise we are to form places in memory in which we put the choirs of angels, the seats of the blessed, Patriarchs, Prophets, Apostles, Martyrs' (Yates 1969: 122).

58 See varied comment on *sabhāgataṃ* see CDB II 1959 n. 355 and Woodward 1930 (KS V): 338, n. 1. The translation 'in the same company as' is a compromise between the two interpretations (and see PED 681). I have taken *ehīti* as an imperative.

59 See also Ap 546; For her life story DPPN II 900–04.

60 See Harvey 1990: 300–21.

61 A V 334–37. He is given just five recollections.
62 See Woodward 1936 (GS V): 215 and nn. 1–3.
63 See DP I 328: *ārādhaka*.
64 See DP I 449: *upaṭṭhitassati*.
65 Translation for *patiṭṭhāya*.
66 Literally 'in a bed crowded with children' (*puttasambādhasayanaṃ*: see PED 693).
67 To live as a householder: *ajjhāvasati* (see DP I 37).

9 THE RECOLLECTIONS: THE FOUR MINDFULNESSES

1 For the standard description of death see M I 49 and Nidd 1 123, 124, PED 524. The meditation on death as described by Upatissa (PF 166–70) and Buddhaghosa (Vism VIII I –41) is primarily a *samatha* practice.
2 For sense-sphere *devas* the imminent falling away from that realm is anticipated rather poignantly by the withering of the tree in front of them: they then take rebirth in accordance with their *kamma*.
3 See, for instance, Harvey 1990: 211–12 and this book, the recollection of generosity (25) 126.
4 See A I 137–42. Yama is described by the commentaries as living in a celestial mansion, where he too is the recipient of his *kamma* (DPPN II 680–1). For more comment on this figure and his meaning, see MLDB 1341–2, nn. 1206–7 and Tin 1993: 87–93.
5 See DPPN II 611–20.
6 The two lists of ten, in the same order, are found later in this *nikāya* listed separately. *Maraṇasaññā* occurs as second in one list and third in another in the section on the 'tens' (see A V 105–6).
7 Other *samatha* practises are also sometimes denoted by *saññā*: the foul (11–20) and loathsomeness in food (39) for instance: see the lists mentioned in previous note.
8 He argues that the *kasiṇa* practice (1–10) leads to *jhāna* because the object is a simple concept, whereas death and the person who experiences it are not (see PP 258 n. 12).
9 The Pāli is: *maranam bhavissati, jīvitindriyaṃ upachijjissatī ti vā maranaṃ, maranaṃ*.
10 In addition, see PF 66–7, 'by way of object'.
11 Buddhaghosa places this text under his seventh heading, as to 'the limitedness of extent' (see Vism VIII 35–7).
12 *Tikkhaṃ*: sharp, acute, clever.
13 *Bahulā kho me paccayā maraṇassa* (A III 307).
14 There is no direct counterpart to Buddhaghosa's list of the ten impediments to meditation in the canon, where he delineates problems connected with (1) dwelling, (2) family, (3) gain (a monk who is too popular and the recipient of many gifts may need to practice where he is not known), (4) a class of students, (5) building (work), (6) travel, (7) kin, (8) illness, (9) books and, (10) supernormal powers, if the meditator wishes to pursue insight rather than calm (see Vism III 29–56).
15 This is most striking in the *Saḷāyatanasaṃyutta* (S IV 1–203).
16 See *Samaññaphala-Sutta* (D I 62–8) and repeated throughout the *suttas* in the first section of the Dīghanikāya.
17 See S IV 158–9 for fishhooks, S IV 197–8 for lute, S IV 175–7 for chariot.
18 See for instance S I 101.
19 See for instance S IV 189–90.
20 This is stressed in the *Indriyabhāvanā-Sutta* (M III 298–9), where the Buddha refutes teachings that advocate cutting off the senses.
21 It should be noted that Buddhaghosa in his instructions makes the number of parts of the body, thirty-two, adding the brain which does not appear as a separate item in the canon. He gives no reason for this.

22 These are the first five of the earth or hard parts of the body: the others are flesh, sinews, bones, bone marrow, kidneys, heart, liver, diaphragm, spleen, lungs, intestines, mesentery, stomach and excrement. The brain is also considered as earth.
23 The formula associated with the practice omits the insight element of the *Satipaṭṭhāna-Sutta*: M III 89 (MLDB 1331 n. 1129).
24 Although Horner dismisses it as 'only a sectional presentation of the *Satipaṭṭhāna-Sutta*' (Horner 1959 (MLS III): 129 n. 1)' it includes, however, a variety of physical analogies, not included there, which lend the text great vitality and substance.
25 See Gethin 1992a: 56.
26 In the *Asaṅkhasaṃyutta*, S IV 359.
27 See DhS 40–51 and this anthology 33–4.
28 This is a tricky passage: it seems that the rebuking monk is like restraint, the one who is rebuked like the lack of it. For comment see Woodward 1927 (KS IV): 130 nn. 6–7 and CDB II 1431 n. 219.
29 *Nānāvisaye nānāgocare*: lit. different distinctions and different grazing grounds.
30 For Anuruddha see A I 23 and DPPN I 85–90.
31 *Indriyāni*: the faculties of sense.
32 Āsabhivācā.
33 PF 64 says that it leads to first four *jhānas*. For Upatissa's account of practice, see PF 156–66.
34 PF 166 and see It 80–1. Vism VIII 238 quotes A IV 353: *Ānāpānasati bhāvetabba vitakkūpacchedāya*. Some mild pejoration is implied in the term *vitakka* in this context. As a factor of the first *jhāna*, the correct application of *vitakka*, both within *jhāna* and in daily life, is equated with the second path factor, right resolve (*sammāsaṁkappa*) in the *Abhidhamma* system (DhS 7 and BPE 8 n. 1). Here it is the tendency to unskilful thought, as in the *Vitakkasaṇṭhāna-Sutta* (M I 118–21).
35 For full account of practice see VIII 145–244. See also BMTP 227–58.
36 But does *assāsa* denote the in or the out-breath? See CPD I 525 for varied interpetration.
37 The extent to which the breath is controlled is one of the many diversities of practise that vary according to tradition and, I understand, even locality. Many Thai *samatha* practices distinguish carefully between a long and a short breath and the meditator needs to learn how to do them differently, rather as a singer needs to learn breathing techniques. See Buddhadāsa 1997: 39–50 and for further variations on length of breath, see Dhammadharo: talks given 1956–60: 28.
38 Called after the white water lilies that blossom then.
39 The four stages of path. The *saṃyojanas* of belief in self, doubt or uncertainty, attachment to rites and rituals, lust and ill-will are the lower fetters (*orambhāgiya*). The higher (*uddhambhāgiya*) ones bind beings to rebirth in *rūpa* and *arūpa* realms.
40 I have followed Bhikkhu Bodhi's translation for *suddhāsāre* (MLDB 942).
41 See also M I 301.
42 See Vism VIII 231–3 and Buddhadāsa 1988: 79–89.
43 The breath is one body amongst others. MA IV 140. This is the body of air amongst the body of fire, water and earth; or, as one of the twenty-five classes of matter, *rūpa* (DhS 585). See Horner 1959 (MLS III): 125 n. 1.
44 The feeling that is pleasant that is associated with the in- and out-breath (MA IV 140).
45 *Viveka*, *virāga*, *nirodhā* and *vossagga*.
46 Mahākappina is considered as foremost amongst the arahats for teaching the monks (A I 250). See DPPN II 473–475.
47 See, for instance, the *Dhammacakkappavattana-Sutta*, S V 420–31.
48 The fullest description of *nibbāna* as the end of suffering is given in S IV 360–72, a text recommended by Buddhaghosa for this recollection (see Vism VIII 245–5).
49 I understand from Dr David Charles that the expression '*tertium non datur*' is the correct term for such antitheses.

50 The placing of the elements, which one associates with the sense-sphere, alongside the formless sphere, does seem at first sight curious, as if the *rupa* realm is being omitted. It was possibly presumed that the four elements may still be present in the *rūpa* realm, in some subtle form, as in the object of the *kasiṇa* practice.
51 Masefield 1994b: 2 1077 n. 100, reads *vācāvatthumattam.*
52 Reading *phuṭṭho* with Norman 1992: 105, 341–2.

10 31–34. THE FOUR DIVINE ABIDINGS (*BRAHMAVIHĀRĀ*)

1 This can be inferred from the early texts. See for instance DhS 1, BPE n. 2 and Asl 128–30, 132–3. For Buddhaghosa's further comments on the four see Asl 192–7.
2 PED 540–1: related to *mitta*/Skst *mitra*, a friend. Buddhaghosa says it is derived from *mid*, to love or to be fat (Asl 192).
3 See BMTP 263–78.
4 See Nyanasampanno 1976: 94–5.
5 See Aronson 1980: 73. Aronson's important study is the best introduction to these practices as they are presented in the canon (Aronson 1980: 60–77).
6 Concerning *Brahmam etam vihāraṃ idha-m-ahu* Norman writes, ' it would be possible to translate as "They say this realm is brahma" ' (GD 177 n. 151).
7 See also A V 150–1 for ten ways of removing ill will.
8 Sympathetic joy is excluded from this list, possibly as it is difficult to arouse in such a case.
9 See DP I 573: *anodhi.*
10 (i) *pīlaṇaṃ*, (ii) *upaghātaṃ*, (iii) *santāpaṃ*, (iv) *pariyādānaṃ*, (v) *vihesaṃ* (for opposite see CPD I 479–80).
11 Ñyāṇamoli translates, 'It is will since it wills that' (Ñyāṇamoli 1982 (PD): 319).

11 35–38. MEDITATION ON THE FORMLESS (*ARŪPASAMĀPATTI*)

1 This is suggested by the close approximation of the order of states to the structure of the heaven realms. The *deva* and Brahma realms are regarded literally as heavenly locations, but they also describe and enact the features of the associated meditation. See Collins 1998: 297–309; Gethin 1998: 112–32; Hamilton 2000: 94–5.
2 The *Vibhaṅga*, to which Buddhaghosa constantly refers, gives the most comprehensive canonical account of these practises (Vibh 245, 261–3).
3 Discussion concerning the formless realms formed the basis of a seminar in Oxford in 2001 that included papers by Dr Alex Wynne, L.S. Cousins, Dr Sue Hamilton and Prof. Johannes Bronkhorst: their papers and subsequent discussion helped to provide background for this section.
4 For their accounts of these see Vism X and PF 113–20.
5 D II 156. See An 2003: 184–7.
6 The first three concern the perception of material shapes, external material shapes in the form sphere, and the beautiful (the pure and bright colours of the *kasiṇa*: MA III 256 and Horner 1957 (MLS II): 213 n. 3). See this anthology 163–5.
7 See for instance, D I 183, M I 174, M I 41–2.
8 DhS 266 also uses *samatikamma*. Buddhaghosa glosses this word (Vism X 12–15) in this section. In the introduction to the objects of meditation, however, he uses it to describe the relinquishment of *jhāna* factors in all *jhānas* after the first (Vism III 103, 108).
9 *Āneñjābhisaṃkhāro*: see Vibh 135: just as in the case of Āḷāra Kālāma who did not see or hear 500 carts passing (see D II 130).
10 He omits the limited space *kasiṇa* (Vism X 1).

11 See Vibh 262: *taṃ yeva ākāsaṃ phutaṃ viññānaṃ*.
12 This sphere can engender a view of permanence (see M II 229–30), as seems to have been the case with the Buddha's earlier teacher, Āḷāra Kālāma (see M I 164).
13 The Bodhisatta is never reborn in a formless heaven as the lifespan would be too long for him to cultivate the perfections.
14 See Hare 1935 (GS IV): 282, n. 1.
15 The Pāli is *ubhato bhaṭṭho ubhato parihīno*.
16 *Anabhihiṃsamāno* VRI/*anabhihaṃsamāno* PTS. See DP I 226, *abhihiṃsamāno*, hurting. See Hare 1935 (GS IV): 283 n. 1 for discussion of word and possible roots. He suggests it is a counterpart to 'not falling' in the case of the foolish monk. I like his suggestion of 'not boggling at': we could say now 'without being fazed'. For this and the rest of the *sutta* I am indebted to Hare's translation (pp. 283–4) and nn. 1–5 on variants. As Hare comments, it is unfortunate that Buddhaghosa does not quote beyond the first *jhāna* (n. 1).
17 Immeasurable (*appamāṇa*), so able to extend to a limitless object (see Asl 164, 188, DhS 181–5, 211–13; BPE 50–1, 55 n. 1).
18 *Sakkhibhabbatā*.

12 THE ONE PERCEPTION AND THE ONE DEFINING

1 The word *paṭikkūla* is translated 'against the slope; averse, objectionable, contrary, disagreeable' (PED 393). For this practice see Vism XI 1–26, PF 205–6; also BMTP 314–17.
2 See A I 41. One list of ten starts with perception of the foul (*asubhasaññā*) and ends with cessation (*nirodhasaññā*); the other, immediately following, starts with impermanence (*aniccasaññā*) and ends with five cemetery contemplations. The two lists of ten, in the same order, are found later in this *nikāya* listed separately (see A V 105–6).
3 Nutrition is regarded as of four kinds: edible, contacts (*phassa*), volition (*cetanā*) and consciousness (*citta*) (see M I 261).
4 For a good modern account of the practice of mindfulness while eating, see James 1986: 55–7.
5 See also A I 114. For behaviour with regard to food exhibited by the Buddha, see M II 138–40.
6 See Thanissaro 1998: 495–504.
7 See Ariyesako 1998: 76–93. The monk who impressed upon me the importance of the *Vinaya* as a means of arousing mindfulness and confidence was Ven Candavanna, who died in 1993 while abbot of the Cambodian vihāra in Washington. He insisted that it was in such small details as the application of the rules in different situations, such as the way that one ate, that mindfulness and investigation were best aroused.
8 For the pleasure of almsgiving see, for instance, M I 236–7.
9 Bhikkhu Bodhidharma at a meal for monks (*dāna*), at the Manchester Centre for Buddhist Meditation.
10 *Anabhiratasaññā*. See DP I 222.
11 *Paricitena*; gathered, accumulated, collected: PED 424.
12 *Paṭikkīlyatā/Paṭikulyatā*; reluctance, loathsomeness: PED 392.
13 In Upatissa's list it is followed by the perception of loathsomeness in food, the sphere of nothingness and the sphere of neither perception nor non-perception. For his account of practice see PF 197–205.
14 The brain is not on the list, though it is included in Buddhaghosa's list for parts of the body associated with earth: see Vism XI 68.

15 So there are upwards winds that cause vomiting and belching, down-going winds which expel excrement and urine, winds outside the bowels, winds in the bowels, winds that course through all the limbs, and those which cause flexing and extending the body by means of a network of nerves.
16 This is described as an object for meditation in the same way as each of other elements in their internal manifestation (see M III 241–2). Buddhaghosa and Upatissa however take space as a meditation object without reference to space within one's own body: for limited space (10), see Vism V 24–16 and PF 129–30; for the sphere of infinite space (35) Vism X 124 and PF 113–16. According to the *Abhidhamma*, the four elements are considered interdependent (*aññamañña*), and so always arise together in all momentary configurations of matter: unlike the four elements space is regarded as derived matter (see (DhS 583–4 and 962–6).
17 See *Maitrī Upaniṣad* 3.2 (Roebuck 2000: 417–18).
18 In Ud 80: quoted in the section on the Recollection of Peace (30). For an excellent analysis of the four elements in Buddhist thought see Hamilton 2000: 155–65.
19 The other *suttas* recommended by Buddhaghosa are the *Mahāhatthipadopamā-Sutta* (M I 184–91), the *Rāhulovāda-Sutta* (M I 420–6 and the text) and the *Dhātuvibhaṅga-Sutta* (M III 237–40).
20 On another occasion Sāriputta describes the elements in terms that echo the *Mahārāhulovāda-Sutta*, as similes for the mind that experiences *mettā* (A IV 373–5).
21 For stages where each practice leads, see PF 64.
22 A cadaver cannot be used for this reason.
23 On Rāhula see DPPN II 737–40.
24 See DPPN II 737, which cites Ja I 160ff. and Ja III 64ff.
25 See DPPN II 738.
26 See MLDB 1266 n. 643. Sāriputta was put in charge of Rāhula after his ordination: he was renowned as a teacher that could bring his students to stream-entry (see M III 248). At this stage Rāhula was neither, but possibly the famous teacher of insight had not seen the boy's need for some other practices before moving on to breathing mindfulness.
27 M I 423. Temperament was felt to be to a certain extent dependent on the balance of the humours or elements, as it was in Western ancient and mediaeval medicine: see PF 58.
28 According to Buddhist cosmology, the universe and world systems are destroyed from time to time by imbalances of the elements of water, wind or fire (see Vism XIII 32–65).

CONCLUSION

1 I have retained the apt English connotations of 'to make much of' for this word, often also, correctly, translated as 'to practise frequently' (see PED 485).
2 See, for instance, Cousins 1984a, Soma Thera 1951 (in Appendix, PF 353–62) and Guneratana 1985: 150–74. For the antiquity of this debate see Gombrich 1996: 96–134.
3 See Keown 1992: 75–82, Cousins 1984a.
4 On the seven stages of insight, employed by some *vipassanā* meditation traditions, see Ñāṇarāma 1993, BMTP 361–96.
5 See M I 420–6. It includes 'opposites' for the divine abidings, comments about the breath at the moment of death and an analysis of space as an internal element. See also advice to Nandiya in A V 336 for the recollection of 'good friends' (23*) and a different formulation of *devatānussati* (26).
6 See Cousins 1984b.

CANONICAL REFERENCES

This is a list of some places in the canon where practices are described, mentioned or implied. The list is neither comprehensive nor statistically representative: many groupings of practices are pericopes which recur in a number of *suttas*. Looking up the Pāli term in the dictionaries gives many references (PED, CPD, DP). The search mechanism in VRI gives all references.

1–10. *kasiṇa*

Ten *kasiṇa*: A I 41; A V 46, 60; D III 268; D III 290; M II 14; Patis I 6.
Eight *kasiṇa*: Dhs 203.
Perception of light (*āloka saññī*): A IV 87; A II 211; A III 321; M I 347.
Earth, water and space: Patis II 208.

11–20. Meditation on the foul (*asubha*)

A I 41 perception of the foul (twice); A I 41 skeleton + four charnel ground; A II 52; A III 83: one of ten *dhammas*; A IV 46: one of seven perceptions; A V 105: one of ten; A V 109: perception of foul in parts of body; Ap 563: hand of corpse eaten by worms; D II 245; D III 290 one of nine perceptions; Dhp 147–50; Dhs 263–4; It 17–18: skeletons of one person over many aeons would make a mountain of bones; It 93; M I 57–8; S IV 111 own body; S V 128: skeleton + four charnel ground; Sn 341: own body; Th 393–8: corpse with worms; Thī 388; Vin III 68 = S V 320.

21–30. Ten recollections (*anussati*)

Ten: A I 41; Nidd 1 360; A I 30.
Six: A III 284; A III 312–14; A V 332–4; D III 250; Nidd 1 492.
Five: Buddha, *dhamma*, *saṅgha*, *devatā* and *sīla*: A I 206–11: various kinds of cleansing.
Five: Buddha, *dhamma*, *kalyāṇamittā*, *cāga* and *devatā*: A V 334–7.
Four: S V 394: Buddha, *dhamma*, *saṅgha* and *sīla*.
Three: Buddha, *dhamma*, *saṅgha*: Dhp 188–92; M I 36–40 compared to washing of cloth ready for dye; Sn 222 –38: *Ratana-sutta*.

21. Recollection of the Buddha (Buddhānussati)

A I 207; Ap 7–54: Buddha visualizes past Buddhas; D II 1–54: past Buddhas, life story of present Buddha, list of 32 marks; D III 142–5: list of 32 marks; Dhp 296; Sn 1133–49: recollection of presence of Buddha; S V 233: practised by arahats.

22. Recollection of dhamma (dhammānussati)

A I 207; A III 379–83: advantages of hearing *dhamma* at death; Dhp 297: recollection of *dhamma*; Dhp 79, 115, 259, 364; Dhp 102: potency of one word of *dhamma*; It 33–4; It 81–2: monk who practises according to *dhamma*; It 90–1.

23. Recollection of the saṅgha (saṅghānussati)

A II 183–5: purity of *saṅgha*; Dhp 106: honour to arahats best; Dhp 298; It 10–12: disunity in *saṅgha*, unity in *saṅgha*; A I 208–9; S I 5: serene appearance.

24. Recollection of generosity (cāgānussati)

A III 34: virtuous man excels all stingy people in generosity (*cāga*); A III 172–3: five gifts (*dāna*) of a good man; It 26: results of giving (*dāna*); J II 112: *saddhā*, *sīla* and *cāga*.

25. Recollection of virtue (sīlānussati)

A I 209–10: compared to cleansing of a mirror; Dhp 54–6: perfume of virtue; Dhp 67–8.

26. Recollection of deities (devānussati)

A I 210–1: some relevant references: D II 253–62: visualization of *devas*; S V 394–5: *devas* delighting in holy life amongst humans; Ud 21–4: Nanda persuaded to stay in holy life.

27. Mindfulness of death (maraṇasati)

A I 41–2: once, with perception of death (twice); A III 83: perception of death (twice); A III 306–8: with every in- and out-breath; A IV 46: perception of death; A IV 148: one of seven *dhammas*; A IV 316–19, 320–22; A V 105: one of ten perceptions; Dhp 235; S III 100–2: 5 ways death may come; Sn 574–593.

28. Mindfulness of body (kāyagatāsati)

A I 43–6; A IV 373–8; D II 290–8; Dhp 293, 299; M I 148; M I 414; M III 237; M III 88; S IV 355.

29. Breathing mindfulness (ānāpāṇasati)

A III 120: 5 qualities with which a monk practising breathing mindfulness will penetrate immovable (*akuppa*); A V 108–12: one of ten perceptions; It 80–1: corrective against discursive thoughts; M I 56–63; M I 426: to be practised on final breath; Patis I 162–96: treatise on breathing mindfulness; S V 320–2; Th 548.

30. Mindfulness of peace (upasamānussati)

A I 42; Dhp 181, 201, 205; It 61–2; M I 164: Buddha leaves first teacher as teachings did not lead to peace; M I 284: practice of immeasurables leading to internal peace; M II 82–3: eightfold path leading to peace; S IV 369: qualities of *nibbāna* include peace. Patis I 16: peace equated to tranquillity (*passadhi*); Patis I 46: keeping precepts leading to peace; Sn 919: peace to be found inside oneself, not by looking at another; Ud 80: attributes of *nibbāna*; Ud 80–1: attributes of *nibbāna*.

31–4. Loving kindness, compassion, sympathetic joy and equanimity (*brahmavihārā*)

A I 10: finger-snap; A II 72: safeguard against snakes and other creatures; A III 290–2: providing escape; A V 342: eleven advantages; D I 76–9; D II 186–7: Universal Monarch practises before death; D III 223–4; Dhs 251–62; M II 207–8; Patis II 130–9; S V 115: with enlightenment factors; Vbh 272–84.
Loving-kindness. Dhp 5; Dhp 368; M I 424: overcomes ill-will; M I 129; S II 263–5 cow's udder; S II 189: not easy to find being who has not been mother, father, brother, sister, son, daughter; Sn 143–52: *metta-sutta*; It 19–21.
Compassion. D II 237–43, 250.
Equanimity. A III 279.

35–8. Formless meditations (*arūpasamāpatti*)

A I 82; D II 112; D II 156: Buddha practises before death; D III 268; Dhs 55–61. It 51: form, formless and *nibbāna*; It 73; M I 41: tranquil abodes; M I 164–5: Buddha leaves teachers; Nidd 2 672; Ud 80: *nibbāna* that base (*tadāyatanaṃ*) where no formless spheres; Vibh183; Ja I 405–7.

39. Loathsomeness in food (*āhāre paṭikkūlasaññā*)

A I 41 (Twice); A III 83: leads to *nibbāna*; A IV 46: one of list of seven; A IV 148: one of list of seven; A V 105: leading to deathless (*amata*).

40. The defining of the four elements (*catudhatu–vavatthānabhāvanā*)

D I 211–22; brahmin ascends to each heaven to enquire about where four elements cease; D II 294; M I 184–91; M I 420–6; M III 237–47.

BIBLIOGRAPHY

Pāli texts

Texts used are those of the Pāli Text Society, 73 Lime Walk, Headington, Oxford. A key to all texts and their translations, *List of Issues*, may be obtained on request: the PTS offer more recent imprints for many translations. The canon is also available in the Chaṭṭha Saṅgāyana Tipiṭika CD-ROM (1997; free distribution from Vipassanā Research Institute, Igatpuri, India) (VRI).

Bibliography of translations

For those unfamiliar with consulting translations from Pāli the abbreviation for the text, such as M I 34, refers to its abbreviated title. In this case it would be *Majjhimanikāya*, volume I, page 34. This reference is found in the square page-reference brackets within any translation, and/or at the top inside corners of a page opening. For ease of cross-reference, the bibliography for translations of Pāli texts has been made separately.

There is not space in this volume to consider all the material now available on the internet. Many good translations of *suttas*, however, can be found by tapping the name of the *sutta* concerned into the search engine.

An, Y.-G. (2003) *The Buddha's Last Days: Buddhaghosa's Commentary on the Mahāparinibbāna Sutta*, Oxford: PTS (commentary and trans. D II 72–167).

Bodhi, Bhikkhu (1989) *Sāmaññaphala Sutta commentary and trans.*, Kandy: BPS (commentary and trans. D I 47–85).

—— (2000) *Connected Discourses of the Buddha*, 2 vols. Oxford and Somerville, MA: Wisdom/PTS (CDB: trans. of S).

Bodhi, Bhikkhu and Nyanaponika Thera (2000) *Numerical Discourses of the Buddha: An Anthology of Suttas from the Aṅguttaranikāya* (copyright 1999) Kandy: BPS (trans. of A).

Burlingame, E.W. (1921; reprint 1990) *Buddhist Legends: Translated from the Original Pāli text of the Dhammapada Commentary*, Harvard Oriental Series 28–30, 3 parts, Cambridge, MA: Harvard University Press/PTS (BL: trans. of DhpA).

Cone, M. and Gombrich R.F.G. (1977) *The Perfect Generosity of Prince Vessantara: A Buddhist Epic Translated from the Pāli and Illustrated by Unpublished Paintings from Sinhalese Temples*, Oxford: Clarendon Press (trans. of Ja VI 479–593).

Cowell, E.B. (ed.) (1895–1907; reprint 2000) *The Jātaka or Stories of the Buddha's Former Births*, 7 vols, New Delhi: Asian Educational Services (trans. of Ja)

Hare, E.M. (1934; reprint 1973) *The Book of the Gradual Sayings (Aṇguttaranikāya)*, III, London and Boston, MA: PTS (GS: trans. of A).
—— (1935; reprint 1978) *The Book of the Gradual sayings (Aṅguttaranikāya)* IV, London: PTS.
Horner, I.B. (1938–66) *The Book of the Discipline*, 6 vols, London: PTS (trans. of Vin).
—— (1954, 1957, 1959) *The Middle Length Sayings of the Buddha*, 3 vols, London: PTS (MLS: trans. of M).
—— (1975) *Minor Anthologies*, III, *Buddhavaṃsa: Chronicle of Buddhas*, London: PTS.
Ireland, J. (1997) *The Udāna and Itivuttaka*: *Two Classics from the Pali Canon*, Kandy: BPS (trans. of Ud and It).
Jayawickrama, N.A. (trans.) (1990) *The Story of Gotama Buddha*, Oxford: PTS.
Masefield, P. (1989) assisted by N.A. Jayawickrama, *Elucidation of the Intrinsic Meaning So Named the Commentary on the Vimāna Stories*, Oxford: PTS.
—— (1994a) *The Udāna*, Oxford: PTS (trans. of Ud).
—— (1994b) *The Udāna Commentary: Paramatthadīpanī I*, 2 vols, Oxford: PTS.
—— (2000) *The Itivuttaka*, Oxford: PTS (trans. of It).
Mellick Cutler, S. (1993) *A Critical Edition, with Translation of Selected Portions of the Pāli Apadāna*, unpublished thesis, University of Oxford.
Ñāṇamoli, Bhikkhu (1952; 6th edn 1998) *Mindfulness of Breathing, Buddhist Texts from the Pali Canon and Commentaries*, Kandy: BPS.
—— (1956, 1964; reprint 1976) *The Path of Purification* (*Visuddhimagga*), 2 vols, Berkeley, CA and London: Shambala (PP: trans. of Vism).
—— (1982) with intro. by A.K. Warder, *The Path of Discrimination* (PD: trans. of Patis).
—— (1991) *The Dispeller of Delusion (Sammohavinodanī)* revised by L.S. Cousins, Nyanaponika Mahāthera and C.M.M. Shaw, 2 vols, London: PTS.
—— (1995; revised edn 2001) Bhikkhu Bodhi (ed.) *The Middle Length Discourses of the Buddha*, London and Somerville, MA: Wisdom/PTS (trans. of M).
Norman, K.R. (1969) *Elders' Verses*, I, London: PTS (trans. of Th).
—— (1971) *Elders' Verses*, II, London: PTS (trans. of Thī).
—— (1992) *Group of Discourses* (*Sutta-Nipāta*), II, revised with intro. and notes, Oxford: PTS (trans. of Sn).
—— (1997) *The Word of the Doctrine (Dhammapada)*, with intro. and notes, Oxford: PTS.
—— (1999) W. Pruitt (ed.) 'Pāli and English', *The Bhikkhupātimokkha*, Oxford: PTS.
Pruitt, W. (1998) *The Commentary on the Verses of the Therīs*, Oxford: PTS.
Rhys Davids, C.A.F. (1900; 3rd edn 1974) *A Buddhist Manual of Psychological Ethics*, London: PTS (BPE trans. of DhS).
—— (1909 and 1937; 2nd edn in one vol. 1980) *Psalms of the Early Buddhists*, Oxford: PTS (trans. of Th and Thī).
—— (1917; reprint 1979) *The Book of Kindred Sayings*, I, London: PTS (KS: trans. of S).
—— (1921; reprint 1995) *Dialogues of the Buddha*, III, Oxford: PTS (DB: trans. of D).
—— (1922; reprint 1982) *The Book of Kindred Sayings*, II, London: PTS (KS: trans. of S).
Rhys Davids, T.W. (1899; reprint 1995) *Dialogues of the Buddha*, I, Oxford: PTS (DB: trans. of D).
Rhys Davids, T.W. and Rhys Davids, C.A.F. (1910; 4th edn 1959) *Dialogues of the Buddha*, II, London: PTS.
Soma Thera (1981; 5th edn) *The Way of Mindfulness, being a translation of the Satipaṭṭhāna Sutta of the Majjhima Nikāya: Its Commentary, the Satipaṭṭhāna Vaṇṇanā*

of the Papañcasūdanī of Buddhaghosa Thera; and Excerpts from the Līnatthapakāsanā Tīkā, Marginal Notes, of Dhammapāla Thera and Commentary, Kandy: BPS (trans. of M I 55–63).
Thittila, Sayadaw, U. (1969) *The Book of Analysis*, London: PTS (trans. of Vibh).
Tin, P.M. (1920–1; reprint 1958) edited and revised C.A.F. Rhys Davids, *The Expositor*, 2 vols, London: PTS (trans. of Asl).
Walshe, M. (1987) *Thus Have I Heard; The Long Discourses of the Buddha: Dīghanikāya*, London: Wisdom (trans. of D).
Woodward, F.L. (1924; reprint 1979) *The Book of Kindred Sayings*, III, London: PTS (KS: trans. of S).
—— (1927; reprint 1979) *The Book of Kindred Sayings*, IV, London: PTS.
—— (1930; reprint 1979) *The Book of Kindred Sayings*, V, London: PTS.
—— (1932; reprint 1979) *The Book of Gradual Sayings*, I, London: PTS (GS: trans. of A).
—— (1933; reprint 1982) *The Book of Gradual Sayings*, II, London: PTS.
—— (1936; reprint 1986) *The Book of Gradual Sayings*, V, London: PTS.

Bibliography

A number of works listed are privately published by monasteries or meditation groups. Contact with a local Theravāda Buddhist Monastery may help in finding some, or tapping the name of the writer, teacher or monastery concerned into the search engine on the internet.

Ariyesako, Bhikkhu (1998) *The Bhikkhu's Rules: A Guide for Laypeople*, Kallista, Australia: Sanghāloka Forest Hermitage.
Aronson, H.B. (1980) *Love and Sympathy in Theravāda Buddhism*, Delhi: Motilal Banarsidass.
Bapat, P.V. (1937) *Vimuttimagga and Visuddhimagga, A Comparative Study*, Poona: Calcutta Oriental Press.
Basham, A.L. (1951; reprint 1981) *History and Doctrine of the Ajivikas*, Delhi: Motilal.
—— (1967; paperback edn 1971) *The Wonder That was India: A Survey of the History and Culture of the Indian Sub-continent Before the Coming of the Muslims*, London: Fontana Collins.
Beyer, Stephan (1973; 2nd edn 1978) *The Cult of Tāra: Magic and Ritual in Tibet*, Berkeley, CA, Los Angeles, CA and London: University of California Press.
Blackstone, K. (1998) *Women in the Footsteps of the Buddha: Struggle for Liberation in the Therīgāthā*, Richmond, Surrey: Curzon.
Bodhi, Bhikkhu (1981) *Going for Refuge: Taking the Precepts*, Wheel Publication, nos 282–4, Kandy: BPS.
—— (ed.) (1990) *Dāna: The Practice of Giving, Selected Essays*, Wheel Publication, nos 367–9, Kandy: BPS.
Boonman, N. (2004) *From One to Nine*, Bangkok: Poonyathiro.
Boowa, Phra Maha (1973) *Forest Dhamma: A Selection of Talks on Buddhist Practice* Bhikkhu Paññavaḍḍho trans., Bangkok: Sathirakoses-Nagapradipa Foundation.
Brereton, J. P. (1987) 'The Lotus' in M. Eliade (ed.), 16 vols, *The Encyclopedia of Religion*, New York and London, 9: 28–31.
Bronkhorst, J. (1993) *The Two Traditions of Meditation in Ancient India*, Delhi: Motilal Banarsidass.

Bucknell, R. and Kang, C. (eds.) (1997) *The Meditative Way: Readings in the Theory and Practice of Buddhist Meditation*, Richmond, Surrey: Curzon.

Buddhadāsa, Bhikkhu (1997) *Mindfulness with Breathing: A Manual for Serious Beginners*, trans. from Thai by Santikaro Bhikkhu, foreword by L. Rosenberg, Boston, MA: Wisdom.

van Buitenen, J.A.B. (1975) *The Mahābhārata*, vols 2–3, Chicago, IL and London: University of Chicago Press.

Carter, J.R. (ed.) (1982) *The Threefold Refuge in the Theravāda Buddhist Tradition*, Chambersberg, PA: Anima.

Chah, Ajahn (1998) *The Key to Liberation and the Path of Peace: Talks on Dhamma Practice*, Ubon Rajathani, Thailand.

Coleman, J.E. (1971) *The Quiet Mind*, London: Rider.

Collins, S. (1982) *Selfless Persons: Imagery and Thought in Theravada Buddhism*, Cambridge: Cambridge University Press.

—— (1987), 'Kalyāṇamitta and Kalyāṇamittatā', JPTS, 11: 51–72.

—— (1998) *Nirvāna and Other Felicities: Utopias of the Pāli Imaginaire*, Cambridge: Cambridge University Press.

Conze, E. (1956; reprint 1975) *Buddhist Meditation*, London: Unwin.

Cousins, L. S. (1973) 'Buddhist *Jhāna*: Its Nature and Attainment according to the Pāli sources', *Religion*, 3: 115–31.

—— (1983) 'Pāli Oral Literature', in Philip Denwood and Alexander Piatigorsky (eds) *Buddhist Studies; Ancient and Modern*, London: Curzon, 1–11.

—— (1984a) 'Samatha-yāna and Vipassanā-yāna', in Gatare Dhammapala, R. Gombrich and K.R. Norman (eds) *Buddhist Studies in Honour of Hammalava Saddhatissa*, Nugegoda, Sri Lanka: Hammalava Saddhatissa Felicitation Volume Committee, 56–68.

—— (1984b) '*Abhidhamma*', in J.R. Hinnells (ed.) *Penguin Dictionary of Religions*, Harmondsworth, Middsx: Penguin, 19.

—— (1996) 'Good or Skilful? *Kusala* in Canon and Commentary', *Journal of Buddhist Ethics*, 3: 136–64.

—— (2001) 'Formless Realms', unpublished talk and paper, Oxford.

Deleanu, F. (1992) 'Mindfulness of Breathing in the *Dhyāna Sutras*', *Transactions of the International Conference of Orientalists in Japan*, 37: 42–57.

—— (1993) '*Śrāvakayāna Yoga* Practices and *Mahāyāna* Buddhism', *Waseda Daigaku Daigaku-in Bungaka kenkyu -ka kiyø*, special issue no. 20, 7, Nouyoshi Yamabe. 'New Fragments of the *Yogalehrbuch*', Bulletin of Kyusyu Ryukoku Junior College.

Dhammadharo, Ajaan Lee (undated: talks 1956–60) Geoffrey DeGraff trans., *Keeping the Breath in Mind: Lessons in Samādhi*, Rayong, Thailand: free distribution.

Dhammasami, Bhikkhu (1999) *Mindfulness Meditation Made Easy*, Penang, Malaysia: Inward Path.

—— (2000) *Different Aspects of Mindfulness*, Penang, Malaysia: Inward Path.

Gethin, R.M.L. (1992a) *The Buddhist Path to Awakening: A Study of the Bodhi-pakkhiyā Dhammā*, Leiden, New York, Koln: Brill.

—— (1992b) 'The Mātikas: Memorization, Mindfulness and the List' in J. Gyatso (ed.) *In the Mirror of Memory: Reflections on Mindfulness and Remembrance in Indian and Tibetan Buddhism*, Albany, NY: State of New York Press, 149–72.

—— (1994) '*Bhavaṅga* and Rebirth according to the *Abhidhamma*', in T. Skorupski and U. Pagel (eds) *The Buddhist Forum*, 3: 11–35.

—— (1998)*The Foundations of Buddhism*, Oxford: Oxford University Press.

Gombrich, R.F. (1971) *Precept and Practice: Traditional Buddhism in the Rural Highlands of Ceylon*, Oxford: Clarendon Press.

—— and Bechert, H. (ed.) (1984) *The World of Buddhism: Buddhist Monks and Nuns in Society and Culture*, London: Thames and Hudson.

—— (1988) *Theravāda Buddhism; A Social History from Ancient Benares to Modern Colombo*, London and New York: Routledge and Kegan Paul.

—— (1996) *How Buddhism Began: The Conditioned Genesis of the Early Teachings*, London and Atlantic Highlands, NJ: Athlone.

—— (1997) 'Religious Experience in Early Buddhism', Eighth Annual lecture, British Association for the Study of Religions, p. 11ff.

van Gorkom, N. (1975) *Abhidhamma in Daily Life*, Bangkok: Dhamma Study Group.

Griffin, J. (1979) *Homer on Life and Death*, Oxford: Oxford University Press.

Griffiths, P. (1983) 'Buddhist *Jhāna*: A Form-critical Study', *Religion*, 13: 55–68.

Guneratana, Mahathera H. (1985) *The Path of Serenity and Insight: An Explanation of the Buddhist Jhānas*, Delhi: Motilal Banarsidass.

—— (1988) *The Jhānas in Theravāda Buddhist Meditation*, Wheel Publication, nos 351–3, Kandy: BPS.

Hamilton, S. (1996) *Identity and Experience: The Constitution of a Human Being According to Early Buddhism*, London: Luzac Oriental.

—— (2000) *Early Buddhism: A New Approach. The 'I' of the Beholder*, Richmond, Surrey: Curzon.

Harrison, P. (1978) '*Buddhānusmṛti* in the *Pratyutpanna – Buddha saṃmukhāvasthita-samādhisūtra*', *Journal of Indian Philosophy*, 6: 35–57.

Harvey, P. (1990) *Introduction to Buddhism: Teachings, History and Practices*, Cambridge: Cambridge University Press.

Hecker, H. and Nyanaponika Thera (1997) Bhikkhu Bodhi (ed.) *Great Disciples of the Buddha, Their Lives, Their Works, Their Legacy*, Somerville, MA: Wisdom.

James, A. and James, J. (1986) *A Meditation Retreat*, Box, Wiltshire: Aukana.

Jerome K. Jerome (1889; 1998 edn) *Three Men in a Boat*, Oxford: Oxford University Press.

Johnson, W. trans. (2001) *Kālidāsa's The Recognition of Śakuntala*, Oxford: Oxford University Press.

Keown, D. (1992) *The Nature of Buddhist Ethics*, Basingstoke: Macmillan.

Khantipālo, Bhikkhu (1980) *Bag of Bones: A Miscellany on the Body*, Wheel Publication, nos 271/272, Kandy: BPS.

—— (1981) *Calm and Insight: A Buddhist Manual for Meditators*, London and Dublin: Curzon Press.

Kuan, J., T-F. (2004) *The Practice of Mindfulness in Early Buddhism*, unpublished thesis, University of Oxford.

Lindop, A. and Cousins, L.S. (1998), unpublished trans. of Dieter Schlingoff, *Ein Buddhisticsches Yogalehrbuch* (Berlin 1964).

MacQueen, G. (1988) *A Study of the Śrāmaṅyaphala-sūtra*, Wiesbaden: Harrassowitz.

Malalasekera, G.P. (1974) *Dictionary of Pāli Proper Names*, 2 vols, London: PTS.

Manné, J. (1990) 'Categories of the *Sutta* in the Pāli Nikāyas and Their Implications for Our Appreciation of the Buddha's Teaching and Literature', JPTS, 15: 9–87.

—— (1995) 'Case Histories from the Pāli Canon: The *Sāmaññaphala Sutta*: Hypothetical Case Histories or How to be Sure to Win a Debate', JPTS, 21: 1–34.

Mellick Cutler, S. (1994) 'The Pāli *Apadāna* Collection', JPTS, 20: 1–42.

Murcott, S. (1991) *The First Buddhist Women: Translations and Commentaries on the Therīgathā*, Berkeley, CA: Parallax.

Ñāṇārāma, Mahāthera (1993; 2nd edn) *The Seven Stages of Purification and The Insight Knowledges: A Guide to the Progressive Stages of Buddhist Meditation*, Kandy: BPS.

Nandargikar, G.R. (1971; 4th edn) *The Raghuvaṃsa of Kālidāsa, with the commentary of Malināthа*, Delhi: Motilal Banarsidass.

Nyanaponika Thera (1961) *The Five Mental Hindrances and Their Conquest: Selected Texts from the Pāli Canon and the Commentaries*, Wheel Publication, no. 26, Kandy: BPS.

—— (1965) *The Threefold Refuge*, Wheel Publication, no. 76, Kandy: BPS.

—— (1962; revised edn 1969) *The Heart of Buddhist Meditation: A Handbook of Mental Training Based on the Buddha's Way of Mindfulness with an Anthology of Relevant Texts translated from the Pāli and Sanskrit*, London: Rider and Company.

—— (1949; revised edn 1998) *Abhidhamma Studies: Buddhist Exploration of Consciousness and Time*, Boston, MA: Wisdom.

Nyanasampanno, Ven. Phra Maha Boowa (1976) trans. S. Buddhasukh, *The Venerable Phra Acharn Mun Bhuridatta Thera: Meditation Master*, Bangkok: Mahamakut Rajavidyalaya Press.

Palihawadana, M. (1997) 'Pāli *Sajjhāya* and Sanskrit *Svādhyāya*: An Inquiry into the Historical Origins of *Parittāna* Recitation' in Bhikkhu Dhammajoti, A. Tilakaratne and, K. Abhayawana (eds) *Essays in Honour of Professor Y. Karunadasa*, Kuala Lumpur: 493–515.

Pandita, Sayadaw U. (1992) trans. Ven U Aggacitta, *In This Very Life, The Liberation Teachings of the Buddha*, Kate Wheeler (ed.), Boston: Wisdom.

Panofsky, E., Klibansky, R. and Saxl, I. (1964) *Saturn and Melancholy: Studies in the History of Natural Philosophy, Religion and Arts*, London: Nelson.

Pradhan, A.P. (1986) *The Buddha's System of Meditation*, 4 vols, New Delhi: Oriental University Press.

Rahula, W. (1967) *What the Buddha Taught*, P. Demieville foreword, 2nd enlarged edn, Bedford: Gordon Fraser.

—— (1981) 'Humour in Pāli Literature', JPTS, IX 156–74.

Randall, D. (1998) 'An Art Therapy Programme Incorporating Buddhist Concepts to Address Issues of Aggression in Adult Male Prisoners', unpublished MA thesis, Perth.

Randall, R. (1990) *Life as a Siamese Monk*, Bradford on Avon, Wiltshire: Aukana.

Roebuck, V. trans. (2000)*The Upaniṣads*, New Delhi: Penguin India.

Rowlands, M. (ed.) (1982) *Abhidhamma Papers*, Manchester, NH: Samatha Trust.

Saddhatissa, H. (1971) *The Buddha's Way*, London: George, Allen and Unwin.

Shattock, E.H. (1958) *An Experiment in Mindfulness*, London: Rider and Company.

Shearer, A. (2000) *The Spirit of Asia: Journeys to the Sacred Places of the East*, photography by M. Freeman, London: Thames and Hudson.

Skilling, P. (2000) 'The Arahats of the Eight Directions', *Fragile Palm Leaves for the Preservation of Buddhist Literature*, no. 6: 12, 22.

Strong, J.S. (2001) *The Buddha: A Short Biography*, Oxford: Oneworld.

Sumedho, Ajahn (1987) *Mindfulness, The Path to The Deathless, The Meditation Teaching of Venerable Ajahn Sumedho*, Great Gaddesden, Hertfordshire: Amaravati.

—— (1992) *Cittaviveka: Teachings from The Silent Mind*, Great Gaddesden, Hertfordshire: Amaravati.

Suvaḍḍhano, Bhikkhu (undated; talks given 1961) *A Guide to Awareness; Dhamma Talks on The Foundations of Mindfulness* (*Satipaṭṭhāna Sutta*), Bangkok: Mrs Thiwasree Piyaphan.

Thanissaro, Bhikkhu (1998) *The Buddhist Monastic Code: The Pāṭimokkha Training Rules*, Valley Center, CA: Metta Forest Monastery.

Thomas, E.J. (1927; paperback 1975) *The Life of Buddha as Legend and History*, London: Routledge Kegan Paul.

Tin, Sayagyi U. Chit (1993) W. Pruitt (ed.) *Buddhist as a Way of Life and other Essays*, Trowbridge, Wiltshire: The Sayagyi U Ba Khin Memorial Trust, UK.

Topsfield, A. and Harle, J.C. (1987) *Indian Art in the Ashmolean Museum*, Oxford: Ashmolean Museum.

Vajirañāṇa Mahāthera (1962, 2nd edn 1975) *Buddhist Meditation in Theory and Practice: A General Exposition According to The Pali Canon of the Theravada School*, Kuala Lumpur: Buddhist Missionary Society (BMTP).

Wickramagamage, C. (1984) 'The Origin of the Buddha Image', *Buddhist Studies in Honour of Hammalava Saddhatissa*, Nugegoda, Sri Lanka: Hammalava Saddhatissa Felicitation Volume Committee, 249–54.

Williams, P. (1989) *Mahāyāna Buddhism: The Doctrinal Foundations*, London and New York: Routledge.

Winney, J. (ed.) (1966) *The General Prologue to The Canterbury Tales*, Cambridge: Cambridge University Press.

Yates, F.A. (1969) *The Art of Memory*, Harmondsworth, Middsx: Penguin.

Zimmer, H.R. (1960) completed by Campbell, J., 2nd edn, *The Art of Indian Asia: Its Mythology and Transformations*, 2 vols, New York: Pantheon.

INDEX

Note: Page numbers in bold indicates where a subject is treated in some detail.